RELIGION, CULTURE, AND PUBLIC LIFE

SERIES EDITORS: ALFRED SEPAN AND MARK C. TAYLOR

The resurgence of religion calls for careful analysis and constructive criticism of new forms of intolerance, as well as new approaches to tolerance, respect, mutual understanding, and accommodation. In order to promote serious scholarship and informed debate, the Institute for Religion, Culture, and Public Life and Columbia University Press are sponsoring a book series devoted to the investigation of the role of religion in society and culture today. This series includes works by scholars in religious studies, political science, history, cultural anthropology, economics, social psychology, and other allied fields whose work sustains multidisciplinary and comparative as well as transnational analyses of historical and contemporary issues. The series focuses on issues related to questions of difference, identity, and practice within local, national, and international contexts. Special attention is paid to the ways in which religious traditions encourage conflict, violence, and intolerance and also support human rights, ecumenical values, and mutual understanding. By mediating alternative methodologies and different religious, social, and cultural traditions, books published in this series will open channels of communication that facilitate critical analysis.

After Pluralism: Reimagining Religious Engagement, edited by Courtney Bender and Pamela E. Klassen

Religion and International Relations Theory, edited by Jack Snyder

RELIGION IN AMERICA

A POLITICAL HISTORY

DENIS LACORNE

TRANSLATED BY GEORGE HOLOCH

COLUMBIA UNIVERSITY PRESS   NEW YORK

COLUMBIA UNIVERSITY PRESS

Publishers Since 1893

NEW YORK   CHICHESTER, WEST SUSSEX

Originally published in French as *De la religion en Amérique* © Edition Gallimard, Paris 2007

English translation copyright © 2011 Columbia University Press

Library of Congress Cataloging-in-Publication Data
Lacorne, Denis.
[De la religion en Amérique. English]
Religion in America : a political history / Denis Lacorne ; translated by George Holoch.
p.   cm.
Includes bibliographical references (p.   ).
ISBN 978-0-231-15100-9 (cloth : alk. paper) — ISBN 978-0-231-52640-1 (ebook)
1. Christianity and politics—United States—History.   2. United States—Church history.
I. Title.
BR515. L2513 2001
261.70973—dc22   2011014314
∞

Columbia University Press books are printed on permanent and durable acid-free paper.

This book is printed on paper with recycled content.

Printed in the United States of America

c 10 9 8 7 6 5 4 3 2

References to Internet Web sites (URLs) were accurate at the time
of writing. Neither the author nor Columbia University Press is responsible for
URLs that may have expired or changed since the manuscript was prepared.

For Maria Ruth Ruegg

CONTENTS

TONY JUDT

THE OUTSIDER, IT IS SAID, sees more clearly. To be sure, there are exceptions: to understand a closed microsociety it helps to be an insider with all an insider's clues and codes. But as a rule, the view from afar has much to recommend it. The French in particular have long specialized in this perspective: some of the best accounts of Russia, for example, are by nineteenth-century French travelers, and it was the French philosopher Montesquieu who displaced himself into the perspective of the "Persian" observer in order to offer perceptive insights onto his own countrymen.

But nowhere have the French trained their sights with such enthusiasm and sustained interest as upon the United States of America. The fascination has been mutual: many of the best historical studies of early modern and modern France have been undertaken by American scholars. But there is a certain asymmetry to the relationship: French historical scholarship has tended to veer south and east rather than west. The French interest in America has been most fully articulated by intellectuals, travelers, and social observers. Since the latter were often among France's most distinguished writers, this has been very much to the U.S. advantage. From the settlement of North America, the country has been visited and discussed by everyone from Voltaire to the Duc de La Rochefoucauld-Liancourt, from Madame de Staël to Alexis de Tocqueville, from Simone de Beauvoir to Bernard-Henri Lévy.

If the quality of the observations thereby culled has varied, the interest has never dulled. There is good reason for this. France, like the United States, was refounded in the late eighteenth century on an Enlightenment and republican basis. In contrast to the United States, the French revolutionary settlement proved unstable and contentious for much of the ensuing two centuries: both the republic and its institutions were challenged by voices seeking a return to the past. On the face of it, America proved a more successful and complete revolution, displacing an imperial monarchy with a republican constitution and a society united behind it—despite the disgraceful paradox of slavery.

But seen through another glass, it was America that proved unstable. From the French perspective, the contrast between organized religion and a republican political culture was clear and unambiguous from the outset. In 1791, even before the monarchy was overthrown, the French revolutionaries began a despoiling of the established (Catholic) church and its material wealth—a process that culminated just over a century later in the complete disestablishment of the French Church and the unambiguous construction of an unbreachable wall of *laïcité* ("laicness" or "ultra-secularism") between church and state.

This established a clear space in which republicanism could define itself not just against the monarchy and the church but against all forms of religious practice and expression. At least until the recent advent of a new minority of practicing Muslims, the French could contentedly suppose that to be republican—i.e., to be French—was to keep faith and religious practice far away from the public place: no crosses, no bibles, no veils. It was thus a source of ongoing wonder and some distaste to look across the Atlantic and see France's fellow enlightened republic (the only other significant institutional survivor from the age of reason) wallowing in apparent public religiosity.

For the paradox of the United States, of course, was that it was founded under the auspices of "a Creator" and was from the outset a world of committed believers—whether Episcopalian, Methodist, Baptist, Catholic, or Jew—but had given itself a constitution in which the very first amendment specified unambiguously that there should be no established religion of any sort. Thus, whereas it took the French more than a century to rid themselves of an established church, the Americans successfully and definitively did so right away. And yet they continue to be quite distinctively religious—more so than any other Western or developed society. How can this be?

Professor Denis Lacorne of France's distinguished Sciences-Po is already well known to readers on both sides of the Atlantic for his writings on American political and cultural life. Unlike most French commentators on American affairs (Voltaire included), he has not only spent time in the United States, he has also lived and taught here. He speaks fluent English—even today a rarity among French scholars and intellectuals—and is more familiar with the ins and outs of American history and politics than most Americans.

In his latest book, *Religion in America: A Political History*, Lacorne does more than just offer an overview of the place of religious practice and religious conflict in the making of America (though he does this in a way that American students and general readers will find extremely helpful); he integrates his story into another story, that of the French fascination with America and the insights and misunderstandings to which it has led. He observes that even the earliest commentators, men like Jean de Crèvecœur, were disposed to conflate the Puritan and republican strands in colonial political culture—whereas, as Lacorne demonstrates, these were juxtaposed and often contradictory elements that surfaced at different occasions and create not so much a complexity of American roots as a tension between alternative models for the good society.

These tensions run through American history, and the contradictions they pose to observers are well illustrated in the work of both the greatest commentators—Tocqueville, most obviously—and the most superficial. Nor do the tensions run conveniently along political lines. The populist tradition that fed into the modern Democratic Party was at least as religious as the more conventionally Protestant Republican heritage: the defense of dissenting Baptists or persecuted Catholics could take radical and oppositional form to the power structure of a republic run by and for a small commercial elite. Indeed, the emphasis on the separation of church and state long favored minority religions frightened at the prospect of their suppression at the hands of the dominant mainstream heritage of the Episcopalians.

Conversely, the established elite—having no need of religion to support their authority from the late nineteenth century onward—were quite content to see religion retreat to the private sphere, but took great care to emphasize the need to keep *all* forms of faith and practice equally clear of public favor. From the point of view of the foreigner, and particularly the French observer with a Cartesian preference for rigorous logic and sustained categories, the periodic resurfacing of these issues in the form of juridical revision of the interpretation of the First Amendment was a source of confusion: surely these things had been settled once and for all in 1789?

But the fungibility of American public affairs, and the shifting sentiments brought about by war and fears of war, have reintroduced God into American politics in ways that confuse foreigners. Here in America we now sign off our coins, our pledges of allegiance, and even our public speeches with invocations of God. Americans today believe in their God (and very often the Devil) to an extent that others find mysterious. Indeed, in these respects the United States has more in common with Islamic or Hindu societies than it does with the rest of the "de-Christianized" West. There are churches everywhere in America and they are full.

And yet: as Denis Lacorne brings out well, this is not a token of the reestablishment of official Christianity. Even the most conservative and faith-based presidents of recent years have taken great care to distinguish between their own born-again or otherwise determined Christian practice, and the amorphous and widely varying commitments of their fellow citizens: "my fellow Americans" clearly addresses a world of Catholics, Jews, Muslims, Hindus, and others besides, not to mention tens of millions of nonbelievers.

Thus it would be a foolish American politician indeed, or one whose sights were firmly set on a local horizon, who sought to emulate those European politicians—from Poland to Italy, from Germany to the Netherlands—who insist upon the "Christian" identity of Europe. In this respect, Americans are far more serious about their *laïcité*, at least collectively, than their unbelieving European confreres. To American observers, the European reluctance to admit Islamic Turkey into the European Union remains a mystery, parochial and self-destructive. And it is perhaps worth observing that French commentators and politicians—the first to damn America for its ultrareligiosity—are in the front line of those defending an implicitly Christian definition of "Europe" against the barbarians without.

The prospects for Jefferson's "wall" separating church from state are perhaps better than people suppose. It doesn't much matter—and Lacorne is very good on just why this is so—whether the occasional provincial courthouse displays the baby Jesus at Christmastime on its front lawn. But it does very much matter whether or not being Christian—or a particular kind of Christian—determines your prospects in public affairs in the republic.

Here, perhaps, Lacorne is rather generous. When Joseph Lieberman was selected by Al Gore as his vice-presidential running-mate in 2000, the American media fell over itself to congratulate the republic in welcoming a Jew as a potential head of state and government. When some pointed out that France, that notorious sinkhole of anti-Semitic prejudice, had to date elected five Jewish heads of government, there were cries of disbelief. So we should not rush to suppose that the real as distinct from the symbolic separation of church and state in America is and always has been unbreached. To the contrary: it took nearly two centuries to elect a Catholic to the White House and may take nearly as long again before we see a Muslim uncontentiously installed there. On the other hand, much the same is true of France.

I cannot recommend this book too highly. We stand always to gain from looking at ourselves through the lens of another, and Denis Lacorne is a reliable and enlightening guide. Moreover, by moving insensibly back and forward between Parisian perspectives and American practices, he pulls us a little closer to the rest of humanity. The illusion of American exceptionalism is one of the more dangerous myths in which this country has wallowed, separating itself in its own eyes from everyone else. If we did not appreciate just how isolating this was in years gone by, we should surely do so now.

Tony Judt
New York City

INTRODUCTION

THERE IS GENERAL AGREEMENT THAT the United States is the most religious of advanced Western democracies. The level of religious observance in the country is unusually high and political language is imbued with religious values and religious references. "In God We Trust" is the national motto of the United States and enshrined on its currency, "one nation under God" was added to the Pledge of Allegiance in 1954, and an impressive number of elected officials—members of Congress, cabinet officers, and presidents such as Jimmy Carter and George W. Bush—have claimed a special relationship with the Almighty following a momentous adult conversion experience. And yet this reality is the source of major misunderstandings, clichés, and misperceptions between the United States and other Western nations regarding the proper role of religion in a modern democracy.

Nowhere is this more evident than in France, where contemporary writers—journalists, political scientists, philosophers, novelists—are particularly disturbed by what they see on the American political scene: the proliferation of religious slogans and allegories; the frequency of worship services, prayer meetings, and thanksgiving celebrations organized by public authorities; the inordinate use of a Manichean rhetoric opposing the forces of Good to the forces of Evil. Such manifestations of an overwhelming public religiosity reinforce the French belief that the United States is an aggressively and unapologetically Christian nation. Its political creed, it is argued, has remained fundamentally Anglo-Protestant, despite an increasing influx of Asian and Latino immigrants whose cultural values are by definition outside the ambit of Anglo-Protestantism.

Based on these assumptions, numerous French observers have concluded that there is no escape from religion in American politics and that, despite its well-established republican framework, American democracy is less advanced because it has not yet completed its process of secularization. The French, they argue, are more authentically "republican" than the Americans, because they have enshrined a secular ideal in the first article of their constitution and have established a long-lasting separation between church and state.

Against the background of these widely accepted continental clichés, I have attempted to do two things in this book. The first is to trace the broad outlines of the role of religion in the formation of a distinct American national identity. The second is to examine, against this background, how key French thinkers, from Voltaire and Tocqueville to Sartre and Bernard-Henri Lévy, have tried to explain the place and significance of religion in American politics.

AMERICA IS UNIQUE IN THAT the foundation of its political institutions preceded the development of its national identity. As the historian John Murrin aptly put it, in the United States, as opposed to most European countries, the "constitutional roof" was built before the "national walls."[1] The American Revolution and its constitutional climax did not deepen a strong, preexisting sense of national identity. It created a new political framework, and the "national walls," including cultural references to a distant past, were built later.

In looking at the history of these attempts to construct a national identity, I argue that there is not, as some historians and political scientists have maintained, one narrative, but at least two major competing narratives of identity formation. These narratives have been crafted by historians, philosophers, novelists, and political leaders, who at certain critical junctures reassess or reformulate the links between the past, the present, and the future.

The first narrative, derived from the philosophy of the Enlightenment, is essentially secular. Associated with the Founding Fathers and reflected in the founding documents (the Declaration of Independence, the Constitution, the Federalist Papers), it is predicated on the necessity of separating religion from politics in order to preserve newly acquired political freedoms from the danger of an overpowering established church. The American attempt to create a genuine "wall of separation" between church and state was embraced by prominent continental thinkers like Voltaire, Tom Paine, and Démeunier, the editor of the *Encyclopédie Méthodique* (1784–1788), who saw the American project as a radical attempt to create a new political regime, detached from religion and liberated from the weight of an ancient history.

The second narrative of American identity, which I call "Romantic" or "Neopuritan," is based on a radically different view of history. It sees the national identity as the climax of a continuous progression of freedom starting with the Reformation and culminating with the first New England Puritan colonies. This alternative vision of America was elaborated by Whig politicians and Romantic historians (most notably Bancroft) in the first half of the nineteenth century. It is still shared by political scientists who, like Samuel Huntington, insist that there is only one core identity for the United States— the "American Creed"—which they describe as a stable ideology based on a unique combination of Protestant and republican values.

DESPITE THE FREQUENCY WITH WHICH these two basic versions of American national identity are still invoked by modern political thinkers, both have undergone significant modifications and adaptations over the course of the last two centuries. Near the middle of the nineteenth century, the rise of Jacksonian democracy and the arrival of millions of non-Protestant immigrants called into question the dominant Neopuritan paradigm and gave rise to various reinterpretations of the American national identity. The most significant of such reinterpretations were fashioned by nativist advocates of the new science of Social Darwinism and by progressive elites eager to facilitate the assimilation of newcomers while respecting their distinct cultures and religious traditions.

In the twentieth century, the secular paradigm so strongly defended a century earlier by Thomas Jefferson was rediscovered and rehabilitated by progressive justices of the Supreme Court. That paradigm continues to define the court's jurisprudence today despite numerous attempts to lower or break down the "wall of separation" between church and state. In stark opposition to this revival of the secular paradigm, a new evangelical antisecular narrative emerged in the South in the 1960s and has profoundly marked the ideology and electoral strategy of the Republican Party.

THE SECOND EMPHASIS OF THIS book is on how French observers have perceived the complex interaction of religion with politics in America. French views of religion in America are surprisingly diverse and idiosyncratic. At the time of the American Revolution, there was a productive exchange of ideas between French intellectuals and American political elites. The consensus, following Voltaire's influence and that of other Enlightenment philosophers, was that religion was not central to the building of a modern American nation; what mattered most was a "government without priests" and a genuine separation between church and state. In the 1830s, this view was generally displaced by a new perspective defended, among others, by Tocqueville: the "spirit of religion" was the root cause of American democracy and the Puritan tradition was acknowledged as structuring the political life, the social mores, and the religious beliefs of the country. There were some dissenting voices expressed by followers of Saint-Simon who questioned the relevance of Puritanism and praised the rising influence of more "democratic" religions derived from the Second Great Awakening. But the perspective adopted by Tocqueville remained dominant in the mid-nineteenth century and was widely shared by other European thinkers and American historians.

It was only a century later, starting in the 1930s, that French perceptions of religion in America significantly diverged from these earlier secularist and Neopuritan currents. Perhaps the most significant example is the influential French Catholic writers who, concerned about the excesses of modern capitalism, came to the conclusion that the "death of God" was the central value of the American polity and that it was Europe's duty to prevent the spread of such a dangerous materialistic ideology to the rest of the world. This radically new perspective placed on an equal footing "Godless America" and "Godless (Soviet) Communism." It marked the beginning of a fundamental divergence between French and American views of religion in America—a divergence which persists to this day, although, paradoxically, with diametrically opposed results. The consensus shared by a majority of French writers and journalists today, which dates to the end of the Second World War, represents a clear break from the 1930s: God is once again back in America and the American identity is fixed once and for all in its Puritan past, as if nothing had changed over the past four centuries.

Twentieth-century French perceptions of America, however contradictory, share a common pessimistic message. The United States is not really a
democracy. It is either a godless nation dominated by the profit motive, or the
very opposite: an intolerant Anglo-Protestant theocracy.

IN REVISITING THE COMPLEX interplay of secular and religious traditions
in America, this book provides a decentered historiographical perspective
based on the confrontation of two distinct literatures: two rival American
exegeses of the "founding of America" and competing visions of the "essence" of America defended by prominent as well as lesser-known French
observers. French perceptions and misperceptions of America do matter: they
have had a definite impact on the formative thought of the Founding Fathers
and Tocqueville's *Democracy in America* remains to this day an inspiring work
for American scholars. But other French writers deserve rediscovery, and a
systematic reading of their works will deepen our knowledge of America's
political and religious development as seen from abroad over the course of
four centuries. Paradoxically, modern French writers do not seem to understand that America is more than the sum of its parts and cannot be reduced
to a fixed Puritan or evangelical ideology, uncritically used to explain what
is wrong with America, from Jimmy Carter's election to the Lewinsky affair
to Bush's war against the Axis of Evil. Perceptions matter, even if they are
distorted and sometimes comical; they influence public opinion on both sides
of the Atlantic. Religion in America can be better understood if it is seen in
the context of an intermittent, often friendly but sometimes hostile dialogue
between French and American thinkers.

IT IS OBVIOUS THAT THE PERIODS chosen for this book—the late
eighteenth century, early and mid-nineteenth, early twentieth, the 1930s, and
the present—follow a chronological order. But this apparent order is interrupted by a series of deliberate discontinuities. They refer to critical moments or "historiographical regimes" that, it is assumed, influence the very
way in which we think about religion in the United States. The authors studied never wrote in a closed world. Their perceptions, real or imaginary, were
necessarily located in a larger historical context that directed their views and
incited them to emphasize certain particular events, sets of great ancestors, or
utopias over others.

Constant and simultaneous reference to French and American sources might seem unnecessarily complicated, but I have found it to be the best way of revealing the common historiographical traditions shared by France and the United States. It has also helped me to verify the accuracy of my sources and establish the necessary critical distance between European and American narratives often wrongly presented as factual. The confrontation of two national literatures dealing with the same subject—religion in the United States in relation to politics—has greatly eased my task. It has allowed me to develop a better understanding of the conflicting accounts presented by French and American witnesses of great American political and religious transformations in all their ambiguities, contradictions, and inaccuracies.

RELIGION IN AMERICA

I

America, the Land of Religious Utopias

AMERICA IN VOLTAIRE'S TIME was a distant and little-known territory. Intriguing reports from travelers, missionaries, soldiers, and adventurers confirmed the idea that the New England settlers were not just merchants or farmers but also ideologues, testing new ideas on a large and still virgin territory. America was seen as a laboratory for political, social, and religious experimentation. And it was above all the blossoming of new religions that drew the attention of French observers looking for a better world. But not all French *philosophes* could travel to America. They either stayed in France, like Abbé Raynal, and imagined the new American religious landscape, or they visited England, like Voltaire, to discover the new faiths that were being exported to North America.

Voltaire set the tone by pursuing his interest in the Quakers, whom he personally met during his three-year visit to England (1726–1729). This short but memorable experience led him to write the "Letters on the Quakers," first published in 1734. His reputation was such that all European visitors to America felt obliged to meet the "Good Quakers" of Pennsylvania after having read the latest edition of Voltaire's *Philosophical Letters*. Voltaire's ideas were discussed, verified on the ground, and accepted by some and rejected by others, depending on the traveler and the circumstances.

The Religion of the Quakers

Voltaire thought he had found in Quaker practices the expression of the true, simple, and primitive religion to which the deists of the time aspired. Quakerism heralded the outline of a natural religion based on a single dogma: "There is a God and we must be just." This was in Voltaire's view "the universal religion established in all times and among all peoples." Quakerism approached this ideal by reviving the practices of the early Christians, all dressed in the same way, "in a coat unpleated at the sides, and without buttons on the pockets or sleeves" and wearing "a large flat-brimmed hat." They rejected any hierarchy, any distinctive signs, and any profession of faith. The pages devoted to the Quakers in the *Philosophical Letters* bring to light the paradigmatic character of that admirable religion in Voltaire's eyes, because it evidenced the real existence of a desacralized church, divested of all the essential sacraments: baptism, communion, penance, and so on. There were no archaic rituals, the *philosophe* remarked, no preaching of the Gospel, no throwing of cold water on the head of an unwilling child.[1]

Voltaire set out to conduct a veritable field study in the London area. He met a famous Quaker to learn about the particularities of this singular religion. What emerges is a striking picture of the clash between two utterly foreign cultures. Voltaire encounters "a fresh-looking old man who had never been ill because he had never known either passion or intemperance." The old man receives the *philosophe* "with his hat on his head . . . without the slightest bow," using "thee" and "thou" with a natural simplicity that matched his appearance. Surprised, Voltaire behaves with exquisite politeness and approaches the old man, "bowing and making a leg as is our custom."[2] With the preliminaries over, they approach the most difficult questions with extraordinary frankness: Jewish rituals, the pilgrimage to Mecca, Paul's Epistle to the Corinthians, the peaceful nature of the true Christian who would be incapable of behaving like a wolf, a tiger, or a dog. The cultural gap is obvious and wide: "'With respect to communion,' I asked, 'what do you do?' 'We do not celebrate it.' 'What! No communion?' 'None, except the communion of hearts.'"[3]

Voltaire's admiration is heartfelt but not without limits. He acknowledges that there are also among the Quakers "contortionists" who speak in a "jumble" inspired by the Gospels that is not very persuasive for a visitor from

France. But his interest in the Quakers is so strong that he feels obliged to embark on the history of the sect, beginning with the curious life of its founder, George Fox, the son of an illiterate worker, "of irreproachable conduct and saintly folly."[4]

In Voltaire's view, this new exotic religion functioned as a model: it offered the image of a perfectly viable counter-religion, a reverse Catholicism including none of the dogmas, rituals, or sacraments of the Roman Church. The exoticism was twofold, in relation both to continental Catholicism and to the two established religions of England and Scotland—Anglicanism and Presbyterianism. The strangeness was further accentuated when transposed to North America, where William Penn, son of an admiral and friend of the Duke of York (the king's brother and the future James II), had established his empire by securing from the British crown the immense territory of Pennsylvania. Voltaire showers the ruler of the new colony with praise: He is a great legislator of exemplary wisdom, a pacifist, the protector of the Indians, and most important the inventor of a new form of state, unprecedented in the annals of humanity—a "government without priests," with no army, and peopled by citizens equal among themselves. Hence this laudatory comment: "William Penn might well have boasted that he brought back the golden age of which so much is spoken and which in fact never really existed save in Pennsylvania."[5]

The notion that the Quakers of Pennsylvania had brought to life the mythical golden age persisted. It shows up in the article "Quaker" in the *Encyclopédie* of Diderot and d'Alembert, in works by Abbé Raynal about America, as well as in the article "Pennsylvanie" in the *Encyclopédie méthodique* of Démeunier, which repeats the bulk of Raynal's remarks.

Updating Voltaire's presentation in his article for the *Encyclopédie*, the Marquis de Jaucourt observes that, whereas Quakerism has declined in England, it is thriving in Pennsylvania. Like Montesquieu before him, Jaucourt makes a striking parallel between Penn and Lycurgus.[6] He claims that the great lawgiver of Pennsylvania holds "the distinction of having formed a population among whom probity seems as natural as bravery was for the Spartans." Like Voltaire, Jaucourt admires this modern government. He praises the virtue, intelligence, industriousness, and wisdom of this "truly great" people, and concludes that Quakerism "is, all things considered, the most reasonable and perfect system yet imagined."[7]

Imitating Voltaire and Jaucourt, Abbé Raynal also expresses his admiration for the Quakers' modesty, probity, and love of work. Convinced that "a people without masters and without priests" enjoyed common prosperity, he believes this new republic is the incarnation of the mythical heroic age of antiquity. Again like Voltaire, Raynal notes the simplicity of the Quakers' way of life, their disdain for titles, fashions, and ceremonies, as well as the modesty of their dress: "Without braids, embroidery, lace, or cuffs, they banned everything they called ornament or superfluity. Their coats were unpleated, and their hats did not even have buttons, because they are not always necessary. This disdain for fashion impelled them to be more virtuous than other men, from whom they distinguished themselves by their modest appearance."[8]

Raynal is struck by the extreme egalitarianism and extreme individualism of a religion in which each believer is a potential priest awaiting illumination from the Holy Spirit to reveal his inspiration to the assembled Friends. For them the gift of speech has a sacramental value and it is, remarkably, shared equally among men and women. Raynal acknowledges, however, that everything is not perfect among the Quakers. Inspiration may sometimes irritate "the sensitivity of the nervous system" so as to provoke convulsions (hence the name Quakers or Tremblers). Indeed, such practices were often severely sanctioned by confinement to the "madhouse, prison, whipping, the pillory, often bestowed on believers whose crime and folly was an excessive desire to be reasonable and virtuous." In fact, Raynal observes, these convulsions are no more shocking than the lack of formality displayed by the members of the Society of Friends. For what is important is the exceptional quality of the human relations cultivated by the inhabitants of Pennsylvania. The same thing is true of the relations of the Quakers with the "natives of the country," based on good faith, trust, and the respect of promises at a time when Native Americans were already being persecuted and wrongly despoiled of their ancestral lands. Finally, Raynal praises the exemplary nature of the religious regime inaugurated by William Penn: "The virtuous legislator built his society on a foundation of toleration. . . . [H]e allowed all people the freedom to invoke the Supreme Being in their own way, permitting neither dominant religion in Pennsylvania, nor compulsory contributions for the building of a house of worship or attendance at religious services which was not voluntary."[9]

Raynal is nonetheless worried about the future of a state with open and undefended borders. He wonders whether the Quakers' radical pacifism is excessively imprudent, and decides that it may not be. After all, what would an enemy have to gain from an invasion of the Quaker republic? Nothing, or very little: fallow land abandoned by its inhabitants, ruined workshops, businesses deserted by a diaspora of Friends who would prefer to emigrate, even if it meant going to the ends of the earth, rather than submit to their enemies or take up arms in their own defense.[10]

The description of the Quakers in the next to last volume of the *Histoire des deux Indes* introduces a welcome pause in the cycle of conquests and tribulations marked by the cruelty of war, the pursuit of wealth, the introduction of slavery, and the extermination of the Native Americans. That rare occurrence in the history of humanity—the triumph of innocence and peace—gives reason for hope:

> At last the writer and his reader can breathe a sigh of relief. At last they can find some compensation for the disgust, the horror, or the sadness inspired by modern history, and above all by the colonization of the New World by Europeans. Up until this point, the only way these barbarians knew of taking possession of it was to begin by destroying its peoples, the only way of cultivating it, to begin by laying it waste. At last we can witness the seeds of reason, happiness, and humanity sown among the ruins and devastation of a continent still reeking with the blood of all its peoples, civilized or savage.[11]

J. HECTOR ST. JOHN DE CRÈVECŒUR (1735–1813), in *Letters from an American Farmer*, published around the same time as Raynal's *Histoire des deux Indes*, also expresses open sympathy for the Quakers. Like all his predecessors, he is impressed by the simplicity and austerity of their way of life. Their religious observance is "without hierarchy, coercive laws, or outward forms of worship." The author is particularly struck by the complete absence of ornament in the meeting house he visits, which is lacking in all the apparatus of a revealed religion. It is a place of exemplary sobriety, with four white walls, benches, and nothing else: "Neither pulpit nor desk, font nor altar, tabernacle nor organ, were there to be seen. . . ." The meeting of Friends that he attends in the small town of Chester is made up of men and women, black and white, in roughly equal numbers. Repeating in his way the experience of Voltaire, Crèvecœur apologizes for his show of antiquated manners that makes him ridiculous in his hosts' eyes: "The involuntary impulse of ancient custom made me pull off my hat. . . ." He swiftly corrects the mistake and puts his hat back on, as is done among Friends. To his great surprise, nothing happens in the meeting house. Absolute silence prevails for about half an hour, until a "female Friend" stands up and states modestly that the spirit has moved her to speak. Her discourse, says Crèvecœur, was of exemplary simplicity. She

> delivered it without theological parade or the ostentation of learning.... Her discourse lasted three-quarters of an hour.... Never before had I seen a congregation listening with so much attention to a public oration. I observed neither contortions of body nor any kind of affectation in her face, style, or manner of utterance; everything was natural, and therefore pleasing, and shall I tell you more, she was very handsome....[12]

Obviously charmed by the beauty of the ritual, Crèvecœur draws up an astonishing inventory of Quaker virtues: modesty, probity, justice, equity, frugality, cleanliness, gentleness, benevolence, charity, and, to crown everything, "tranquil and wise manners"; in short, an extraordinary "calm of passions," unknown in Europe and the rest of America. Crèvecœur like Raynal was among the first French observers to note the important place granted to women, treated on an equal footing with men, participating in all the activities of the Society of Friends, and even encouraged to teach others "when they feel inspired." He also pointed out certain prohibitions against "swearing, gambling, and debauchery" and emphasizes that Quakers abhor the "taking of oaths," so that they refuse any employment requiring a religious oath according to the Test Act.[13] But he fails to note that the Constitution of Pennsylvania, although in existence for some time, takes full account of this situation by allowing all applicants for public employment to "swear" or to "affirm" (for those who reject oath-taking) that they will be "true and faithful to the commonwealth of Pennsylvania" (Section 40, 1776 Constitution of Pennsylvania).

Other writers expressed great admiration for the politics of the Quakers and particularly for their noble and courageous commitment to the emancipation of the slaves. Anthony Benezet, the "distinguished Quaker and apostle of humanity," was singled out for praise by the Geneva banker Étienne Clavière and the French publicist and future leader of the Girondins Jacques-Pierre Brissot in a travel narrative they published in 1787. Benezet was a preacher of a new kind, who spoke in favor of Negro emancipation and converted both his fellow-worshipers and members of other churches in other states to that cause. The Quakers indeed belonged to a new humanity "destin[ed] to regenerate the dignity of man."[14]

Anticipating Tocqueville, Rabaut Saint-Étienne, a Protestant minister, deputy to the Assemblée Nationale (1789–1791) and future Girondin, thought he had found in the Quakers the practice of an "equality of the moderns"[15]: not the impossible dream of complete equality of wealth, but a relative equality characterized as "moral equality." This, he thought, was particularly useful for the survival of a modern society. "The Quakers," Rabaut writes, "live as brothers, and yet they are of unequal wealth; but the haughtiness of the rich and insulting vanity are absolutely unknown among them ... a man of little wealth lives in the company of a wealthy man ... women have the same rights as men."[16] The religion of the Friends hence represents much more than a utopia: it is a utopia that has already been realized, the moderation of which—a remarkable ability to mitigate social, sexual, and economic differences—guarantees its survival and constitutes a model for the new French Republic.

Other writers, such as Volney, were more skeptical. After three years in the United States, from 1795 to 1798, Volney was probably the first French *philosophe* to criticize the "romantic mistake of the writers who give the name *new and virgin people* to a collection of inhabitants of old Europe." He did not believe in the "essential goodness" of American laws nor the inherent wisdom of the government of the country.[17] But while he had no illusions about the "exceptionalism" of the New World, Volney nonetheless found admirable qualities among the Quakers of Pennsylvania, beginning with a theoretical and practical morality that was particularly propitious for improving the fate of humanity. The importance the Quakers accorded to the education of children was in his view the very emblem of a great religion that would "merit the title of *church* of all reasonable men," had it not retained a major defect for a man of science: the refusal to teach the natural and physical sciences on the pretext that such knowledge is too "*profane.*"[18]

Could there be anything better than the Quakers? Was there another religion that was simpler, more austere, and even purer than that of the Society of Friends? So asked the anonymous author of the article "Pennsylvanie" in the *Encyclopédie méthodique*. While attaching great importance to Raynal's arguments (quoted at length), he thought he had discovered the answer in the sect of Dumplers, settled in the community of Euphrates, fifty miles from Philadelphia.[19] Even more disinterested than the Quakers, the Dumplers "are through religion what the Stoics were through philosophy, indifferent to insults." Dressed with extreme simplicity, they wear "coarse shirts, full trousers, and heavy shoes," all covered by a long white robe topped by a simple hood. "Enemies of blood," they are all vegetarians and live in a kind of primitive communism, sharing the fruits of their labors. Like the Quakers, they preach only when they feel inspired. And unlike mainstream Protestants, they believe in neither original sin nor eternal punishment, which does not keep them from frequent prayer: twice in the evening and twice during the day. In short, they are modern contemplatives. Men and women live chastely apart. Marriage is not forbidden, but those who do marry settle outside the community.

According to the *Encyclopédie méthodique*, Pennsylvania is not the place where the Golden Age has returned to earth, but the location of innocence and virtue. The isolation of communities, the large size of parishes, the dispersion of churches, and the multiplicity of sects offers little room for dogmatism: "Innocence and lack of science protect their morals more certainly than precepts and controversies."[20]

The Disenchantment of Skeptics

Other late eighteenth-century travelers demonstrated less enthusiasm. The exoticism of North American religions continued, naturally, to be a source of fascination, and Quakerism gave rise to further detailed and impassioned descriptions. But it was also a source of alarm, because the religion of the Friends seemed to liberate uncontrollable passions that threatened public order and the smooth functioning of a still patriarchal society.

In his *Voyage dans les États-Unis d'Amérique*, the Duke de la Rochefoucauld-Liancourt, an émigré from the French Revolution, was troubled by the power attained by Gemaima Willkinson [Jemima Wilkinson], who "believed herself called to a higher destiny, and came up with a plan to become the leader of a sect." The visitor found this feminization of religious authority startling, and he decided to track her down in her lair in the new religious community of "Jerusalem" on Lake Seneca. He attended one of the meetings held by the prophetess in her own house. He found everything about it surprising, beginning with her clothing: she wore a man's dressing gown, jacket, and collar, a white silk tie, and her hair was cut short. To look at, this pleasant woman, who seemed younger than her years, had a "handsome, very youthful face, good teeth, and beautiful eyes." But she had a suspect appearance and her conduct with converts was just as troubling: she was said to prohibit young women from marrying and "it was rumored that she took a personal interest in the women around her." But the honor of the sect was preserved because a masculine presence, a "strapping lad, quite young and well built," dressed in a white robe and claiming to be the reincarnation of the prophet Elisha, was said to be periodically "admitted to the intimacy of the *universal friend*."[21] This extravagant behavior, which the duke apparently found shocking, induced him in turn to discredit the validity of the prophetess's preaching. Apart from misogyny, the French visitor had good reasons for being surprised at the odd cast of mind of a woman who, according to recent research, claimed to have been reborn after her "death" in a typhus epidemic and frequently asserted that her disincarnated body, neither masculine nor feminine, had become the "tabernacle" of a perfect spirit: the Public Universal Friend. Her identity, she claimed, had been transformed by contact with the divine, and her message, largely based on the Book of Revelation, had a resolutely millenarian cast. Hence, she was preparing her congregants for the Second Coming of Christ. Many contemporary witnesses reported that her fiery preaching attracted large crowds in Philadelphia.[22]

Another political expatriate, Ferdinand Bayard, who was a follower of Rousseau, undertook a systematic critique of his predecessors in the name of a history based on the verification of facts and the rejection of literary impressions: "The century of beatifications has passed," he asserted, and then demonstrated that William Penn was not the modern Lycurgus imagined by Montesquieu and the Encyclopédistes.[23] The treaty Penn had signed with the "natives" of the colony was indeed not just and magnanimous as Abbé Raynal and Chevalier de Jaucourt claimed. William Penn had bought the Native Americans' land for a pittance, and his son Thomas, not bound by any of the promises made by his father, committed the worst atrocities against these now impoverished populations, justifying these atrocities with dubious "theological subtleties." The "atrocious and despicable conduct" of Penn's disciples, Bayard decreed, destroyed any illusion the unfortunate Indians may have had about the moral gentleness of a supposedly peaceful religion.[24]

When he visited Philadelphia, Bayard was surprised to discover strong social hierarchies firmly rooted in custom that were completely contrary to the principles of equality advocated by the Quakers. Observing the growth of luxury and artificial needs, the visitor revealed the basic hypocrisy of men who may well have worn shirts without cuffs, but owned clothes of fine cloth, and of women who "wore no feathers" but wore "cloth as magnificent as that of their husbands." Even worse, the Quakers were threatening the foundations of a healthy political economy because they slowed the growth of monetary resources by "display[ing] much silver on their tables. This great luxury is especially harmful because it absorbs, like a miser, the metals that circulation alone uses and that in turn accelerate circulation."[25]

Bayard's attack is ferocious: behind the superficial brilliance of a religion without priests—a religion that is tolerant, peaceful, simple, and modest, he sees only deceptions and atrocities against Native Americans, the frantic pursuit of luxury by city dwellers, and a new infatuation for what the critics of America called, a century later, the almighty dollar. In this respect, Bayard anticipates future critics of modern America: "I sense that in a country where everything, including a man, is only a sign for a bag of money, where talents and virtues are assayed on a scale, *strongboxes are everything and moral individuals nothing.*"[26] Comparing the way of life of the Ancients to that of the Moderns, he asserts that the only virtue for a Philadelphian is a head for business which guides all his actions to the detriment even of the "duties of propriety." In emergencies, the Romans apologized to their interlocutors: "My gods, my country, call me to the Capitol, to the battlefield." But, Bayard observes, "the merchants of Philadelphia say with the same feeling of urgency: 'I'm wanted in the shop.'" The former can truly be considered men and citizens, the latter are only dealers or usurers. There is no new Lycurgus in Pennsylvania, no probity, or ancient virtue, and certainly no golden age. To Bayard, the country offers only the distressing spectacle of commerce, luxury, and usury, with the inescapable consequence that the great moral and republican virtues of antiquity have disappeared.[27]

In his *Essai sur les révolutions*, published in the same year, Chateaubriand also expresses sharp disappointment and draws conclusions similar to those of Bayard: the commercial immorality of these strange beings who wear "large hats and coats without buttons" clearly prevails over the legendary virtue and generosity of the Friends so often praised in the literature of the Enlightenment.[28] As witness to the new age, Chateaubriand is obliged to acknowledge the facts: he must renounce his preconceived notions derived from the great authors he had read in preparing for his journey to North America:

> When I arrived in Philadelphia, full of Raynal, I begged the favor of being shown one of those celebrated Quakers, a virtuous descendant of William Penn. Imagine my surprise when I was told that if I wanted to be cheated, I simply needed to enter the shop of a Friend; and that if I was curious to see how far the spirit of self-interest and commercial immorality could go, they would show me the spectacle of one Quaker wanting to buy something from another and each trying to deceive the other. I saw that

this society, which had been so much praised, was for the most part nothing but a collection of greedy merchants, without warmth or sensitivity,
who have achieved a reputation for honesty because they wear different
clothing from other men, never answer yes or no, and never have two
prices because the monopoly of certain merchandise forces you to buy
from them at the price they want, in a word, cold actors always perform-
ing a farce of probity, calculated at a huge rate of interest, and for whom
virtue is a matter of speculation.[29]

THE FRENCH VIEW OF THE Quakers had been completely transformed
in the course of half a century. Establishing parallels and moving back and
forth between the Ancients and the Moderns, Montesquieu, Voltaire, and
Jaucourt (none of whom had ever set foot in North America) believed they
had found a reincarnation of Lycurgus in the founder of the state of Pennsylvania. But the infatuation with Quakerism, the ultimate exotic religion, was
short lived. The first French visitors, Crèvecœur and Brissot, no doubt influenced by the myth of the Good Quaker and by the intellectual authority of
their predecessors (who would dare to contradict Voltaire?) merely confirmed
the truth of the myth with their own eyes. Other travelers with a more critical
perspective, such as La Rochefoucauld-Liancourt, Bayard, and Chateaubri-
and, set out to dismantle the myth and found nothing but cruelty, deception,
and hypocrisy behind the virtuous façade of the Society of Friends. In their
view, the new religion had in no way changed human nature and the alleged
virtue of the Moderns had not eliminated the vices of the Ancients.[30] Beneath
an appearance of exemplary probity, the Quaker regime of Pennsylvania presented the distressing spectacle of a decadent Europe populated with Tar-
tuffes. And the disillusion was even greater because it thereby afflicted other
symbols of republican virtue. When Chateaubriand landed in Philadelphia
in 1791, "full of enthusiasm for the [A]ncients," he expected to encounter in
what was then the capital of the United States the new Cincinnatus, General Washington, first president of the Federal Republic. He was disappointed
when he saw the great man riding in an elegant phaeton: "Cincinnatus in a
carriage slightly disturbed my Republic of the year of Rome 296 [sic]. Could
the dictator Washington be anything but a peasant prodding his oxen with a
goad and holding on to the shaft of his cart?"[31] Philadelphia, with its display
of luxury, "elegant dress," "inequality of wealth," and "immorality of banking
and gambling houses," was after all only a city like other cities, a mere colonial

transplantation of an English town. Chateaubriand sadly observed: "Nothing indicated to me that I had moved from a monarchy to a republic."[32]

The repetitive character of the arguments made by French visitors lies behind the stereotypes that were endlessly repeated by later visitors and anticipates modern anti-Americanism. But the criticisms were neither thoughtless nor systematic. Chateaubriand's opinion, for example, remained nuanced, despite his criticisms. His general impression was positive, because he acknowledged that he was in the presence of a modern republic—"a republic of an unknown kind foreshadowing a change in the human spirit."[33] Moreover, Chateaubriand concluded that freedom was a precious treasure bequeathed by America to the rest of the world. And not just any freedom, because it was the "daughter of Enlightenment and Reason," based on a political innovation unknown to the Ancients, the system of a representative republic.[34] The best representative of the new American democracy was indeed its president, General Washington, whom Chateaubriand finally met in his home in Philadelphia, where the French visitor was fully reassured by the "old Roman simplicity" of the great man.[35]

The Religion of the Savages

American religions seemed exotic to French observers in two contradictory ways. The first, just analyzed, was as the harbinger of a utopian ideal. Thus the "natural" religion of the Quakers appeared to belong to a distant, perhaps unlikely, future. The second was as the survival of a very distant past, dating back to the origins of humanity.

For some writers, such as Corneille de Pauw, the oldest known religion in North America, the religion of the Savages, was strictly speaking not yet a religion, but mere superstition, even less developed than the beliefs of the Ancients of the European continent, the Germans and the Gauls. A product of the extreme ignorance of "timid, credulous, and consequently superstitious" people, it was a religion of fear: "If they hear thunder, if something new frightens them, today they worship a stone, tomorrow a tree; they have the most absurd ideas about the divinity, and almost always portray him as an evil being, which they strive to appease and calm by sacrifices and offerings; they have sorcerers rather than priests."[36]

Other writers, not so harsh in their view of the natives of the country, discovered in the founding myths of the natives obvious similarities with ancient religions. In Volney's view, the history of the ancient Greeks recounted by

Thucydides matched at every point the history of the Hurons and Algonquins of America. Wandering "naked in the forests of Hellas and Thessaly,"
the "ancient Greeks were true savages, of the same kind as those of America."
Climate, vegetation, eating habits, and religious ideas were the same. The
Great Manitou of the Indian tribes was analogous to the "Jupiter of the heroic
age," while the subaltern manitou bore some resemblance to the *daimones* of
antiquity, "spirits of the woods and fountains, honored with the same superstitious worship." Where did such ideas come from? Volney first considers the
hypothesis of a "primeval source" for all human religions, based on shaman-
ism, that spread around the world. But he rejects it in favor of the theory of
probable coincidence, connected to similar physical and climatic conditions
as well as to the state of development of a single human species. The foundation myths of the Savages and the Ancients are similar because they result
quite simply from the "natural production of the human mind."[37]

Chateaubriand formulates the same analogies in his *Voyage en Amérique* and
is particularly interested in the "system of religious fables" invented by the
Indians. He finds in it "traces of Greek fictions and Biblical realities."[38] After
devoting five pages to the fables of the Savages and their accounts of the creation of the world, he expresses surprise and wonder at observing that a long
journey through a huge "ocean of forests," in search of "a few noble savages,"
returned him metaphorically to his point of departure.[39] "Moses, Lucretius,
and Ovid, each seemed to have made a bequest to these populations, the first
his tradition, the second his incorrect physics, the third his metamorphoses. In
all of this there was enough religion, falsehood, and poetry for one to learn, go
astray, and find consolation."[40] One can see at work in Volney and his contemporary Chateaubriand a Copernican conception of history: the apparent exoticism of the religion of the Savages is merely the repetition of a distant past
that is already known and has been overcome. But Volney goes even further
in his rereading of the classic sources: the ancient peoples of the Peloponne-
sus did not live through the golden age so much praised by classical writers.
They were "true savages," "vagabonds like the Hurons and the Algonquins,
the ancient Germans and the Celts," and their civilization came from outside,
from the other side of the Mediterranean. It was in fact imported by "colonies
of foreigners . . . from the shores of Asia, Phoenicia, and even Egypt," who
had behaved toward the Greeks exactly as the first English colonists of Virginia and New England had toward the Indians. The clever interplay of three
elements—Ancients, Moderns, Savages—developed by Volney leads him to
offer a fundamental revision of Greek history as it was taught in the schools of

Europe.[41] The discovery and observation of the mores of the Savages by the Moderns enables him to correct retrospectively existing knowledge about the earliest Ancients. From this perspective, to adopt the terms of an argument presented by François Hartog, history was no longer the circular reproduction of a *historia magistra*, of models to imitate, taken from the past and projected into the present and future, but rather the reverse: the projection of the present onto the past advanced the knowledge of history, thereby challenging "a mass of illusions and prejudices,"[42] wrongly defended by the best students of the classical sources.[43]

Anglo-American Puritanism

In the religion of the Quakers, French travelers saw the emergence of an exemplary utopia: a religion without priests. With the religion of the Savages, they felt transported to an ancient past—their own—displaced to North America. The religious practices of the Puritans posed a problem for them: Puritanism was obviously well adapted to the modern age and yet the extreme religious zeal displayed by the first New England settlers was reminiscent of the barbarism of the Savages. Coming out of a dark period of the history of England, this religion was for French observers an archaic formation. The Puritans were a perfect contrast to the Quakers. The latter were pacifists, so much so that they would die rather than fight; the former were fanatical and violent. In this instance too, Voltaire and the Encyclopédistes set the tone. They described the English and Scottish Puritans as madmen full of furor, prepared to commit frightful horrors.[44] These "perverse fanatics"[45] had so little respect for the existing authorities that they conducted themselves like mutineers on a ship in distress, stirred up by their priests against the civil authorities, prepared to commit crimes with sword in hand for the greater glory of God.[46] In his *Examen de Milord Bolingbroke* (1736), Voltaire denounces "the imposture and stupidity of fanaticism" and all the Christian millenarians, the *Christicoles* who took literally the text of the Book of Revelation and made the demented prediction that a new Jerusalem would descend upon the earth. It was for such foolishness, concludes Voltaire (who claims to be presenting Bolingbroke's doctrine) that "Europe drowned in blood and our King Charles I died on a scaffold!"[47]

The same theme was taken up in almost identical terms in the article "Puritains" in the *Encyclopédie*. For Enlightenment *philosophes*, Puritanism was at bottom nothing but a barbarism of the Moderns leading directly to the excesses of Cromwell's supporters: "those sectarians, blinded by their fiery zeal," were responsible for the "civil wars that inundated [Great Britain] with the blood of its citizens" and led to the execution of its unfortunate king.[48]

Lying behind such fanaticism, according to the article's author, was the insufficient *purity* of the Anglican religion under the reign of Elizabeth. He provides a striking analysis of the effects of this fanaticism of small religious differences:

The animosity of these new sectarians against the Catholic religion led them to find the established religion of England insufficiently distinct from the religion of the Pope, which they called the *religion of the Antichrist, the whore of Babylon,* and the like. The episcopal order seemed hateful to them, a vestige of Popery; they condemned the wearing of surplices by churchmen; the confirmation of children; the sign of the cross in baptism; the custom of exchanging rings in weddings; bowing when speaking the name of Jesus, and so on. These were objects of *hatred* for the Puritans. They enable us to see the extent to which the most insignificant of ceremonies can inflame people's feelings when they provide material for disputes among theologians.[49]

Most writers, however, granted that the Pilgrim Fathers had many virtues. Martyrs for the good cause, they had to have had a great deal of audacity and courage to leave the ease and comfort of their home country to emigrate to the bleak lands of New England. Yet they were not at all discouraged because religious faith steeled their determination.

Raynal's *Histoire des deux Indes* provides a clear sense of the epic nature of the voyage of the first Pilgrims: "They sailed from Plymouth on September 6, 1621, in the number of 120 persons, flying the flags of enthusiasm, which, whether based on error or truth, always accomplishes great things." The first winter turned out to be disastrous: half the Pilgrims died of cold or malnutrition; but "the remainder sustained themselves with the strength of character that religious persecution aroused in victims who had escaped from the spiritual sword of the bishops."[50] And yet, neither strength of character nor religious enthusiasm alone was sufficient to ensure the survival of the colony of New Plymouth. The friendship of sixty Indian braves who had come to meet them saved them from disaster by teaching them how to grow corn and to catch fish on the coast of the future New England. The success of the Moderns, according to Raynal, was inseparable from the very welcoming presence of the Savages. The less civilized provided the art of survival to the more civilized, thereby reversing the traditional hierarchy of the opposition between Moderns and Savages.

Left to their own devices in a new world, saved by the providential intervention of a few Noble Savages, the Puritans nonetheless were unchanged:

brutal and intolerant fanatics capable of committing monstrous atrocities against the very people to whom the first generation of colonists owed their lives. Raynal describes a veritable Savage hunt launched in the Boston region in 1724, crowned by the massacre of a group of Indians peacefully sleeping around a fire. He notes with horror that the authors of the massacre, organized by a man named John Lovewell, received 2,250 livres for each Indian scalp. The atrocity of the spectacle leads Raynal to venture a comparison with an earlier period of the colonization of the Americas and issue this terrible judgment of the new Pilgrims: "Anglo-Americans, do you now dare to address reproaches to the Spanish? What have they done, what could they have done that was more inhuman? . . . And you were civilized men? And you were Christians? No. You were monsters of extermination."[51]

Victims of their own rigid morality—men, for example, were forbidden to wear their hair long like the "Indian Barbarians"—the New England Puritans in Raynal's book are transformed into fearsome tyrants whenever a dissident dares to challenge the truth of their faith. This explains the establishment of a cruel system of intolerance aimed particularly against the Quakers, sometimes banished, and sometimes even hanged for violating a banishment order.[52] The atrocities committed against the witches of Salem in 1692 illustrate better than any other example the consequences of the insatiable feverishness that fed the fanaticism of the Puritans:

Three citizens chosen at random were put in prison, accused of witchcraft, and sentenced to hanging; their corpses were left to wild beasts and birds of prey. A few days later sixteen people suffered the same fate. . . . The frailty of age, the infirmities of the old, the honor due the fair sex, the dignity of office, wealth, virtue were all unable to shelter the victims from hateful suspicion in the minds of people obsessed with the phantoms of superstition. They sacrificed ten-year old children; they stripped young women, searching with impudent curiosity all over their bodies for signs of sorcery; and the torturers themselves dictated the confessions they wanted to hear. . . . Ghosts, visions, terror, and alarm increased these prodigies of madness and horror. Prisons were filled, scaffolds remained standing. All citizens were seized by grim terror. The wisest, groaning, fled a cursed, bloody land; and those who remained asked only for a grave.[53]

Although Raynal acknowledged that this excess of enthusiasm faded in the end, he asserted that the New England Puritans, at the very moment of his writing, remained forever marked by the ferocity of their ancestors' fanaticism.[54] Other writers, such as La Rochefoucauld-Liancourt, writing in 1798, were still surprised at the harshness of the laws adopted in a New England state like Connecticut. Sunday amusements of any kind, for example, were banned, horse racing was subject to punishment, and "any man or woman who wears the costume of the other sex" was fined seventy-five dollars.[55] The law, finally, called for the punishment of adultery by publicly administered whipping and branding the face with a hot iron.[56] The same laws, La Rochefoucauld explains, theoretically protect freedom of conscience. But, in fact, nothing of the kind is true, and "Presbyterianism still prevails, with all its harshness, despotism, and intolerance."[57] For French observers, intolerance and religious fanaticism were the primary characteristics of the America of the seventeenth century.

Of course, Raynal acknowledges, fanaticism finally died out in the eighteenth century, but traces could still be found in "the outrageous harshness" of the legislation of the New England states.[58] If there was a tolerant system, it had to be looked for elsewhere: in the Carolinas or the mid-Atlantic states of New York, New Jersey, Pennsylvania, and Maryland.

ON THE EVE OF THE French Revolution, it was no longer the fashion to describe the fanaticism and austere conduct of the Puritans or the atrocities they committed. It was agreed that the epidemic had been eradicated and extenuating circumstances were sought to explain it, beginning with certain physiological causes: scurvy perhaps, the change in climate, or even the "vapors and exhalations of newly plowed land."[59] Conscious of Puritan history, an intelligent traveler such as Chateaubriand had no hesitation in employing a detached and cruelly ironic tone in speaking of these people supposedly chosen by God who had been betrayed by a capricious Providence. It had led the first Puritans to Cape Cod, allowed most of them to die from hunger, and, a few months later, permitted their mortal enemies the Catholics to land in the same province, followed by a curious "cargo of solemn lunatics," the Quakers. It was almost as though the Moderns, "poor humans who were the playthings of their own folly," had become Barbarians.

The tragedy of the European wars of religion had been followed by another history that took on the colors of farce before the eyes of the astonished natives of the country: "What was an Indian supposed to think," Chateaubriand wondered, "as he contemplated one by one the strange performers of this *great tragicomic farce* that the society constantly enacted?" The spectacle was clearly amazing: New England Puritans persecuting dissidents, going so far as to "immolate their brothers ... for the love of heaven"; Quakers who were such extreme pacifists that they "allowed themselves to be slaughtered without fighting back"; Anglicans in Virginia, "persecutors in fancy dress," accompanied by their black slaves; Catholics in Maryland, guided by "priests in bright raiment covered with crosses speaking gibberish and professing universal tolerance...." The spectacle was undoubtedly simultaneously depressing and amusing for the observer, "who could not imagine that all these people came from the same country ... the small island of England."[60]

Religious Tolerance

The Puritans, then, seemed to be Barbarians whose fanaticism remained incompatible with the modern age of reason. Hence, it was better to turn the page and describe the more recent advances of post-Puritan America. It was in this context—the description of a modern America, emancipated under the influence of Enlightenment philosophy—that Encyclopédistes, *philosophes*, and travelers discovered another form of American exoticism: religious tolerance. In his *Treatise on Tolerance* (1763), Voltaire observes, of course, that the Quakers of Pennsylvania are the most peaceful of men, and he describes with amazement the extreme tolerance practiced in Carolina, where "you need only seven heads of families to establish a religion approved in law."[61] Starting from these premises and bolstered by new travel narratives, nine years later, Voltaire thought it legitimate to generalize his observations by asserting that "in all of English America, which amounts to approximately one-fourth of the known world, complete freedom of conscience is established. And provided one believes in God, any religion is welcomed, in return for which commerce flourishes and the population increases."[62]

Crèvecœur's "American farmer" provides the most precise and enthusiastic description of multiethnic, multinational, and multireligious American tolerance. He invites the reader to imagine a visit to a rural county in New York:

> We observe that in this house, to the right, lives a Catholic, who prays to God as he has been taught and believes in transsubstantiation. About one mile further on the same road, his next neighbor may be a good, honest German Lutheran, who addresses himself to the same God.... [He] believes in consubstantiation; by so doing, he scandalizes nobody.... Next

to him lives a seceder, the most enthusiastic of all sectaries; his zeal is
hot and fiery, but separated as he is from others of the same complexion,
he has no congregation of his own to resort to where he might cabal and
mingle religious pride with worldly obstinacy.[63]

Religious tolerance, in Crèvecœur's view, is a direct consequence of
the immensity of the territory of America. The geographical dispersion of
churches is enough to explain the phenomenon. With more perspicacity, Voltaire proposes another kind of explanation. American tolerance is, in his view,
primarily the expression of a philosophical principle the tenor of which he
sets out in the *Treatise on Tolerance*. He notes that this principle was really put
into practice in a particular region of North America—Carolina—"whose
legislation," he informs us, "was framed by the philosopher John Locke."[64]
But tolerance is much more than a principle; it is also an effect of modern English economic practice transplanted to the United States. The best place to
observe tolerance in action is the London Stock Exchange, of which Voltaire
paints a memorable picture:

> Go into the Royal Exchange in London, a building more respectable
> than most courts; there you will find deputies from every nation assem-
> bled simply to serve humankind. There, the Jew, the Mohammedan, and
> the Christian negotiate with one another as if they were all of the same
> religion, and the only heretics are those who declare bankruptcy; there
> the Presbyterian trusts the Anabaptist, the Anglican accepts the word of
> the Quaker. Leaving this peaceful and liberal assembly, some go to the
> synagogue, others go to drink; this one is baptized in a great font in the
> name of the Father, the Son, and the Holy Spirit; that one has his son
> circumcised while some Hebrew words that he does not understand are
> mumbled over him; still others go to their church with their hats on their
> heads to await the inspiration of God, and all are content.
>
> Were there only one religion in England, despotism would be a threat;
> were there two, they would be at each other's throats; but there are thirty,
> and they live happily and at peace with one another.[65]

This very pragmatic view of religious pluralism had an undoubted influence on the work of the delegates to the Constitutional Convention in Philadelphia who drafted the Federal Constitution of 1787. Its principal architect,
James Madison, frequently quoted the concluding passage of the "Letter on
the Presbyterians" to his friends.[66] In Federalist 51, Madison argues like a true

disciple of Voltaire when he worries about the danger posed by the proliferation of political factions. The solution, for Madison, consists of transposing
into the political realm what already exists in the religious realm. To prevent
one faction from asserting dominance by wrongly claiming to act in the name
of the general will, it is imperative that there be in the state a "multiplicity
of interests," as there is in religion a "multiplicity of sects."[67] For the fewer
the factions, the greater the risk the rights of anyone who does not share the
ideas of the majority of the moment will be undermined. Political pluralism
is consequently the best way to protect the rights of minorities. This system,
which is of course imperfect, at least makes it possible to achieve the general
interest to the greatest degree possible, by means of the interplay of conflict
and rivalry between particular interests.[68] In this sense, then, the religious
diversity of eighteenth-century America helped give birth to the basic principle of American pluralism.

For Thomas Paine, the greatest English propagandist of American ideas,
the explanation was even simpler. It lay in the principle of equality on which,
in his view, the entire architecture of the American government was based.
Indeed, how could men belonging to different nations, speaking different languages, and devoted to rival religions understand one another? A traditionalist
like Burke "would have tortured his invention to discover how such a people
could be governed."[69] Paine, Burke's great contradictor, offers an empirical
and rational explanation. Religious tolerance, so striking to foreign observers in the late eighteenth century, was the product of two complementary
phenomena, one social, the other political. On the one hand, the difficult and
trying experience of colonizing a "wilderness" impelled the first immigrants
to cooperate among themselves, despite their religious divergences. On the
other, there were the direct effects of the political institutions of a country
that offered on a grand scale a representation of what Athens was "in minia-
ture."[70] This is why, Paine asserts, the largest denomination in the country,
that of the Presbyterians, had been unable to maintain for long its status as the
established church. In a democracy, he concluded, "no one sect is established
above another, and all men are equally citizens."[71] The American democratic
system had put an end to the religious monopoly of the successors of the first
Puritans.

FOR THE FRENCH OF THE ENLIGHTENMENT, American religion was
indeed an object of astonishment, the expression of a certain idea of progress
and modernity. The Quakers seemed to embody for them something like the

end of religion: a disenchanted religion, lacking hierarchy, devoid of any sacramental substance. This was what Voltaire and his disciples so much admired
as the "religion without priests." Conversely, the religion of the Savages offered an example of a religion of the Ancients acclimatized to the particular natural conditions of the New World. Between these two extremes was
situated the archaism of the Puritans whose confirmed fanaticism called to
mind another rhetorical figure of history: barbarism. While Puritans aroused
admiration for their strength of character and the purity of their way of life, it
was nonetheless their fanaticism that drew the most attention and discredited
them. Such fanaticism was frightening because it was systematic and universal; it targeted those who thought differently, who were driven into exile, as
well as the Indians, who were hounded to near extinction. But this fanaticism,
so disparaged and so contrary to the ideals of the Enlightenment, was observed and judged over the long term. It evolved; the Puritan regime shifted
imperceptibly toward a regime of tolerance that became widespread in the
late eighteenth century and much more vigorous than the tolerance that existed here and there in old Europe.

Tolerance was beneficial not only in moral terms; it also had material consequences, and this is what troubled the advocates of religious modernity. For
it facilitated commerce, which the Quakers of Philadelphia used and abused,
foreshadowing, in the view of the Romantics, the rise to power of a new form
of vice, unknown in old aristocratic societies: "commercial immorality," in
Chateaubriand's expression. This late critique of the effects of religious modernity anticipates in turn a historiographical shift fully adopted by the great
historians of the nineteenth century: the rehabilitation of Puritanism in the
name of a new religious conception of democracy.

2

The Rehabilitation of the Puritans

IN THE EIGHTEENTH CENTURY, *philosophes* such as Voltaire, Diderot, and Raynal, and scholars, essayists, and travelers such as Démeunier, Brissot, Volney, and La Rochefoucauld-Liancourt were skeptics often accused by their opponents of being deists or atheists. Religion occupied a negative place in Enlightenment thought because it was seen as an obstacle to the progress of humanity. Left to itself, religion could lead only to anarchy and to the bloody disorders of the wars of religion resulting in an endless struggle between the forces of "superstition" (Catholicism) and "enthusiasm" (Protestantism).

If civil society was not pacified by the introduction of new modes of behavior, if commerce and industry did not experience strong growth, and if political institutions were not able to impose respect for a regime of tolerance, the ideal of progress would be compromised. Montesquieu had shown the way in *The Spirit of Laws*: the sources of a modern political system even more virtuous and effective than the ancient Roman system lay in the complementary evolution of laws and mores softened by the moderating effects of commerce. Other writers tried to establish a connection between this modernity and

Protestantism. They produced a new political and moral history centered on the real or presumed effects of a unique Protestant spirit.

The Puritans: From Robertson to Tocqueville

The new Enlightenment historiography reached its apogee with the works of the Scottish historians and philosophers: David Hume, William Robertson, Adam Smith, and Adam Ferguson, each influenced in his own way by Montesquieu and Voltaire. The monumental *History of the Reign of the Emperor Charles the Fifth* (1769) by William Robertson was one of the first systematic histories of Europe. Its author was, according to J. G. A. Pocock, a "modernist," whose *View of the Progress of Society in Europe* anticipated the works of Marx and Braudel.[1] In Robertson's view, the advent of a modern society was inseparable from the progress of commerce and closely related to the development of cities and the replacement of a feudal aristocracy that was warlike, heroic, and licentious, with a bourgeoisie that was urbane, disciplined, morally austere, calculating, and cautious with its wealth.

Robertson is of particular interest here for his *History of America*, published in 1777 and translated into French the following year, which transposed to the New World a historical method first developed to explain the economic and social progress of the Old World.[2] A vehement adversary of monocausal interpretations of contemporary history, Robertson criticized writers such as Buffon and De Pauw because of the excessive importance they attributed to climate and other physical phenomena to demonstrate the alleged degeneration of the Savages of North America and their supposed "weakness of body" and "coldness of soul." This approach, according to Robertson, neglected the influence of moral and political causes that were decisive in explaining the aptitude for work, relations between the sexes, and the political organization of native peoples. In the last part of his *History of America*, published posthumously in 1796 on the basis of notes assembled by his son, Robertson speculated about the nature and political effects of the first English colonies in North America. He presented a particularly harsh assessment of the conduct of the first colonists of Jamestown, Virginia (1609–10), portrayed as "indigent adventurers," "dissipated, hopeless young men," "so profligate or desperate that their country was happy to throw them out as nuisances in society."[3] Unfit for work, pursuing phantom wealth (imaginary gold mines), unable to cooperate among themselves or to find the means of subsistence, the five hundred colonists of Jamestown were in six short months down to sixty, "reduced to such extremity of famine, as not only to eat the most nauseous and unwholesome roots and berries, but to feed on the bodies of . . . their companions who sunk under the oppression of such complicated distress."[4] The social conditions created by these first immigrants were nothing but a "horrible anarchy," unworthy of a modern nation, a regression of civilization to barbarism.

In contrast, Robertson discovered among the New England colonists an unusual cast of mind completely unlike that of the Virginia adventurers. What could have induced mostly well-off Englishmen to leave their native soil to "endure innumerable hardships under an untried climate, and in an uncultivated land, covered with woods, or occupied by fierce and hostile tribes of savages"?[5] Robertson answers the question by a process of elimination: they were not impelled to act by a desire to serve the nation, nor by a thirst for wealth. It took a much stronger principle to transform men into entrepreneurs in spite of themselves, able to withstand all the dangers that had undone the first colonists at Jamestown. Robertson defines this principle as "a spirit," the spirit of zeal and innovation characteristic of Puritanism, more simply the Puritan spirit.[6] Robertson was the first Enlightenment historian who set about rehabilitating the Puritans, making them into something more than mere fanatics: colonists able to succeed in their undertaking despite the obstacles, whose spirit bestowed a veritable "character" on the people of New England, and gave a "peculiar tincture" to the civil and religious institutions of the colonies.[7]

And yet, Robertson was fully aware of the Puritans' excesses: their reputed intolerance, their persecution of Quakers, Baptists, and other nonconformists, the cruelty of a penal system based on the Old Testament, and so on. But he saw the decisive point as the undeniable economic and political success of the Puritan establishments and the extraordinary spirit of mutual assistance that enabled enthusiasts to confront every danger so that they could better propagate their doctrine. It was indeed the Pilgrims—the Brownists,[8] first refugees in Holland and then settlers in North America—who most successfully established a preliminary form of modern democracy: "the levelling genius of fanaticism," abolishing all religious hierarchy in the name of a return to original Christianity.[9] The intrinsic democracy of this new ecclesiastical order had a decisive impact on the political institutions of the Plymouth colony. They were based on the idea of natural equality among men: any free man who was a member of the church was admitted into the supreme legislative body.[10] In the late 1620s the same spirit of innovation led the Puritans to exceed the rights granted them by the British crown in the Charter of the Massachusetts Bay Company. [11] "Animated with a spirit of innovation in civil policy as well as in religion; and by the habit of rejecting established usages in the one, they were prepared for deviating in the other."[12] As soon as they landed in New England, the Puritans disregarded the content of the charter and declared themselves to be free individuals united in society solely according to the principles of natural law—which gave them the freedom to choose the "mode of government" best suited to them and the laws "they deemed most conducive to general felicity." This declaration was manifestly illegal, but Charles I, happy to remove such turbulent men from his kingdom, was finally "disposed to connive at the irregularity of a measure which facilitated their departure."[13] A pattern was set: Americans did not hesitate to defy royal authority when it was contrary to their interests and, most important, they established a preliminary form of a regime based on popular sovereignty.

The rebellious spirit of the Puritans contained in embryonic form the political conditions for the War of Independence of which Robertson was able to witness only the early stages. Both cautious and prophetic, the Scottish historian asserted: "in whatever manner this unhappy contest may terminate, *a new order of things* must arise in North America."[14]

IN THE FIRST PART OF *Democracy in America*, published in 1835, Tocqueville reinvented and developed Robertson's argument in his own way.[15] Tocqueville was the first modern thinker to give explicit content to the new order of things anticipated by Robertson. Like most Enlightenment philosophers and historians, and unlike Joseph de Maistre, for whom America was an "infant in swaddling clothes" about which too little was known to be able to draw any conclusions, Tocqueville was convinced that the *character* of a nation was contained in embryo in its origins. "In a manner of speaking, the whole man already lies swaddled in his cradle."[16] Tocqueville's approach is to begin with the present and then to look as far back into American history as possible to discover the "point of departure" of modern America.[17]

Where does Tocqueville locate such a point of departure? At first he follows a historical chronology, noting that Virginia was the first English colony, settled in 1607. Like his English and Scottish predecessors, he acknowledges that these emigrants did not have a very good reputation. They were "men without resources or discipline," unscrupulous seekers of wealth, pursuing gold like modern conquistadors. The unhappy experience of these colonists, "not much above the lower classes of England," was accompanied by the early introduction of slavery, which "was to exert an immense influence on the character, laws, and entire future of the South." But this was not the real point of departure for what formed "the basis of the social theory of the United States." Tocqueville found this basis in the later Puritan colonization of New England. Unlike their Virginia predecessors, the Puritans did not come from the lower classes of the mother country; nor were they wealthy landowners, like some of the English who settled Virginia in the late seventeenth century. "Neither rich nor poor," they "belonged to the well-to-do classes," and most important, they were distinguished from the other colonizers because they were acting "in obedience to a purely intellectual need." They were pursuing an idea that had nothing to do with "improving their situation or enhancing their wealth," but was rather focused on the spiritual enterprise of ensuring the victory of the religious doctrine of the Levellers. The aims of this doctrine went beyond religion in the narrow sense and "coincided with the most absolute democratic and republican theories."[18] The true founders of the new order of things—the Pilgrims in Tocqueville's view—carried democracy with them to the New World. In a sense, they were doubly democratic, because of their social condition and because they professed democratic ideas.

Differentiating himself from the interpretations offered by French travelers of the late eighteenth century and from the ironic and mocking complaints Chateaubriand directed against the New England colonists, Tocqueville rehabilitated the Puritan adventure by emphasizing their "purely intellectual need."[19] Interestingly, he used the same historical sources as Robertson[20] and not surprisingly came to the same conclusion: The Puritans adopted "without debate and put into practice" the eminently democratic principle of the sovereignty of the people. "Free from all political prejudice," their democracy resembled that of ancient Greece. For example, in Connecticut all citizens were entitled to vote. Equality of wealth was "almost perfect," and, "*as in Athens*, matters affecting everyone's interests were discussed in public places and in general assemblies of citizens." These "ardent sectarians and impassioned innovators" succeeded in establishing democracy in the most natural way, because their religious ideas were inseparable from their political ideas. The *point of departure* identified by Tocqueville was not confined to a point in space or time; it was a theoretical point of departure, the "victory of an idea," or rather the harmony of two apparently contradictory ideas: "the spirit of religion" and "the spirit of liberty."[21]

Tocqueville agreed that the Puritans' conception of democracy was incomplete, pointing out that the early Puritans enacted "bizarre and even tyrannical laws," for example prohibiting the use of tobacco, forbidding long hair, and severely punishing (at least in theory) blasphemy, witchcraft, adultery, and "even social intercourse between unmarried individuals," as well as idleness, drunkenness, and the refusal to attend Sunday services.[22]

A FREQUENT MISTAKE, ONE THAT Tocqueville does not make, consists of mistaking political liberty for religious liberty and of picturing the Puritans as strong advocates of religious liberty. According to the historian John Murrin, this mistake is an integral part of one of the oldest American myths, namely, that the first New England colonists were fleeing religious persecution in England to establish a regime of religious liberty in North America. The myth does not stand up to empirical investigation, since the Puritans had a single overriding interest: to establish a genuine and durable religious orthodoxy. They succeeded brilliantly in New England, despite a few famous conflicts with supporters of rival religious orthodoxies such as Anne Hutchinson and Roger Williams, who were swiftly excommunicated and expelled from the colony. Punitive laws, arrests, and convictions, along with a few executions, served to terrorize dissenters, primarily Quakers and Baptists, and to hasten their move to more tolerant states such as Pennsylvania and New York.

At the same time, the Chesapeake Bay states of Maryland and Virginia quickly came under the domination of another religious orthodoxy that was introduced later but also proved influential because it was generously financed by the mother country: the Anglican Church. In 1743, nearly two-thirds of the residents of New England and the Chesapeake Bay region remained subject to the authority of a single religious establishment—Congregationalism in one region and Anglicanism in the other. In neither case was there true freedom of worship. The institutionalization of religious liberty was not made possible until much later, with the adoption of the Bill of Rights in 1791. A well-informed observer would have found it exceedingly difficult to detect a current of opinion favoring the free exercise of religion or the creation of a real separation between church and state.[23]

The absence of religious liberty did not prevent the unprecedented flowering of political liberty. The first Pilgrims founded this liberty on solemn pacts (covenants or compacts) entered into, they believed, with God's blessing. The most celebrated of these agreements was the Mayflower Compact, drawn up after a hazardous crossing of the Atlantic that took them not to the "northern parts of Virginia" (today New York) as they had initially intended, but to the harbor of Cape Cod. Rediscovered by Romantic historians who were passionately interested in historical origins, the Mayflower Compact was often described as an act of political sovereignty, a draft Constitution conceived for a colony destined for a radiant future. This is the complete text:

> In the name of God, Amen; we whose names are underwritten, the loyal subjects of our dread sovereign King James, having undertaken, for the Glory of God and advancement of the Christian faith and honour of our king and country, a voyage to plant the first colony in the northern parts of Virginia, do by these presents, *solemnly and mutually, in the presence of God and one of another, covenant and combine ourselves together into a civil body politic,* for our better ordering and preservation, and furtherance of the ends aforesaid; and by virtue hereof to enact, constitute, and frame, such *just and equal* laws, ordinances, acts, constitutions and offices, from time to time, as shall be thought most convenient *for the general good of the colony.* Unto which we promise all due submission and obedience (11 November 1620).[24]

It is important to understand that the founding compact of the first Protestant community in Plymouth, in which Tocqueville saw a genuine social contract along the lines dreamed up by Rousseau in the following century,[25] was really a civil pendant to earlier religious compacts signed by the Pilgrims. These covenants followed previous religious pacts, which I would characterize as "original covenants."

The first of these covenants were signed by Robert Browne's disciples, who advocated a radical break from the Church of England and were therefore known as "Separatists" or "Brownists." A covenant was a consensual and voluntary act whereby a community of worshipers decided to constitute themselves as a "true" church. Contrary to Anglican tradition, a church of this kind could not be created by an established ecclesiastical authority, decree, or an act of Parliament. It was a local, autonomous decision carried out by individuals who came together to form a sovereign congregation, the only body with the power to select and ordain its own pastors. Far from being open to all, the original covenants of the early Congregational churches were exclusive, valid only for confirmed believers.

How then were the authenticity and sanctity of the beliefs of a new Congregational church to be judged? It was a difficult question and the answers varied, although the goal remained the same: to bring the visible church of the community of worshipers as close as possible to the invisible church of the elect, that is, to increase the probability—with no certainty, of course—that the new congregation would be made up of "saints."[26] Robert Browne described in this way the original covenant leading to the formation of his church in Norwich:

> So a covenant was made. . . . There were certain chief pointes [of doctrine] proved unto [the future members of the church] by the scriptures, all which being particularlie rehersed unto them with exhortation, thei agreed upon them and pronounced their agreement to ech thing particularlie, saiing: to this we geve our consent.
>
> First therefore thei gave their consent to joine them selves to the Lord in one covenant and felloweshipp together and to keep and seek agrement under his lawes and government; and therefore did utterlie flee and avoide such like disorders and wickednes as was mencioned before.[27]

In Browne's Separatist argument, the Church of England was anything but a church, because it brought together a heterogeneous collection of pious and impious people, regenerate Christians and nonbelievers. Carried to extremes, Separatism led to the denunciation of other Protestants in unusually vehement terms. They were "dogs and Enchaunters, and Whoremongers, and Murderers, and Idolatours," who displayed their irreligion in "Atheisme and Machiavelisme on the one side, and publique Idolitrie, usuall blasphemie, swearing, lying, kylling, stealing, whoring, and all maner of impietie on the other side."[28]

The covenant with God that Browne described was relatively undemanding. It merely enumerated the doctrinal elements of the members' profession of faith. No evidence of inner authentic faith touched by grace was required. For the early Separatists, the presence of such a faith among the members of the congregation was not discernable. A pure gift of God, it could be known only by Him, and to claim otherwise would have meant contravening the very principle of predestination.[29] The Calvinism of the Puritans, however, was not a closed or predetermined system. The ways of the Lord were, of course, impenetrable, but the believer was permitted to "detect virtual signs of his election" on the basis of sustained declared faith, made manifest by a successful professional life in harmony with his vocation.[30]

Little is known about the original covenant that the Pilgrims from the Separatist community of Leiden made, except that it very probably followed the pattern invented by Robert Browne. Their church was a "company of the faithful," and their faith, attested by public confession and exemplary conduct, amounted, according to Edmund Morgan, simply to "acceptance of the truths of Christianity." Later covenants made in New England by other Puritan communities carried the search for external signs of probable election to extremes. For example, the members of the new churches of the Massachusetts Bay colony had to describe their slow progress toward a state of grace and sanctification by setting forth their doubts, their sins, the sincerity of their faith, their thorough knowledge of scripture, and their submission to and acceptance of the will of God. Certainty was not allowed; indeed, the best evidence that one was a member of the elect was one's very uncertainty about one's election.[31] The important thing for admission into a community of "saints" was to persuade one's peers that one had respected the terms of the covenant made with them under the auspices of Providence, by proclaiming one's faith publicly and supplying countless details of one's laborious path to sanctification.

The New England Puritans manifested some degree of originality by making the practice of religious covenanting more complex. Their covenants were not modest professions of faith along the lines of an old Anglo-Puritan practice first described by Robert Browne, but rather interminable critical narratives, subjected to inquisitorial examination by those who saw themselves as the elect, despite their doubts (those doubts being the very sign of their election).

The original covenants of a purely religious nature were followed by political contracts instituting systems of sovereignty, the prototype of which was the Mayflower Compact. These covenants displayed the spirit of liberty that so surprised Tocqueville and which he carefully distinguished from another essential aspect of the American character, the spirit of religion. The Puritans' spirit of liberty was practically unlimited, since it enabled them "to do what is just and good without fear," as John Winthrop asserted in a speech quoted by Tocqueville.[32] This explains the Puritans' marked tendency toward political innovation and their extraordinary "knowledge of government"[33] with respect to matters as varied as popular sovereignty, public education, and public welfare. Some emigrants, Tocqueville explained, did not hesitate to violate the founding charters of their colonies in order to assert their sovereignty, for example by choosing their own political leaders, drafting their own penal laws, and even deciding on questions of war and peace. In short, like the great legislators of antiquity, they legislated "as if answerable to God alone."

Political life was therefore intense: "real and active, wholly democratic and republican."[34] For Tocqueville this democracy of the Moderns, reinvented on New England soil, echoed the great myths of antiquity, since it "leapt full grown and fully armed from the middle of the old feudal society"[35]—like Athena the goddess of liberty, who had sprung fully armed from the head of Zeus.

The Pilgrim Fathers: Between Myth and Reality

Did Tocqueville's idyllic description of the New England political system correspond to the facts? Or was the French visitor mistaking his desires for realities in order to justify his theory of the point of departure, emphasizing the gap between semifeudal old Europe and new America, the quintessential experimental site for modern democracy? It would be more accurate to say that Tocqueville was somewhat prone to exaggeration, like most American historians of the time, beginning with the most renowned among them, George Bancroft.

The Mayflower Compact did not in fact describe the democracy Tocqueville imagined. Its signatories were a small group of forty-one "free" men (eighteen Pilgrims and twenty-three "strangers" out of a total of 102 passengers—women, children, and servants were excluded from the group of signatories). Considered in context, the Mayflower Compact was a circumstantial document intended to appease certain passengers who did not consider themselves under any obligation to remain in New England because the territory initially selected by the Virginia Company was located at the mouth of the Hudson. The compact bound together the members of a very heterogeneous colony made up of two distinct groups: "saints," whose motivations were above all religious, and "strangers," whose military, agricultural, and other skills were meant to facilitate the settling of the Pilgrims. When the Mayflower Compact promises just and equal laws for all, it is merely guaranteeing equal treatment for Pilgrims and adventurers to avoid any risk of mutiny. Rather than the founding document of a democracy unprecedented in the annals of humanity, the Mayflower Compact was primarily intended to maintain the cohesion of a group of immigrants at the moment they were planning to settle on bleak terrain for which they had no clearly established right of ownership.[36]

Ten years later, in 1630, when nearly one thousand Puritans[37] landed in North America to take possession of the Massachusetts Bay Company's land, there was nothing particularly democratic about the political contract binding them together. In accordance with a royal charter that defined the powers of the company, only about ten of the principal shareholders (freemen)[38] had the right to vote and could elect a governor and his deputies in a general assembly. John Winthrop fully shared this narrowly aristocratic conception of government. He believed the best possible government was a government "of the least part," which he desired to be "the wiser of the best."[39] This was somewhat at odds with what Tocqueville believed he had found in New England: "democracy such as antiquity had never dared to dream of."[40]

Yet some forms of "avowed republicanism"[41] finally arose, on the initiative of Winthrop and his assistants. For example, at the general assembly of October 19, 1631, Winthrop decided to expand the community of voters by adding all of the colony's male residents to the small number of shareholder voters— about one hundred people. In addition, these new electors could initiate legislative measures and appoint the members of the colony's executive council. But this practical experiment of democracy in action was of short duration, because another general assembly meeting a year later reversed course and declared that only members of the officially recognized church would have the right to vote.[42] This provoked vigorous protests from "highly respectable persons" who belonged to other churches: withholding the right to vote from them, they considered, meant they were deprived of the fundamental rights of Englishmen.[43] The province of Massachusetts, in the view of Chief Justice John Marshall of the Supreme Court, was less democratic in the Puritan period than the mother country: "The rigid adherence of Massachusetts to withholding the privilege of a freeman from all who dissented from the majority in any religious opinion could not fail to generate perpetual discontents."[44]

In short, the Puritans' political revolution was rather modest: as Bancroft remarked, the colony moved in one short year from an "elective aristocracy" to a "sort of theocracy."[45] The change was nonetheless real; freemen were no longer only the rich, that is, shareholders or owners of Massachusetts Bay Company land, but also colonists with no resources who contributed nothing but the sincerity of their faith. In this way, a simple commercial enterprise gradually changed into a small republic of believers.[46]

From 1634 on, the freemen no longer participated directly in decision making in the colony's general assembly; they were represented by elected deputies who alone had the right to appoint the governor and his assistants and to pass the necessary legislation to govern the colony. Was this new representative regime a theocracy in the full sense of the term? Yes, if theocracy means controlling the opinion of the faithful, since dissenters were not tolerated in New England. No, if theocracy means government by clergy, as pastors had no political power. In Winthrop's time they were not permitted to run as candidates in elections, nor could they exercise the slightest political or civil responsibility.[47]

In other words, the New England Puritans invented neither republic, nor democracy, nor the principle of popular sovereignty, because their definition of the electorate remained too restrictive and too imbued with religious convictions. Their great originality lay in their capacity for innovation and experimentation. "In their hands," wrote Tocqueville, "political principles, laws, and human institutions seem to be malleable things, capable of being shaped and combined at will."[48] This did not prevent the Puritan colonies from coming under the control of metropolitan Britain forty years later. Indeed, the American Puritans had never challenged the sovereignty of the English king. Their power existed by default, until royal charters imposed by the mother country clarified the situation. It therefore cannot be argued that the great principles of the Declaration of Independence of 1776 or the Federal Constitution of 1787 already existed in embryo in the political experiment of the early Puritans. Their *spirit of liberty*, very real and vigorously asserted, represented only an ephemeral moment in the history of New England.

A "New Grammar" of Liberty

It was not until after 1776 that true popular sovereignty made its appearance in America with the creation of thirteen independent republics and the adoption of constitutional conventions that established new political rules, soon ratified by town meetings. In June 1779, for example, the Massachusetts legislature called on all men twenty-one and older to form a convention to adopt the articles of a new constitution that was later to be adopted by two-thirds of the same electorate.[49] According to Thomas Paine, these new electoral practices revealed the birth of a "new grammar" of liberty. The constitutions of the new American states "were to liberty what a grammar is to language."[50]

This new grammar was based on readily observable facts connected to the very origin of political power. Everything is simple in America, Paine asserts: "We have no occasion to roam for information into the obscure field of antiquity, nor hazard ourselves upon conjecture. We are brought at once to see the point of seeing government begin, as if we had lived in the beginning of time. The real volume, not of history, but of facts, is directly before us, unmutilated by contrivance, or the errors of tradition."[51] Paine's argument contains no Puritan mythology. If there was a "bible" at the origin of each of the thirteen American states, it was a political document, an artifact produced by delegates of the people meeting in a constitutional convention, such as the 1776 Pennsylvania convention that Paine analyzes in detail.

How did this new grammar of liberty work? Paine provides a vivid description in the second part of *The Rights of Man*, published in 1792 and dedicated to Lafayette:

> Here we see a regular process—a government issuing out of a constitution, formed by the people in their original character, and that constitution serving, not only as an authority, but as a law of controul to the government. It was the political bible of the state. Scarcely a family was without it. Every member of the government had a copy; and nothing was more common, when any debate arose on the principle of a bill, or on the extent of any species of authority, than for the members to take the printed constitution out of their pocket, and read the chapter with which such matter in debate was connected.[52]

For the generation of the Founding Fathers, as Paine's writings attest, political liberty was not the invention of the Ancients—in this case, the Puritans. It was, in the full sense of the term, a liberty of the Moderns that could be dated precisely to 1776, the outset of the War of Independence. This liberty was the result of the progress of natural reason, and as Hamilton maintained in *Federalist* No. 22, "The fabric of American empire ought to rest on the solid basis of *the consent of the people* . . . that pure, original fountain of all legitimate authority."[53]

American political thought of the late eighteenth century was in complete harmony with the spirit of the Enlightenment. *The Federalist Papers*, the most influential political work of the time, frequently mentions Plutarch, Montesquieu, Grotius, Locke, Hume, and Mably, and completely omits accounts of the Puritans, although they were known and available. The progress of philosophy, deism, and reason had finally overshadowed the old fantasies of Puritanism. The federal Constitution of 1787, ratified by the requisite majority of nine states on June 21, 1788, was indeed a daughter of the Enlightenment, a constitution without God.

THE REDISCOVERY OF PURITANISM in the first half of the nineteenth century was closely linked to a thorough critique of the excesses of Enlightenment philosophy. This critique was particularly intense during the presidential elections of 1796. John Adams, elected that year, summed up the political feelings of the time: from 1778 to 1785, the nations of Europe appeared "to be advancing by slow but sure Steps towards an Amelioration of the condition of Man, in Religion and Government, in Liberty, Equality, Fraternity, Knowledge, Civilization, and Humanity." But everything changed with the excesses of the Terror, which set Europe back "for at least a Century, if not many Centuries."[54] Many American historians and essayists, of course, made similar arguments, vehemently denouncing the "deranged principles" of the French *philosophes* that precipitated France into the fatal experiment of Jacobinism, with its deplorable consequences: the abolition of religion, the persecution of priests, the prohibition of all belief, and even worse, the worship of a "Prostitute" called goddess, Reason.[55]

In France, the same criticism was not confined to the advocates of the Counterrevolution. It was also expressed with more finesse by a major liberal figure such as Guizot. Deploring the failure of the French Revolution, Guizot proposed to turn for inspiration to an unjustly neglected past. The considerable progress accomplished by the human spirit, he explained in the fourteenth lecture of his *General History of Civilization in Europe* (1828–1830), made the eighteenth century one of the greatest centuries in history—indeed, probably the century that had contributed the most to the progress of humanity. But, Guizot went on, the course of history had been perverted, so that "the absolute power exercised at this period by the human mind corrupted it, and it entertained an illegitimate aversion to the subsisting state of things, and to all opinions which differed from the prevailing one—an aversion which led to error and tyranny."[56] This provides a glimpse of a novel philosophical history that grants tradition a privileged place while not denying the achievements of the recent past. Guizot, like Tocqueville, who followed his lectures with keen interest, gave pride of place to historical continuity and thereby returned to a tradition initiated by Burke and continued by liberals such as Mme de Staël and Benjamin Constant. In their view, the Reformation was the source of all human progress; it reconciled religion and Enlightenment, and served as an underlying principle that explained the progress of European civilization from Luther to the first phase of the French Revolution.[57]

By dissociating religion and Enlightenment, the French Revolution in its Jacobin phase momentarily interrupted this marvelous historical continuity. But like all general phenomena identified by Guizot, this continuity would necessarily resurface sooner or later, in a France at peace that would at last realize the great synthesis of tradition and revolution.

EARLY-NINETEENTH-CENTURY historiography questioned the very idea of the Enlightenment. The excesses of the French Revolution, the extravagances of the cult of Reason, and the ravages of the Napoleonic wars impelled historians to rediscover (and often to reinvent) a glorious medieval past. Romantic historiography praised the virtues of religion, the irrational, and mysticism while defending the cult of heroes and honoring great ancestors: the Germans, the Saxons, and the Gauls.

Romantic historians in the United States, most of whom had studied in Europe, exhibited similar tendencies and patterns of thought. Rediscovering their own great ancestors—the first English emigrants—they rehabilitated Puritanism at the same time. Fortunately, the democratic and republican passions of the Puritans enabled historians to reconcile the political progress of the Enlightenment with the anachronisms of a religion of enthusiasts and fanatics. In dividing the Puritan spirit into a "spirit of religion" and a "spirit of liberty," Tocqueville reasoned like his contemporary George Bancroft, who had just published the first volume of *History of the United States* (1834), one year before the first volume of *Democracy in America*. Had Tocqueville read Bancroft's manuscript before he finished his own? Did the two have discussions? There is no evidence, although Tocqueville did later correspond with Bancroft. For my purposes, the essential point is the similarity in their approaches, derived from the same historical sources.

Like Tocqueville, Bancroft rehabilitated the Puritans, but he was more rhapsodic and he paved the way for a new American patriotism based on the cult of ancestors. The Puritans had not, of course, overthrown empires like the heroes of antiquity. But they had done something even better by scattering on the soil of a virgin country "the seminal principles of republican freedom and national independence." And, convinced of the power and correctness of their ideals, "they enjoyed, in anticipation, the thought of their extending influence, and the fame which their grateful successors would award to their virtues."[58]

Bancroft overthrew the very foundations of American Enlightenment historiography: the inventors of political democracy were not the Founding Fathers but the Pilgrims, whose history was made up of "events by which Providence leads to ends that human councils had not conceived."[59] From this perspective, the engine of history, the "mysterious influence" which "enchains the destinies of states ... [and] often deduces the greatest events from the least commanding causes,"[60] is not, as Thomas Paine and the authors of *The Federalist Papers* imagined, human will liberated from the fetters of old political and religious traditions. It is rather the slow providential movement of the Reformation that, by detaching the human spirit from religious despotism, made possible the propagation of the doctrines of liberty from the recently discovered continent to distant and even newer countries: Chile, Oregon, Liberia. These doctrines, of which Enlightenment France was a "proselyte," disturbed all the monarchies of Europe, "by awakening the public mind to restless action, from the shores of Portugal to the palaces of the czars."[61]

It would be hard to find a better description of the ineluctable march of humanity toward democracy. For Bancroft, as for Tocqueville, the Puritan point of departure of American democracy was only one link in the great providential chain, although it had a different meaning for each of the two writers. Bancroft, like Guizot and Quinet before him, gave the Reformation a central position. Tocqueville minimized its import, although he did agree that Protestantism accelerated the march of equality, because it "held that all men are *equally* equipped to find their way to heaven."[62] But it is clear that, for Tocqueville, equality of conditions, "the original fact from which each particular fact seemed to derive," preceded the Reformation. It went back to the "Crusades and the wars with England" (that weakened the nobles and brought about the division of their estates), the establishment of municipal institutions (which "introduced democratic liberty into the heart of feudal monarchy"), the invention of printing (which equalized the conditions for the acquisition of knowledge), and the invention of firearms, whereby "peasant and noble became equal on the field of battle."[63]

Tocqueville's complex and nuanced conception of Providence is not confined to any particular religion. It is the result of an irresistible historical process—a process as irresistible as the waters of the biblical Flood, indeed so irresistible that Tocqueville feels that he is "in the grip of a kind of religious terror."[64] Tocqueville's democratic providentialism does not close off the future, but opens up a multitude of possibilities requiring constant vigilance, because it is impossible to halt the march of equality: "We must learn," Tocqueville writes, "to consider the future with a firm and open gaze. Instead of attempting to erect useless dikes, let us rather build the sacred ark that will carry the human race on this boundless ocean."[65]

TOCQUEVILLE'S RELIGIOUS SENSIBILITY, remarkable for a man who admitted he had suddenly lost his faith at the age of sixteen,[66] is inseparable from a philosophical approach intended to be both comprehensive and objective, able to evaluate human progress from above, like God himself, whose "eye necessarily encompasses all things." To this end, Tocqueville abandons his aristocratic prejudices in order to get a better grasp of the paradox of an immanent justice that lowers the great to elevate the poor and the ignorant. Deploring the spectacle of democratic uniformity and mediocrity, afflicted with a vision of "this innumerable host of similar beings, among whom no one stands out or stoops down," Tocqueville concedes that from the point of view of the creator of the universe, the prosperity of the majority requires social justice, that is, "the greater well-being of all." Tocqueville forces himself to side, all things considered, with Providence: "What seems decadence to me is therefore progress in [God's] eyes; what pains me pleases him. Equality is less lofty, perhaps, but more just, and its justice is the source of its grandeur and beauty." And he decides to internalize the perspective of the "Almighty Eternal Being" by putting himself in His place: "I am doing my best," he writes in the conclusion to the second part of *Democracy in America*, "to enter into this point of view, which is that of the Lord, and trying to consider and judge human affairs from this perspective."[67]

At once historians, philosophers, and demiurges, Bancroft and Tocqueville did not seek to rehabilitate the Puritans in the same way. Bancroft intended to celebrate the heroism of the Pilgrims and thereby invented a patriotic ancestor cult. Tocqueville was less lavish in his praise but nonetheless also exaggerated the political importance of the Puritans and their covenants. Tocqueville's point of departure was arbitrary: he was aware that the first colonization of North America had been carried out by the adventurers who settled in Virginia. On the basis of that experience, he might have considered another point of departure: a political tradition detached from religion that was deeply inegalitarian, aristocratic in its values, and antidemocratic because it was in favor of slavery. He may well have been tempted by the idea of a dual narration of the political history of the United States—Puritan and egalitarian on one side and Anglican and inegalitarian on the other.[68] It would no doubt have provided a better explanation for the great tragedy of the second half of the nineteenth century, the Civil War. But it would also have complicated the task of a philosophical historian who was attempting to innovate by connecting apparently very different phenomena: Puritanism, religious liberty, and the political and social equality of a people in the process of formation. Only the political and religious experience of New England was able to nourish his fertile imagination, because of the strong religious impressions it created, and because it "breathe[d] the air of antiquity and [was] redolent of a kind of biblical fragrance."[69]

3

Evangelical Awakenings

IN THE PRECEDING CHAPTER, I attempted to show that the birth of American democracy could not simply be inferred from a narrowly defined Puritan "point of departure," as argued by Tocqueville. The Puritans did not understand "democracy" as we understand it today, and it is the political experience of the elites of the revolutionary period that gave the United States its truly republican character and its modern national identity.

The most prominent Founding Fathers—Thomas Jefferson, John Adams, George Washington, James Madison—were not very religious (most of them were deists) and their primary concern was not to build a "City on a Hill" but a more prosperous nation, once the break with England was consummated. The religious past of the United States and the heroic behavior of the New England Puritans held little interest for them. What mattered was the glorification of a heroic present[1] and the revival of a nonreligious, post-Puritan British past. The rights the Americans claimed at the beginning of the War of Independence were the *rights of Englishmen*: the right to representation (no taxation without representation); the right to a fair trial; protection from arbitrary imprisonment in accordance with the long-standing principle of habeas corpus. American national identity was at the time a fragile construction that came out of the War of Independence, a republican artifice based on classical models, with new heroes—the Founding Fathers—a new separation of powers, new procedures for the creation of political institutions (constitutional conventions), all culminating in the federal Constitution of 1787.[2] But as John Murrin has written, this "constitutional roof" lacked the support of solid "national walls."[3] Those walls were gradually built in the course of the nineteenth century by a new political class that was able to strengthen American democracy by encouraging the great mass of white male citizens to participate in the political life of the new federal Union. This political democratization was inseparable from the democratization of religion, which was marked by a huge growth of evangelicalism throughout the country, reaching the most remote regions of a constantly expanding frontier. The idea of a Christian nation is a later myth propagated by Romantic historians such as George Bancroft, evangelical preachers seeking massive conversions, and politicians who were quick to condemn the atheism or the alleged Jacobinism of Jefferson's supporters.

The Great Awakenings

The origin of American evangelicalism goes back to the first Great Awakening initiated in 1734 by Jonathan Edwards (1703–1758), preaching in Northampton, Massachusetts, and the most brilliant British evangelical, George Whitefield (1714–1770), on his repeated tours of Georgia, Pennsylvania, and New England. Jonathan Edwards's sermons had two major themes. The first, with egalitarian implications, was that every man, even the least educated, had a spiritual sense more acute than "all the knowledge of philosophers or statesmen." This spiritual sense enabled them to apprehend the spiritual light emanating directly from God and to appreciate its "ineffable beauty." This experience of mystic conversion undergone by hundreds of the young preacher's parishioners was supposed to "reach the bottom of the heart and change its nature."[4] Edwards's second major theme, found in a series of sermons titled *A History of the Work of Redemption*, was the epic and age-old battle between the forces of Christ and the forces of Satan—a battle that was ended by the redemptive force of the Gospel whose message had to be spread at all costs, with emphasis on its eschatological aspect: the certain defeat of the Antichrist and the imminent advent—1,260 years after the founding of the papacy—of Christ's millennial Kingdom.[5]

George Whitefield, for his part, had perfected a new type of "Methodist" preaching,[6] open to all and generally conducted outdoors in public meeting places: markets, parks, public squares, coal pits, or large pastures made available to the crowds. Whitefield sought primarily to reach the lower classes. It was said that he was able to hold the attention for an entire day of as many as thirty thousand worshipers in the great cities of England. He achieved great success using the same method of preaching in seven visits to North America beginning in 1738. Whitefield played directly to the emotions of his audience. He began all his sermons with the ritual question: "Are you saved?" Unable to answer in the affirmative, troubled by the question, filled with a vague feeling of guilt, his audience was ready to listen. Whitefield had the habit of first speaking about the dark side of a life of temptation and sin, and then describing the torments of Hell in such striking terms that his audience was reduced to tears. He then focused on the need for sincere repentance and ended his sermon by speaking of the ineffable joys of a new birth marked by the acceptance of the grace of God. An unquestionably brilliant and charismatic orator, Whitefield was a veritable entrepreneur of religion who was able to transform the art of preaching into a magnificent theatrical display. For that reason, he might be considered the spiritual ancestor of such great swayers of crowds as Charles Finney in the nineteenth century and Billy Sunday, Billy Graham, Robert Schuller, Pat Robertson, Jerry Falwell, and Rick Warren in the twentieth. Televangelism and preaching to crowds in gigantic megachurches are merely updated versions of an oratorical art developed in England in the middle of the eighteenth century.[7]

Whitefield's preaching had a decisive influence on the Wesley brothers, the founders of the Methodist Church, who understood, as he did (along with many Baptist imitators), that an effective religion at the time of the first industrial revolution could no longer be a formal religion with rigid traditions and a learned doctrine inaccessible to the masses. The new faith was a *religion of the heart*, based on an adult conversion experience. The conversion of the Wesley brothers was in this respect exemplary. On Pentecost Sunday, May 21, 1738, Charles Wesley suddenly felt a "strange palpitation of heart" that led to his writing a famous hymn:

> Outcasts of men, to you I call
> Harlots, and publicans, and thieves!
> He spreads his arms to embrace you all;
> Sinners alone His grace receives:

No need of him the righteous have;
He came the lost to seek and save.[8]

Three days later, his elder brother John had a comparable experience during a visit to the religious community of Aldersgate Street in London. A few minutes after listening to a reading of Luther's "Preface to the Epistle to the Romans," John Wesley experienced his true conversion that traditionally marks the origin of the Methodist faith: "I felt my heart strangely warmed. I felt I did trust in Christ, Christ alone for salvation, and an assurance was given me, that he had taken away *my* sins, even *mine*, and saved *me* from the law of sin and death."[9]

DOCTRINALLY, THE PREACHERS OF the First Great Awakening were not all Arminians, that is, critics of the Calvinist doctrine of predestination. Jonathan Edwards and George Whitefield, for example, remained close to Calvinism in the sense that they did not believe that divine grace (and hence the possibility of salvation) was given to all men. For the Wesley brothers, in contrast, saving grace had universal reach: it applied to all men, even the most depraved, provided only that they acknowledge their sins. It was therefore impossible to imagine that God, who is love, could have determined in advance the fate of all men by distinguishing the elect from the damned, unless one subscribed to what the Wesley brothers called the "horrible decrees" of Calvinism.[10] Their message was of a different kind. It was a message of love, regularly repeated in *The Arminian Magazine*, published by John Wesley from 1778 on. The argument was impeccably logical: since God is love and that love is universal, "it necessarily follows that God intends salvation for the whole world."[11] The lived experience of a new birth was the demonstration of a possible dialogue between God and his creatures. All the evangelical preacher needed to do was to stimulate the imagination of the faithful by showing them the possibility of this kind of saving exchange. And, from 1771 onward, this is what Methodist missionaries sent to North America proceeded to do.[12]

THE EVANGELICAL REVIVAL OF the early nineteenth century can only be understood in the context of the democratization of religion in the United States.[13] This democratization had an immediate consequence usually ignored by historians of the nineteenth century: a rejection of the orthodoxy of the major established churches, and especially a challenge to the very principle of predestination that was so dear to the Puritans and their direct heirs. It is this theological particularity that has made the history of the relations between religion and politics in the United States so complex—a history made up of breaks and continuity, doctrinal purity and political accommodation, institutional consolidation and fragmentation, religious battles and great ecumenical movements, rigid orthodoxies and charismatic revivals.

Of all the contemporary forms of American religiosity, evangelicalism is probably the least understood. The proliferation of churches and sects creates confusion and American political leaders who call themselves born-again Christians, such as George W. Bush, are often taken for Puritans or fundamentalists. But they are neither. Evangelicalism in the United States is not a pacified and democratized form of Puritanism, nor the radical expression of a new millenarianism. Nor does it represent a marginal phenomenon. And it deserves something better than the mockery of French observers so facilely expressed in the travel narratives of the Duke de La Rochefoucauld-Liancourt, the Marquise de La Tour du Pin, and her English counterpart, Fanny Trollope.

Solidly rooted in the American landscape by the middle of the nineteenth century, punctuated by cycles of exuberant revivals, evangelicalism became the most common and banal form of American Protestantism.

> [Revivals] have become, if I may so speak, a constituent part of the religious system of our country. Not a year has passed without numerous instances of their occurrence, though at some periods they have been more powerful and prevalent than at others. They have the entire confidence of the great body of evangelical Christians throughout our country. There exists, indeed, a diversity of opinion as to the proper means of promoting them.... But ... all, or nearly all, agree that such a revival is an inestimable blessing: so that, he who should oppose himself to revivals, *as such*, would be regarded by most of our evangelical Christians as, *ipso facto*, an enemy to spiritual religion itself.[14]

The success of these repeated revivals can be precisely measured. It has been estimated that in 1850, for example, Methodist and Baptist churches were three times more numerous than the places of worship of the old Congregationalist, Presbyterian, and Episcopalian communities. But the number of churches is deceptive: it does not reveal the real scope of a wave of enthusiasm able to operate outside any religious enclosure, because of the new practice of camp meetings assembling thousands of worshippers for one or more days to listen to an itinerant preacher. The growth of evangelicalism should therefore be measured by people rather than church buildings. In 1850, there were ten times as many Methodist preachers as there were Congregational ministers; the Freewill Baptists, a small sect of the Baptist movement, trained as many ministers as the Episcopal Church, and the Disciples of Christ produced as many preachers as the Presbyterian Church. A recent study estimates that approximately ten million Americans, 40 percent of the total population, were reached by the evangelical revival.[15] Expanding rapidly, in 1813, the Baptists had 2,633 places of worship, 2,142 preachers, and 204,185 worshippers—that is, ten times what they had at the outset of the American Revolution. In 1840, the most dynamic of the evangelical churches, the Methodist Church, had nearly one million members and 9,752 preachers; that is, nearly as many as the total number of postal employees in the territory of the Union.[16] This was indeed a tidal wave that deserves explanation.

One way of understanding evangelicalism is to see it as the result of a social transformation—the religious conversion of those who did not accept Calvinist predestination and could not have been "saints" in the Puritan sense of the term. Common people no longer accepted the arrogance and aristocratic pretensions of gentlemen. The democratization of political life, the proliferation of cheap newspapers reflecting all viewpoints, the great mobility of labor, and the rapid conquest of the West combined to end the social control of small urban communities. Men were free to change jobs, workplaces, and religion. Since the Declaration of Independence they had known they were "created equal," and, in the words of the Methodist preacher "Crazy" Lorenzo Dow, they couldn't see why they shouldn't have the right to "think, and judge, and act for [themselves]" in matters of religion. It was the fashion to denounce traditional religious elites, often compared to the scribes and Pharisees of the New Testament. The most radical Boston Republicans, such as Benjamin Austin, advised the artisans and small farmers of Massachusetts to give up all respect for the "lawyers or priests" who had contempt for the dignity of the people and threatened freedom of expression, if not freedom of conscience itself.[17]

THE SECOND GREAT AWAKENING was unquestionably populist in character: strongly marked by the republican rhetoric of Paine and Jefferson, this revival entailed the rejection of all hierarchy and religious orthodoxy. It also facilitated a challenge to certain religious truths previously taken for granted. Evangelicals, as noted previously, did not believe in predestination. Or rather, they believed that *all* men, without exception, could be saved as long as they experienced as adults a moment of conversion. Such a belief necessarily provided a release from the anxieties expressed by their Calvinist fathers (or themselves in their youth).

The experience of a sudden conversion was sufficient to establish an unshakable faith disconnected from the old precepts, tiresome declarations of faith, and laborious recitations of belief before an audience of certified ecclesiastical authorities. Everything now became simple, clear, blindingly true, as illustrated by the remarks of Henry Alline, who had been brought up in the strictest Calvinist orthodoxy but was willing to sever his religious roots to join a Baptist church. Transported by divine love, he said, his soul had been "ravished with a divine ecstasy beyond any doubts or fears, or thoughts of being . . . deceived."[18] A Presbyterian farmer named Abbott similarly rejected the Calvinism of his adolescence in a heroic moment of conversion to Methodism: " 'Why do you doubt? Is not Christ all-sufficient? Is he not able? Have you not felt his blood applied?' I then sprang upon my feet, and cried out, not all the devils in hell, nor all the predestinarians on earth, should make me doubt; for I know that I was converted: at that instant I was filled with unspeakable raptures of joy."

Another convert expressed the same astonishment and the same jubilant exuberance when a Methodist preacher explained to him the falsity of a system of predestination as unjust as it was arbitrary in its mysterious selection of the elect: "Why, then, I can be saved! I have been taught that only a part of the race could be saved, but if this man's singing be true, all may be saved."[19]

The evangelical passions of the nineteenth century should therefore be understood as the expression of an anti-Calvinist *revolt*, as Nathan Hatch has convincingly demonstrated in his book on the democratization of American Christianity. These passions were propagated by churches that are now prosperous—such as the Baptists, Methodists, and Unitarians—and other "unevangelical sects" such as "Hicksite Quakers, Swedenborgians, Tunkers or Dunkers, Shakers. . ."[20] not to mention the very special evangelicalism of the readers of the *Book of Mormon* transcribed on golden tablets supposedly discovered by the prophet Joseph Smith Jr. in 1827.[21]

Beneath a surface of great institutional cacophony, the evangelical preaching of the Second Great Awakening articulated some simple truths that guaranteed its success and duration. It offered an unprecedented experience of democratization of religion "from below": itinerant preachers with little or no training emphasized spontaneity, hymns, dance, trances, public confession, and cries of joy and glossolalia. The great political ferment of the Enlightenment and the disorders of the American Revolution had weakened old political and religious hierarchies. No civil or religious authority was now in a position to censure the religious experiences inspired by a new generation of traveling preachers.

There was vigorous competition among the new religious entrepreneurs, particularly because no synod, bishop, or central theological school existed that could establish order among the explosion of vocations, the diversity of the subject matter preached, and the fluidity of beliefs. Each new church had its heroes: Elias Smith, Barton Stone, and Alexander Campbell, founders of Christian Connection and Disciples of Christ; Francis Asbury, Lorenzo Dow, and Charles Finney, the major evangelical reformers of the Methodist Church; John Leland, the most dynamic of the Baptist preachers; Richard Allen, founder of the African Methodist Church; William Miller, founder of the Adventist Church; Brigham Young, the most influential Mormon of the Church of Latter Day Saints, and so on.

The central idea in this period of religious renewal was that faith no longer had to be regulated: enthusiasm—guided, of course, by preachers—replaced the formalized creeds, rituals, and commentaries of learned theology. Simple knowledge of the Bible, with no mediation by an interpreter recognized or certified by religious authorities, was considered sufficient. *Sola scriptura* was the leitmotif of the time, and everything that derived from exegesis based on knowledge of the languages of the Bible and a rational and critical reading of the Old and New Testaments was consigned to the attic of stale ideas from a predemocratic age. The proliferation of mystical experiences—trance, ecstasy, and trembling—fervent attention to apocalyptic texts, and literal interpretation of Biblical passages presented as absolute truths were the new forms of a religious eclecticism unprecedented in American history.

"A Cheese for Jefferson"

The *spirit of liberty* was now considered even more inseparable from the *spirit of religion* than it had been at the time of the Puritans. Barton Stone, for example, a former Presbyterian preacher and one of the initiators of the Cane Ridge Revival in Kentucky, vehemently denounced all established churches in the name of "Gospel Liberty" and accepted only the name "Christian" for his denomination. He experienced his break with the Presbyterian Church as a veritable declaration of independence and he claimed to be so imbued with the spirit of liberty that he "could not hear the name of British or Tories, without feeling a rush of blood through the whole system."[22]

Despite his deism and irreligion, Thomas Jefferson remained the major political reference for the new evangelical preachers, in part because he had written the Declaration of Independence, but primarily because he had defended the Baptists of Virginia against the state's established Anglican Church. His bill to establish religious liberty in Virginia, adopted in 1786, earned him grateful recognition from evangelical preachers struggling against established churches in Virginia and well beyond. For example, the small Baptist community of Cheshire, Massachusetts—a state dominated by Federalists who supported John Adams and the maintenance of an established Congregational Church—decided to hold a public celebration of Jefferson's victory over Adams in the presidential election of 1800. With this in mind, Baptist farmers got together to make a colossal cheese weighing over twelve hundred pounds from the milk of nine hundred "republican" cows as a gift for the new occupant of the White House. The journey of the Mammoth Cheese on a carriage pulled by six horses took more than a month, and it was delivered to its illustrious recipient as planned on the morning of January 1, 1802.[23] The reward was sizable for Jefferson, since it crowned years of effort in support of religious liberty. It also demonstrated he was not the dangerous atheist so frequently disparaged by his political adversaries during the 1800 presidential campaign. He was the friend of religion, particularly of minority and oppressed religions.

This display of sympathy put an end, once and for all, to the vicious propaganda of Adams's supporters who had not hesitated to accuse the great patriot of every possible and imaginable impiety. President Timothy Dwight of Yale College, for example, who had a reputation for delivering Congregational sermons of high quality, had warned his compatriots against the candidacy of a man who, if elected, would not fail to institute a "Jacobin regime" with frightful consequences: "the Bible cast into a bonfire, the vessels of the sacramental supper borne by an ass in public procession, and our children ... chanting mockeries against God ... [to] the ruin of their religion, and the loss of their souls."[24] The publishers of a Federalist newspaper in Hudson, New York, went even further when they predicted that the election of the "infidel Jefferson" would certainly bring about the death of religion, because "some infamous prostitute, under the title of the Goddess of Reason, will preside over the Sanctuaries now devoted to the principles of the Most High."[25] The great question, according to another Federalist newspaper, the *Gazette of the United States*, was: "Shall I continue in allegiance to **God—and a religious president** [John Adams]; or impiously declare for **Jefferson—and no God!!!**"[26]

The majority of voters chose Jefferson to succeed Adams, and the victory was due in large part to the votes of evangelicals among the common people who considered themselves bullied by the Federalist elites associated with established churches.

THESE HEROIC BATTLES BETWEEN religion and irreligion, established churches and the new sects of born-again Christians, were soon forgotten with the growth of evangelicalism, which was dominant from the 1840s on in the Middle States, the South, and the new territories of the West. The small sects had become dominant churches. But that did not deter European visitors from describing in great detail the religious practices that were so different from those they knew in their home countries and so contrary to the hierarchy and rituals of the Catholic Church in France and the Anglican Church in England.

The Marquise de La Tour du Pin and her husband, contemporaries of Talleyrand and of the Duke de La Rochefoucauld-Liancourt, who like them emigrated to America after the fall of the French monarchy, bought a small farm near Albany, New York, where they lived happily from 1794 to 1796. Their stay gave them the opportunity to venture into the forest where, like Chateaubriand, they encountered Indians and Quakers settled on a large isolated farm. Invited by the Quakers into a large room, the Marquise was astonished to discover a beautifully made floor on which were set "lines of copper nails, shining with polish, their heads so well buried in the wood they were level with it."[27] What could be the purpose of this curious arrangement? She heard the sound of a bell, doors opened, and fifty young women entered from one side of the room and fifty young men from the other.

> I noticed then that the women stood on the lines of nails, taking care to let not even the tips of their toes pass beyond them. They remained motionless until the woman sitting in the armchair gave a sort of groan or shout which was neither speech nor chant. Then they all changed places, so I concluded that that rather stifled cry must have been some form of

command. After several manoeuvres, they again stood still and the old woman muttered a fairly long passage in a language which was quite unintelligible to me, but in which I thought I caught a few English words. After this, they left in the same order as they had entered.[28]

The interest of this excerpt from the Marquise's memoirs lies in its juxtaposition with another passage describing an encounter with squaws. Exoticism is not where one would expect it. The Indians seem to her to be perfectly rational beings, since they speak English well enough and engage in commercial transactions that Ricardo would have approved of: woven baskets in exchange for a "jar of buttermilk."[29] The Quakers, in contrast, although they are all colonists of English origin, symbolize a return to a state of barbarism that creates a distance, a mystery, and a sense of discomfort between the observer and the observed. Their movements are incomprehensible, guided by lines traced on the floor like so many arcane signs; their inarticulate language is unintelligible; their hospitality, unlike that of the Indians, is so lacking in warmth that the best thing to do is to get away from this bizarre sectarian group as soon as possible.

The true savage of the story, paradoxically, is a famous visitor, the Duke de La Rochefoucauld-Liancourt, who stayed with the Marquise and was invited to meet notables of the city of Albany. But his coarse appearance shocked his hostess who had continued to cultivate a kind of French elegance.

> I ... had to say that nothing would persuade me to take him to call on Mrs Renslaer and Mrs Schuyler unless he did something to improve his appearance. His clothes were covered in mud and dust, and torn in a number of places. He looked like some shipwrecked sailor who had just escaped from pirates. No one would have guessed that such an odd collection of garments clothed a First Gentleman of the Bedchamber![30]

The Duke, of course, did everything possible to improve his appearance. But the demanding Marquise found that the result sill left a good deal to be desired. "I reproached him bitterly, especially for the patch on the knee of the pair of nankeen breeches, which must have come all the way from Europe, so worn were they from laundering."[31] The Indians at least had a sense of decoration and they did what was expected of them by wearing "old artificial flowers, feathers, ends of ribbon of all colours, balls of blown glass" that the Marquise generously distributed to them.[32]

THE HUGE SUCCESS OF ANOTHER TRAVEL BOOK, *Domestic Manners of the Americans*, published in London in 1832, is also worth considering. The author, Fanny Trollope, daughter of an Anglican vicar, was married to a highly educated but impecunious lawyer who had sought to make his fortune in the United States with a store selling English fashions in Cincinnati. The venture was a failure but Fanny Trollope's travel notebooks, written between 1827 and 1831, were to create a great stir. Their author became famous and they no doubt helped foster the literary career of her fourth son, Anthony. Fanny Trollope's account is important because, with her own particular sensibility, it matches the contemporary account by Tocqueville and Gustave de Beaumont.

Like many other European visitors, Fanny Trollope remarked that "the whole people appear to be divided into an almost endless variety of religious factions," which she proceeds to enumerate. She observes that these congregations, often headed by "intriguing and factious" individuals, distinguish themselves from one another by a "queer variety of external observance," the excesses of which have "the melancholy effect of exposing *all* religious ceremonies to contempt." From these unfortunate characteristics, she draws the conclusion that a country such as England, with an established church, offers great advantages; she does, however, note the relative superiority of American Catholicism, which is "exempt from the fury of division and subdivision that has seized every other persuasion."[33] Continuing her survey, she naturally seeks out an example of the great religious innovation of the time, a camp meeting. Her wishes are fulfilled when English friends take her to "a wild district on the confines of Indiana." There she sees "four high frames, constructed in the form of altars ... on these were supported layers of earth and sod, on which burned immense fires of blazing pinewood. On one side a rude platform was erected to accommodate the preachers, fifteen of whom attended this meeting, and with very short intervals ... preached in rotation, day and night, from Tuesday to Saturday."[34] At midnight on the day of her visit, Mrs. Trollope found herself at the foot of the platform among two thousand of the faithful to hear one of the preachers. He "began ... and, like all other Methodist preachers, assured us of the enormous depravity of man as he comes from the hands of his Maker, and of his perfect sanctification after he had wrestled sufficiently with the Lord to get hold of him, *et cætera*. The admiration of the crowd was evinced by almost constant cries of 'Amen! Amen!' 'Jesus! Jesus!' 'Glory! Glory!' and the like."[35] The "solemn and beautiful effect" of the crowd's responses was fleeting. Upon completing his sermon, the preacher summoned the "anxious sinners" to join him and his brothers at the foot of the platform. The chorus in response provoked a powerful collective emotion:

> The combined voices of such a multitude, heard at dead of night, from the depths of their eternal forests, the many fair young faces turned upward, and looking paler and lovelier as they met the moon-beams, the dark figures of the officials in the middle of the circle, the lurid glare thrown by the altar-fires on the woods beyond, did altogether produce a fine and solemn effect, that I shall not easily forget; but ere I had well enjoyed it, the scene changed, and sublimity gave way to horror and disgust.
>
> [More than one hundred participants, mostly women] were soon all lying on the ground in an indescribable confusion of heads and legs. They threw about their limbs with such incessant and violent motions that I was every instant expecting some serious accident to occur.
>
> But how am I to describe the sounds that proceeded from this strange mass of human beings? I know no words which can convey an idea of it. Hysterical sobbings, convulsive groans, shrieks and screams the most appalling, burst forth on all sides. I felt sick with horror.[36]

Fanny Trollope's terrors and her biting irony explain the success of her book, particularly because she flattered the sense of superiority of her cultivated readers who were able to control their emotions and adhered to discreet and subdued forms of religion. She made no real attempt, however, to understand the reasons for the enthusiasm of the followers of American evangelicalism.

THE SAINT-SIMONIAN MICHEL CHEVALIER, a contemporary of Trollope and Tocqueville, was one of the very few Europeans who expressed sympathy for American evangelicalism while recognizing its political and social effects. "The United States," he wrote in *Lettres sur l'Amérique du Nord*, "have innovated in both religion and politics."[37] The widespread practice of revivals, he remarked, underlined the distance that separated American religiosity from its European counterparts. Everything in America was more democratic, beginning with religion: pastors were appointed and dismissed by worshipers, and weighty episcopal hierarchies were replaced by flexible organizations that gave an important place to lay members. The Methodists' invention of the system of "traveling ministers"—famous for their fiery proselytizing and theatrical camp meetings—was particularly well adapted to a constantly growing society of pioneers. It enabled one to understand, Chevalier observed, why the traditional churches, Episcopalian and Congregationalist, were declining in comparison to the new "sects," the Methodists and Baptists, who were now in the majority.[38]

Rather than merely describing a great revival, like Trollope or La Tour du Pin, Chevalier presented a veritable work of comparative sociology by juxtaposing the political demonstrations of the new Democratic Party and the revivals organized by Methodist preachers. Indulging in paradox, he demonstrates that the most visible aspects of politics are inseparable from religion, and that religion, in the ritualized form of the camp meeting, is in fact the expression of modern democracy in action.[39] In the wake of the election victory of Andrew Jackson's supporters in New York, Chevalier witnessed a huge "procession" of Democrats passing before him:

> The democrats marched in good order to the glare of torches; the banners were more numerous than I had ever seen them in any religious festival.... On some were inscribed the names of the democratic societies or sections; *Democratic young men of the ninth or eleventh ward*; others bore imprecations against the Bank of the United States.... Then came portraits of General Jackson afoot and on horseback; there was one in the uniform of a general, and another in the person of the Tennessee farmer, with the famous hickory cane in his hand. Those of Washington and Jefferson, surrounded with democratic mottoes, were mingled with emblems in all tastes and of all colours. Among these figured an eagle, not a painting, but a real live eagle.... The imperial bird was carried by a stout sailor, more pleased than ever was a sergeant permitted to hold the strings of the canopy, in a catholic ceremony.[40]

And yet, Chevalier insists, these "constitutional ceremonies" were quite inferior to revivals, because only half the citizenry participated. Women, who could not vote, were excluded, and the result could only be disappointing: "Any celebration without women is only half a celebration." The organization of camp meetings, in contrast, was deeply democratic because women played the same role as men: "They are as active participants as the most fiery preachers. For that reason, American democracy flocks to these meetings," and a majority of Americans had converted to Baptism or Methodism.[41] If women were removed, religion would lose all its power to fascinate:

From camp meetings take away the *anxious bench*, remove those women who fall into convulsions, shriek, and roll on the ground, who, pale, dishevelled, and haggard, cling to the minister from whom they inhale the holy spirit, or seize the hardened sinner at the door of the tent, or in the passage-way, and strive to melt his stony heart; it will be in vain that a majestic forest overshadows the scene, of a beautiful summer's night, under a sky that need not fear a comparison with a Grecian heaven; in vain will you be surrounded with tents and numberless chariots, that recall to mind the long train of Israel fleeing from Egypt; in vain the distant fires, gleaming amongst the trees, will reveal the forms of the preachers gesticulating above the crowd; in vain, will the echo of the woods fling back the tones of their voice; you will be weary of the spectacle in an hour. But the camp-meetings, as they are now conducted, have the power of holding the people of the West for whole weeks; some have lasted a month.[42]

This was an eloquent defense of Jacksonian democracy, with the implication that, for Chevalier, the forms of public ceremony, whether political or religious, would build the character of a great nation and compensate for the absence of a past in such a young country.[43] From this point of view, evangelical religion was eminently democratic because it created idealism and a social bond where they had been lacking. This is why Chevalier had a resolutely optimistic view of the future of the United States. The superiority of American democracy lay in its capacity for enthusiasm and imagination in contrast to the situation in France, where:

Imagination is treated as a lunatic. Noble sentiments, enthusiasm, chivalric loftiness of soul, all that made the glory of France ... is regarded with contempt and derision. The public festivals and popular ceremonies have become a laughing-stock of the free thinkers. Love of the fine arts is nothing more than a frivolous passion. We make the most desperate efforts to starve the heart and soul, conformably to the prescriptions of our religious and political Sangrados.[44]

The tragedy of contemporary France, he contends, is its irreligion inherited from the Enlightenment. It is true that the philosophy of the eighteenth century functioned like a new Protestantism, because it introduced true freedom of thought into France. But, Chevalier concludes, the "Protestantism" of the philosophes is inferior to Anglo-American Protestantism. The former is ephemeral because it is elitist, inaccessible to the common people. The latter is solid and durable because it relies on the psychology of the people. The great strength of American democracy lies, then, in a particular philosophy of the heart that mobilizes all citizens, men and women alike. In France, Chevalier insists, the parliamentary regime does not stimulate the imagination; it creates no emotions. There may well be ceremonies and festivals, "but these smell too much of the parchment not to disgust our senses."[45]

Tocqueville and American Evangelicalism

Less taken by the political virtues of religious enthusiasm, Tocqueville did not see evangelicalism as an organizing religion in the same way that Puritanism had been. He saw it rather as an epiphenomenon, a form of spirituality that one finds "scattered throughout American society," affecting a small number of individuals, whose strange manifestations cannot be interpreted as a decisive step forward in the great march toward democratic equality. Evangelical religion, in Tocqueville's view, is merely an incidental byproduct of Protestant modernity seeking to relieve souls from their dominant passion: the quest for material goods. Evangelicalism is thus a reaction, a safety valve for the excesses of capitalism, a "brief interval" of respite for spirits "trammeled unduly by the fetters the body would impose on them" in its quest for the pleasures of this world.[46] None of this could be taken very seriously.

Tocqueville apparently failed to grasp the spread and especially the rising power of this new and soon to be dominant religion. Nor did he understand that what was involved in the phenomenal proliferation of sects was the future of American Protestantism itself.[47] The rise of political and religious populism responded to public taste and emotions, to the anxieties provoked by the remnants of the theology of predestination. Tocqueville reproduces all the stereotypes of the French travelers who came to America before him. He epitomizes the opinion of his compatriots when he sees in the gospel hawked by itinerant preachers "an impassioned, almost wild spiritualism that one seldom encounters in Europe." Unlike his traveling companion, Gustave de Beaumont, he did not attempt to inventory all the new churches. He noted the existence, still rare in his opinion, of "bizarre sects" claiming to lead the faithful to eternal happiness, and he concluded that in them "various forms of religious madness are quite common."[48]

Tocqueville said nothing more on the subject in the second volume of *Democracy in America*. He was more forthcoming in a very interesting manuscript that was long unpublished, in which he accentuates the difference between the extreme sobriety of a Quaker service and the frenetic agitation of

a Methodist service. One Sunday in an unnamed city, Tocqueville's curiosity
takes him first to "a large house" that does not look like a church. The traveler
notices the deep silence that prevails in the house. All the worshipers, even
the children, wear the same clothing and the same hats. Nothing happens
for nearly two hours. Intrigued, Tocqueville asks the man who brought him
to this place of meditation whether he has not been brought "to a meeting
of the deaf and dumb." Not in the slightest offended by the impertinence of
the question, his companion replies: "Dost thou not see that each of us waits
for the Holy Spirit to illumine him; learn to moderate thine impatience in a
holy place." Soon, writes Tocqueville, "one of those present got up and began
to speak; his accents were plaintive and each of his words was separated by
a long silence and he said in a very lamenting voice some quite consoling
things, because he spoke of the inexhaustible goodness of God and of the
obligation of all men to help one another, whatever their belief and the color
of their skin."[49]

Going next to a Methodist church, Tocqueville is surprised to be exposed
to great tumult:

> I saw first of all, in an elevated place, a young man whose thundering
> voice made the vault of the building reverberate. His hair was bristling;
> his eyes seemed to hurl flames; his lips were pale and trembling; his en-
> tire body seemed agitated by a general trembling. How I wanted to go
> through the crowd to the aid of this unfortunate man. But I stopped upon
> discovering that he was a preacher. He was speaking of the perversity of
> man and of the inexhaustible treasures of divine vengeance.... He was
> portraying the Creator as occupied unceasingly with heaping up gen-
> erations in the pits of hell and as tireless in creating sinners as he was in
> inventing torments. I stopped, very disturbed; the congregation was even
> more so than I. Terror was painted in a thousand manners on all faces and
> repentance continually took the form of despair and furor. Some women
> were raising their children in their arms and letting out lamentable cries;
> others were beating their brows on the ground; some men were twisting
> themselves in their pews while accusing themselves of their sins in a loud
> voice or were rolling themselves in the dust.... I fled full of disgust and
> penetrated with a profound terror.[50]

Instead of expressing interest in the democratic virtues of preaching that
gave each individual the chance finally to receive divine grace, Tocqueville

limits his interpretation to the social effects of Methodist preaching and presents here a point of view in stark contrast to that of his contemporary Michel Chevalier. The blatantly public nature of acts of repentance, manifested with equal fervor by men and women, delighted Chevalier. But it deeply shocked Tocqueville, who saw in it an abuse of the pedagogy of terror that was degrading for human beings. He found the vulgarity of the proceedings unbearable, and he had trouble believing that the "Author and Guardian of all things" could allow such practices: "Is it necessary to degrade man by fear in order to raise him to Thee, and can he mount to the ranks of Thy saints only by delivering himself to transports which make him lower than the beasts?"[51]

Tocqueville, who insisted that the Puritan experience was the point of departure of American democracy, was unable to accept that its point of arrival was Protestant evangelicalism, however popular it might be. Protestantism, as he observed it in America, had ceased to represent the ideal religion. He therefore continued his search for a reasonable doctrine able to stabilize human conduct while facilitating the flourishing of true democracy. After fleeing the Methodist service and venturing out of the city into wooded territory, Tocqueville comes upon the most surprising of sects, the *Dansars*, whom he alludes to in his book. They have set up a kind of convent that practices primitive communism intended to dissolve all individualism and all desire for the pleasures of this world.[52] The *Dansars* he observed were most likely the Shakers of the small community of Niskayuna, described in great detail by Gustave de Beaumont in an appendix to his novel, *Marie, ou l'Esclavage aux États-Unis*. Beaumont, with some surprise, observed women dressed in white and "men in violet costumes wearing broad-brimmed hats," sitting separately on either side of a central aisle. Silent at first, the worshipers rose and began to intone a religious hymn with discordant voices. That was when the peculiar movements of the Shakers occurred: agitated bodies stirring themselves up for the greater glory of God. "You see them," Beaumont writes, "dancing pell-mell amid violent clamor and with disorderly gestures."[53] Tocqueville depicts more or less the same scene, with more dramatic effects:

> At one end of the room, already lined up, were about fifty men of different ages but all wearing the same costume. It was that of the European peasants of the Middle Ages. Opposite was found an approximately equal number of women wrapped from head to foot in white clothes. Moreover one saw neither pulpit, nor altar, nor anything which recalled a place consecrated by Christians to the worship of the Divinity. These men and

women were singing hymns of a gloomy and doleful tone. From time to time they accompanied themselves by clapping their hands. At other times they began to move and made a thousand turns without losing the beat, sometimes marching in columns, sometimes forming a circle. At other times they advanced toward each other as if to fight and then drew back without having met. . . . They finally stopped; and one of the oldest of the company, after wiping his brow, began in a broken voice: "My brothers, let us give thanks to the Almighty who . . . has finally deigned to show us the way of salvation and let us pray to Him to open the eyes of this crowd of unfortunates who are still plunged in the shadows of error and to save them from the eternal torments which perhaps await them."[54]

Tocqueville refrains from judging the folly of the Shakers; his description speaks for itself. More rigorously analytic, Beaumont first offers a brief sketch of the origins of the sect and its founder Ann Lee, the "Second Messiah," born in 1761. He then goes on to denounce the "vanity" of the Shakers, the "strangeness" of their worship, the "absurdity" of a communal system that despoils the richest of the faithful for the benefit of the poorest, and the impossible rigor of a vow of chastity imposed on all. Beaumont concludes: "in the presence of such a spectacle, one cannot help but deplore the misery of man and the weakness of his reason."[55]

Fanaticism and Irreligion

Less philosophical than Tocqueville, with a more sociological cast of mind, Beaumont drew up an interesting typology of American religions—from the most dogmatic to the least, from the most authoritarian to the most open to free thought. At one end of the spectrum he places Catholicism, at the other Unitarianism. The Catholics, he explains, ban any right of free investigation; the Unitarians, in contrast, abuse the practice to the point of denying the divinity of Christ and emptying Christianity of any content, making it into a mere moral philosophy, simple deism, or "a natural religion based on reason." Between these two extremes, Beaumont sees

a huge expanse occupied by a multitude of other sects: countless intermediary steps appear between authority and reason, faith and doubt; countless efforts of thought always reaching toward the unknown, countless attempts by pride that will not resign itself to not knowing. The human mind runs through all these steps, sometimes driven by the most noble passions, sometimes cast into error by the love of truth, sometimes into madness by the counsels of reason.[56]

Whereas Tocqueville bases his argument on historical and philosophical considerations and proceeds by way of broad generalizations, Beaumont seeks out details at the risk of losing his way in the kaleidoscope of American religions. According to Beaumont, the Presbyterians, the harshest critics of the Catholics and the Unitarians, are followed pell-mell by Methodists, Anabaptists, Episcopalians, Quakers or Friends, Universalists, Congregationalists, United Churches, Dutch Reformed Churches, German Reformed Churches, Moravians, Evangelical Lutherans, and so on. The Anabaptists are split into Calvinists and associates, Mennonites, Emancipators, Dunkers, and so on.[57] The spectacle was enough to make the apprentice sociologist dizzy, because he saw in this prodigious fragmentation "the picture of all [the] aberrations and all [the] infirmities of human intelligence, which turns ceaselessly in a circle where it never finds the point of rest it is seeking."[58]

Tocqueville was similarly dizzied but drew different conclusions: "I firmly believe," he writes, "in the necessity of forms. I know that they enable the human mind to contemplate abstract truths with a steady gaze and, by helping it grasp such truths firmly, allow it to embrace them ardently. I do not imagine that religion can be maintained without external practices...."[59] His distress arises not so much from the existence of "palpably false and patently absurd" religions as from the uncontrolled proliferation of innovative practices, barring the faithful from any critical examination of the abstract truths that make up the dogma of a religion.[60] The proliferation of sects and the increasing complexity of religious practices, with their hymns, rituals, dances, and preaching styles, risk discouraging the masses from any lasting attachment to religion. The danger looming on the horizon in democratic societies is religious indifference: "A religion that became more obsessive about details, more inflexible, and more concerned with petty observances at a time when men were becoming more equal would soon find itself reduced to a band of fanatical zealots surrounded by an incredulous multitude."[61] Tocqueville therefore hoped that, in the interest of religion, the Americans would limit the number of sects and more successfully control the triumph of form over substance that he had found so deplorable.

Tocqueville was worried about the future because he was convinced that religion was necessary for the proper functioning of a democratic system. Religion is helpful to democracy because it moderates the passions aroused by growing equality: "the passion for well-being" and "love of wealth."[62] In this view, religion is the bridle on the democratic horse. In its absence, society would grow unmanageable, giving way to disorder or powerlessness, once men had stopped having "very definite ideas about God, the soul, and their general duties toward their Creator and their fellow man." Only a few philosophers or "minds truly emancipated from life's ordinary preoccupations" would be able if necessary to do without that kind of certainty. But skepticism is particularly dangerous for a free people, because it leads to bad habits that are incompatible with the pursuit of the common good: "Individuals become accustomed to making do with confused and fluctuating notions about the matters of greatest interest to themselves and their fellow men."[63] In the end, widespread doubt

> inevitably enervates the soul; it weakens the springs of the will and prepares citizens for servitude.... When no authority exists in matters of religion, any more than in political matters, men soon become frightened in the face of unlimited independence. With everything in a perpetual state of agitation, they become anxious and fatigued. With the world of the intellect in universal flux, they want everything in the material realm, at least, to be firm and stable, and, unable to resume their former beliefs, they subject themselves to a master.[64]

According to Tocqueville, democracy consequently faces a twofold peril for the future: irreligion and religious fanaticism. The former, as the preceding passage indicates, risks creating a state of perpetual agitation disastrous for the nation's future. The latter seems just as deplorable because it terrifies the people by subjecting them to "intellectual orgies"[65] and sometimes reducing them to a condition lower than that of the beasts. In such instances, the human mind may reach such heights of exaltation that it literally becomes unhinged: "He does not know where to stand and often runs without stopping beyond the bounds of common sense."[66] In the face of the danger posed by exacerbated skepticism and exalted spiritualism, Tocqueville asserts that to preserve the social bond in a democratic system, it is desirable and necessary to encourage the preservation of "dogmatic beliefs in regard to religion."[67] He says nothing about the content of those beliefs, but he suggests that Catholicism is probably the most reasonable religion and the most compatible with the future of American democracy. On that point he differed profoundly with American historians of the time, for whom Catholicism was the principal obstacle to a nation reinvented as simultaneously republican and Protestant.

4

The Bible Wars

THE READER MAY RECALL TOCQUEVILLE'S assertion that the spirit of liberty was fully compatible with the spirit of religion, as the New England Pilgrims, he believed, had demonstrated. In maintaining that religion and civil liberty were, despite appearances, not contradictory phenomena but rather seemed "to support each other," Tocqueville was repeating in his own fashion the predominant view of American historians and political leaders in the first half of the nineteenth century.[1] He was also confirming the views of the major liberal thinkers of his time. Before Tocqueville, Mme de Staël, Benjamin Constant, and François Guizot had all asserted that Protestantism was the religious creed most compatible with the flourishing of democracy and most able to reconcile faith with reason. But, later, Tocqueville called into question the idea that Protestantism was fully compatible with democracy and put forth a thesis that was very surprising for the time: Catholicism, despite its dogmatic and authoritarian character, was a profoundly egalitarian religion that should in the long term also foster democracy.

The reason for this change of view is Tocqueville's increasing conviction that the new Protestant sects were unstable: they unleashed the "fury

of division and subdivision" and revealed an "exalted spiritualism" that was
not compatible with the democratic form of government and could only lead
to the spread of indifference, skepticism, or deism.[2] This unfortunate development, so contrary to the ambitions of the early Puritans, seemed to have
already conquered the intellectual elite, who had rallied to a "sect that is
Christian only in name": Unitarianism. Unitarians, according to Tocqueville's
letter to Kergorlay, "see in Jesus Christ only an angel, others a prophet, finally
others a philosopher like Socrates."[3] They were really deists who "speak of
the Bible because they do not want to shock opinion too strongly, as it is still
completely Christian. They have a service on Sunday; I have been to one.
There they read verses of Dryden or other English poets on the existence of
God and the immortality of the soul. A speech on some point of morality is
made, and the service is over."[4]

Unitarianism seemed to him perfectly suited to the inclinations of "the
upper ranks of society" and the "argumentative classes." It was the visible
symbol of the future decay of Protestantism. Although no doubt sufficient
for the upper classes, deism or "natural religion" could not be suitable for all
social classes, "especially for those who have the most need to have the bridle
of religion." For Tocqueville, the success of the democratic experiment was
inseparable from a religion capable of moderating the passions of the dangerous classes, while at the same time preventing them from falling into "the
single doctrine of self interest." In other words, a religion was required that
was strong and organized enough to serve as a counterweight to the erring
ways of reason, and to "the mental condition, so common with us, in which
men leap over every obstacle, *per fas et nefas* to gain their point."[5]

Tocqueville found this ideal religion in Catholicism, and he admired its
rapid growth in the American working classes. But this exemplary Catholicism was not the religion found in France and the rest of Europe; it was an
"Americanized" Catholicism, unconnected to any system of alliance between
throne and altar, and hence compatible with the republicanism of the Founding Fathers.[6]

The great interest in Tocqueville's argument lies in its prophetic aspect.
Today no one would challenge the idea that Catholicism is compatible with
democracy or that a Catholic can assume the highest political or judicial
offices in the nation. And yet this argument, which was radically new for a
French reader in the 1830s, was just as disconcerting for an American reader, at
a time when a powerful nativist movement was growing in the United States
that warned of the danger of "Catholic tyranny." Corresponding to the "war
between the two Frances," the confrontation between clerical and anticleri-

cal forces, liberals and reactionaries, Revolution and Counterrevolution, was a "war between the two Americas," a conflict between Protestant elites and the Catholic hierarchy, drawing in their wake masses of White Anglo-Saxon Protestants (WASPs) and Irish Catholic immigrants. This was not only a religious war but also and above all a class war coupled with an ethnic and cultural conflict.

The Coming of the Irish Catholics

Catholicism was at a turning point at the time Tocqueville and Beaumont visited the United States. Catholics who had been established in Maryland and Pennsylvania since the seventeenth century were joined by new co-religionists, primarily from Ireland. The first generation of American Catholics had settled Maryland in 1634, a territory granted by royal charter to Cecil Calvert (Lord Baltimore), the eldest son of a great Catholic family ennobled by King James I. These first Catholics belonged to the English aristocracy; great landowners, they came with farmers and servants recruited in southern and eastern England. The Catholics of Pennsylvania were more modest and diversified; they were primarily German and had been readily accepted in the Quaker state noted for its religious tolerance. Along with the Quakers of English origin, they rubbed shoulders with Pietists from their own regions of Central Europe. These first waves of immigration were joined by small colonies of Irish Catholics, which were still atypical because the majority of Irish immigrants at the time were Scotch-Irish Calvinists from Ulster.

At the end of seventeenth century, Catholics made up a small religious community lost in a sea of Protestant sects. There were only about two thousand five hundred of them in Maryland in 1700 (out of a total population of thirty-four thousand), and they were even less numerous in Pennsylvania. In a little less than a century, their population increased tenfold, thanks to new immigrants from southern Ireland and German Catholic states.[7] The total number of American Catholics reached twenty-five thousand in 1790 according to the estimate of John Carroll, the first Catholic bishop in the United States, who presided over the diocese of Baltimore. They were distributed as follows: sixteen thousand in Maryland, seven thousand in Pennsylvania, one thousand five hundred in New York, and two hundred in Virginia.[8] Despite its growth, the American Catholic Church remained very limited, the size of a single French or Spanish diocese. Sixty years later, in 1850, it had more members than the largest Protestant denomination, the Methodist Church.

TABLE 4.1 Growth of the Catholic Population

	TOTAL POPULATION	CATHOLICS	PERCENTAGE OF TOTAL
1790	3,929,214	35,000	0.9
1820	9,638,453	195,000	2.0
1830	12,866,020	318,000	2.5
1840	17,069,453	663,000	3.9
1850	23,191,876	1,600,000	6.9

Source: Statistical Abstract of the United States, 2000, table 1, p. 7; George J. Marlin, The American Catholic Voter (South Bend, IN: St. Augustine Press, 2004), 37.

As table 4.1 shows, Catholics represented less than 1 percent of the total population of the United States in 1790; they exceeded 2 percent in the 1820s, and then doubled their numbers in the two decades prior to 1850.

How is this sudden growth to be explained in a country that is still seen today as fundamentally Protestant? The main reason is to be found in the conjunction of two separate but complementary factors: the expansion of the American economy under the presidency of Andrew Jackson, with major projects requiring large numbers of unskilled workers for the building of roads, railroad lines, canals, and houses; and a succession of agricultural crises in Ireland accompanied by periods of famine driving thousands of the poor to leave. In the twenty years between 1820 and 1840, two hundred and sixty thousand Irish immigrants settled in the United States. The great potato famine hastened the movement, with more than one million new immigrants between 1846 and 1851. In total, more than 4.3 million Irish immigrants settled in the United States in between 1820 and 1920. They were joined over the same period by 1.6 million German Catholics, and more than three million Italian Catholics (half the Germans arrived after 1880, and the vast majority of the Italians after 1900). From 1880 to 1920, they were joined by two million Polish immigrants, one million French Canadians, and hundreds of thousands of Czechs and Lithuanians, most of whom were Catholics.

Marked by these great waves of immigration, American Catholicism in the nineteenth century was at first largely Irish. The "old Catholics," born in the United States and firmly led by clergy of French origin, often recruited among émigrés from the Revolution, were gradually "submerged" by Irish

Catholics who brought with them new forms of religiosity and a conception of hierarchical relations that were very different from the democratic spirit that prevailed in the diocese of Baltimore in the late eighteenth century. But most important, the majority of these new Catholics were young, poorly educated, and willing to accept the lowest-paying jobs in cities, which required little skill.[9] In the unkind words of Archbishop Ambrose Maréchal of Baltimore, they were simply "*la canaille irlandaise.*"[10]

In the view of the New England Protestants, fostered by intense anti-Catholic propaganda of English origin, the newcomers represented a threat to the fragile American Republic. Their attachment to an antirepublican papacy, their ignorance of the Protestant tradition specific to the New World and New England, and their visibility in the poor neighborhoods of large cities like Boston inevitably provoked an anxious reaction from Protestant elites. These elites did not easily accept competition from a Church whose declared aim was "to convert all Pagan nations, and all Protestant nations" and in the United States itself, to convert "the people of the cities, and the people of the country, the officers of the navy and the marines, commanders of the army, the Legislatures and the Senate, the Cabinet, the President and all!"[11] By 1830, newspapers with revealing titles—*The Protestant, The Reformation Advocate, Priestcraft Unmasked, The Downfall of Babylon, The American Protestant Vindicator*—and associations for the defense of Protestantism such as the New York Protestant Association took on the task of relentlessly criticizing the deceptions of papists, the corruption of the lackeys of the Holy Father and his acolytes, monastic plots, and other horrors attributed to the "Romanists." The avowed aim was to prevent the "subversion of Christianity" by the importation of papist ideas. Newspaper readers were urged, for example, to "look the monster in the face" and consider the nature of Catholicism and its leader on the banks of the Tiber. Was he not, as a prospectus for *The Protestant* claimed, the living embodiment of the prophecies of the Book of Revelation: the Great Whore of the mystical Babylon?[12] And as the inventor of the telegraph, Samuel Morse, asserted, wasn't there a "foreign conspiracy" against American liberties, organized by the pope and his fabulously wealthy foreign missions, in the pay of European monarchs?[13]

The enemies most frequently attacked by the propagandists of a free Protestant nation were the Jesuit order, which had recently been reestablished; the Association for the Propagation of the Faith, founded in Lyon in 1822; and especially the Leopold Association of Vienna. According to sermons by fashionable preachers, there was obvious collusion between the Vatican and the

Austrian monarchy—an Austro-Roman Holy Alliance—whose avowed goal was the conquest of the United States and whose subversive agents were the Irish immigrants, "papal serfs" with the mission of establishing the Inquisition in America—the first necessary step in a campaign of forced conversion of Americans to Catholicism.[14]

The anti-Catholic atmosphere fostered by the press and evangelical preaching inevitably encouraged xenophobic actions directed against the Irish immigrant community. Riots in Boston in 1829 and again in 1833 led to the looting of Irish neighborhoods. The most serious episode occurred one day in August 1834, with the destruction of the main buildings of the Ursuline convent recently built on Mount Benedict in Charlestown, a few miles from Boston. The pretext for the attack was the "imprisonment" of a nun, Elizabeth Harrison, who had managed to escape from the tyranny of her superiors for a few days before being captured and locked up, it was said, in an underground pit hidden in the cellars of the convent. Her "flight," which had indeed occurred, was due to her disturbed mind, although the nun voluntarily decided to return to the site of her monastic order. Rumors circulated, fanned by the announcement of a tour of inspection by elected officials at the scene of the "crime," as a hundred rioters headed toward the convent shouting "No Popery!" and demanded the immediate liberation of the unfortunate prisoner. When there was no answer (it was nighttime and the young residents were asleep), the mob set fire to the convent and a week later attacked an Irish immigrant slum located in another part of the city.[15] Fortunately, these riots caused no deaths, but they indicated the virulence of anti-Catholic feeling at a time when Irish laborers, who were badly paid and demanded little, were beginning to compete against native New England artisans and workers.

A NEW LITERARY GENRE AROSE: "the pornography of the Puritan,"[16] in the words of historian Richard Hofstadter. The genre was quite acceptable because the pornography in question was not very explicit and it laid claim to a higher religious truth. Its undeniable success was such that one contemporary noted that "the compilation of anti-Catholic books . . . has become a part of the regular industry of the country, as much as the making of nutmegs, or the construction of clocks."[17] The rules of this new literary genre were very simple: find a defrocked monk, or better, a defrocked nun; have her re-create daily life in a monastic order; emphasize all the failings, jealousies, and torments inherent in a closed society; and, to give the reader his money's worth, reveal some real or imaginary salacious details. Finally, show that beneath the appearance of holiness and propriety lie real perversions and, even worse, crimes and abominations. Popular titles—such as *The Thrilling Mysteries of a Convent Revealed* (1836) or *The Confessions of a French Priest, to which are added Warnings to the People of the United States* (1837)—indicate the popularity and repetitiveness of the genre, the masterpiece of which was unquestionably Maria Monk's *Awful Disclosures*, continually reprinted up to 1870, which sold more than five hundred thousand copies, almost as many as the best-selling book of the time, *Uncle Tom's Cabin*.

In this autobiographical work, Maria Monk, a nun who had fled from the Hôtel-Dieu nunnery in Montreal, describes her life in this institution of the Sisters of Charity, dedicated to the care of the poor and the ill. Her English and Scottish family origins, her education, her four-year novitiate, her hesitations, and her taking of the veil are all described in great detail. Everything goes well until the day she takes her vows. The ceremony of monastic vows, the wearing of a black veil, and the silent meal in the refectory are all exotic enough to stimulate the curiosity of a Protestant reader. It is not until page forty-two that we discover the first terrifying revelation: on the very evening that she takes her vows, Maria Monk, now known as Sister Saint Eustace, is summoned to the private apartment of a priest, Father Dufresne, who treats her "in a brutal manner," and she receives "similar treatment" from two other priests. Discretion is required in this anti-Catholic literature: the author, Maria Monk, does not "speak on such subjects except in the most brief manner," in order not to "offend the virtuous ear" or "corrupt the heart" of her readers. She will say no more, while suggesting the unimaginable: "Few imaginations can conceive deeds so abominable as [the priests of the Seminary] practised, and often required of some of the poor women, under the fear of severe punishments, and even of death."[18]

Discreet about the sexual practices of the lecherous priests who enter the convent of the "Black Sisters" through secret underground passages connected to their seminary, Maria Monk's narrative really has nothing pornographic about it. But it is full of details about the deadly consequences of the sacrilegious practices supposedly encouraged by the Catholic hierarchy. For example, Maria Monk soon discovers that illegitimate children are born in her convent and that they are baptized, then executed by being thrown into pits of quicklime. She is also informed that sisters who are reluctant to accede to the demands of the Mother Superior or of a vicious priest are locked up in cells from which they do not always come out alive, and that the most "disobedient" are tortured and sometimes even executed. The tortures they are supposed to have suffered include kneeling on sharp stones, being hanged by the feet or gagged so tightly that the lips bled, having cheeks pierced with long needles, wearing a hair shirt whose steel points penetrated the skin of the thighs, being branded with hot irons, wearing a mysterious leather hood that caused burns and provoked convulsions, being required to swallow pieces of glass and grind them to powder with painful chewing, and so on.[19] Punishment might also include a severe and disgusting diet, consisting exclusively of garlic and badly cooked eels, sometimes accompanied, in the guise of a soup, with the dirty water from a bowl in which the Mother Superior, Sister Bourgeoise, had washed her feet.[20]

Maria Monk also claims to have witnessed the murder of another nun, Sister Saint Frances, who had confessed to a friend her disgust at the idea of eliminating any illegitimate child that might be born in the convent. She would disobey, she had said, if she were given the order. Her confession was soon reported to the Mother Superior and the bishop of the diocese, who summoned her for a "trial" on the charge of having violated her vows of obedience. Questioned at length by her improvised judges, Sister Saint Frances said "that she would rather die than cause the murder of harmless babes. 'That is enough, finish her!' said the bishop."[21] In a provocative scene worthy of *Justine ou les Malheurs de la vertu*, the designated victim is immediately gagged and tied to a bed, and another bed set on top of it. Priests and nuns jump eagerly onto the bed, and try to disfigure the victim with kicks and knee blows, until she finally dies crushed beneath the weight of her tormenters. At the very moment at which she gives up the ghost, one of the participants in this *danse macabre* laughingly says, "She would have made a good Catholic martyr."[22] Then her body is covered with quicklime, corrosive acid poured over it, and it is thrown into one of the pits dug in the cellar of the convent.

Maria Monk's narrative was presented as an authentic account of the habitual perversion of the Catholic hierarchy. It was intended as a warning against the deleterious effects of a foreign Catholicism imported by thousands of new Irish immigrants, and it signaled the point of departure for a large-scale anti-Catholic campaign that culminated in the founding in 1854 of a political party dedicated to the defense of a Protestant American nation. This party, the Order of the Star Spangled Banner, usually known as the Know Nothing Party, barred its members from revealing their membership in the fraternal order, which was limited to native Americans born of Protestant parents and co-opted by other Protestants. In their quasi-Masonic initiation ritual the Know Nothings promised to use their influence to place "in all offices in the gift of the people, whether by election or appointment, none but native-born Protestant citizens."[23] This xenophobic party achieved considerable success: one hundred members of Congress, eight governors, and several mayors, including the mayors of Boston, Chicago, and Philadelphia, claimed adherence to it on the eve of the Civil War.

The Catholic Church challenged *Awful Disclosures* when it was published, claiming it was a gross forgery or plagiarized from an English anti-Catholic pamphlet, *The Gates of Hell Opened*. But the Protestant press, backed by the testimony of witnesses, fiercely defended the book as a truthful document based on the authentic testimony of a nun who had escaped from the Hôtel-Dieu convent in Montreal and taken refuge in New York.[24] The author of the controversial book was prepared to confirm the truth of her story before a judge.[25] It is now known that *Awful Disclosures* was, as the Catholic authorities had claimed, an apocryphal memoir concocted by Methodist ministers and attributed to a poor woman who had escaped from a Montreal insane asylum. This new popular genre, much imitated at the time, illustrated the strength of Protestant propaganda and its fundamental goal: to protect the hegemony of a Protestant American culture based on the myth of a Puritan foundation. This myth, rediscovered and embellished by early nineteenth-century Romantic historians, was not incompatible with the idea of a nonsectarian, secular republic, detached from all established churches. But it gave no place to the Catholic perspective. The American Creed, as it existed then, offered a strange mixture of xenophobia, Protestantism, and republicanism.

The Bible War

The Bible was at the heart of the conflict between the Protestant and Catholic conceptions of religion, and, by implication, the nation. Teachers in the public education system recommended that the Bible be approached from a "secular" perspective; that is, unconnected to any interpretation derived from any particular faith. The major difficulty was that the Catholics did not use the same version of the Bible as the Protestants (regardless of denomination). Catholics favored the Douai Bible, the first Catholic translation of the Vulgate, published between 1582 and 1602 by Catholic priests exiled from England. Protestants were unanimously attached to the King James Version, first published in 1611 by a group of translators working for the Anglican monarchy. In the preface of the King James Version, the translators did not hesitate to denounce the "calumniations ... of Popish persons," who were too forgetful of the word of God and desired to keep the people in a state of "ignorance and darkness." They saw themselves as the "poor instruments [of] ... God's holy Truth." As defenders of the English monarchy—"our Sion"—they claimed to be the faithful servants of the English language and hoped that their translation would be the most accurate and the closest possible to the "original Sacred Tongues." As for Catholics, they were denounced in the same preface as "selfconceited Brethren, who run their own ways, and give liking unto nothing, but what is framed by themselves, and hammered on their anvil."[26]

Since the Protestant elites had always supported free public education for all, it is not surprising that school programs gave a privileged place to the Bible and that some lessons on morality were based on the reading and recitation of brief passages from the Old Testament, such as the Ten Commandments. Paradoxically, this simple exercise based on a few Christian precepts understandable to everyone, was at the heart of the war between the two Americas, with Protestants and Catholics each defending *their* version of the Decalogue.

In the Protestant tradition, as in the Jewish tradition, the list of commandments—taken from Flavius Josephus and Philo and adopted by Calvin and most evangelical pastors—includes a second commandment stating in its complete version:

> Thou shalt not make unto thee any graven image, or any likeness *of any thing* that *is* in heaven above, or that *is* in the earth beneath, or that *is* in the water under the earth: Thou shalt not bow down thyself to them, nor serve them: for I the Lord thy God *am* a jealous God, visiting the iniquity of the fathers upon the children unto the third and fourth *generation* of them that hate me.[27]

In the Catholic tradition, inspired by the writings of Saint Augustine, the second commandment, formulated in these terms, was omitted to avoid any embarrassment about the cult of saints and the representations in painting and sculpture of their lives and the lives of Jesus and Mary. However, to respect the format of the Decalogue, Catholics to this day compensate for the omission of the second commandment by splitting the tenth in two (see table 4.2).

Comparison of the two versions provided weapons to the Protestants who wanted to demonstrate the "inadequacies" of the Catholic Church: its lack of rationality, its ignorance of Biblical truths and divine prohibitions, and

TABLE 4.2

THE TEN COMMANDMENTS	PROTESTANT VERSION*	CATHOLIC VERSION†
First Commandment	I am the Lord thy God, which have brought thee out of the land of Egypt, out of the house of bondage. Thou shalt have no other Gods before me.	I am the Lord thy God; thou shalt not have strange gods before Me.
Second Commandment	Thou shalt not make unto thee any graven image . . . Thou shalt not bow down thyself to them nor serve them.	Thou shalt not take the name of the Lord thy God in vain.
Third Commandment	Thou shalt not take the name of the Lord thy God in vain.	Remember thou keep holy the Lord's day.
Fourth Commandment	Remember the sabbath day, to keep it holy.	Honor thy father and thy mother.
Fifth Commandment	Honour thy father and thy mother.	Thou shalt not kill.
Sixth Commandment	Thou shalt not kill.	Thou shalt not commit adultery.
Seventh Commandment	Thou shalt not commit adultery.	Thou shalt not steal.
Eighth Commandment	Thou shalt not steal.	Thou shalt not bear false witness against thy neighbor.
Ninth Commandment	Thou shalt not bear false witness against thy neighbour.	Thou shalt not covet thy neighbor's wife.
Tenth Commandment	Thou shalt not covet thy neighbour's house, thou shalt not covet thy neighbour's wife, nor his manservant, nor his maidservant, nor his ox, nor his ass, nor anything that is thy neighbour's.	Thou shalt not covet thy neighbor's goods.

*I use here the King James Version, Exodus 20.2–17. On the Protestant numbering, see, for example, Lois Rock, *The Ten Commandments for Children* (Elgin, IL: Lion, 1995). For a systematic comparison of the Calvinist, Catholic, and Jewish versions, see Félix Garcia Lopez, "Le Décalogue," *Cahiers Évangile* 81 (1992), and Marc-Alain Ouaknin, *Les Dix Commandements* (Paris: Seuil, 1999).

†As presented in *The Baltimore Catechism*. It should be noted that Lutherans preserve the Catholic numbering derived from St. Augustine.

its idolatrous tendencies; in short, its generally superstitious character. The forms of worship of Irish immigrants, the countless images of Saint Patrick, the Virgin, and the Sacred Heart of Jesus; the conspicuous display of the rosary and of blessed medals; religious processions for the adoration of the Holy Sacrament or the Cross; and exuberant funeral processions all inevitably underlined, in the view of American evangelicals, the retrograde character of a religion that subjected its faithful to the absolute authority of an all-powerful clergy and encouraged them to cultivate idolatrous practices. Hadn't Calvin himself denounced Catholics who clothed the statue of the Virgin in an even more extravagant and vulgar fashion than "prostitutes in brothels"?[28]

For a Protestant, the knowledge of God excludes any intercession or mediation based on examples or images. The culture of the Reformation churches was rooted in the doctrine of *sola scriptura*: nothing must come between the believer and the presence of the Word, immediately revealed by reading the Scriptures—the only possible source of "illumination." The second commandment could therefore not be taken lightly. A graven image was nothing but trickery conceived by Satan to trouble men and entangle them in superstition.[29] From a Protestant perspective, a nonsectarian reading of the King James Bible, taught without comment, was perfectly adequate for moral instruction. But it was precisely this type of instruction that the Catholic clergy rejected out of concern to preserve its version of the Decalogue and its control over the content of the Scriptures. The two rival versions of the Decalogue were the stakes in this tumultuous war between the Catholic community and the Protestant majority in the middle of the nineteenth century.

THE MOST EMBLEMATIC INCIDENT IN THIS Bible war was probably the March 1859 revolt of the Catholic pupils of Eliot School, a Boston public school. The immediate cause of the crisis, widely commented on in the press, was the refusal of Thomas Whall, a ten-year-old pupil, to read the Ten Commandments at the beginning of the morning class, as his teacher Miss Shepard demanded, in accordance with Massachusetts law. Thomas Whall repeatedly refused to comply on the grounds that the Bible excerpts in his textbook were taken from the King James Version, and he was harshly reprimanded by the school's assistant principal, who "whipped" him on the hands with a rattan stick until his fingers were bleeding. Nothing worked: Thomas stood fast until he fainted, encouraged by his fellow Catholics. They, too, refused to obey the teachers' instructions, and hundreds of them were expelled on the day they demonstrated their solidarity by bringing their copies of the "Catholic" commandments to class after openly tearing out the pages in their textbooks containing the Protestant commandments.[30]

The affair ended up in court after mediation organized by the school's principal failed. Whall and his father sued the assistant principal who had done the whipping for the use of excessive force, but he was vindicated by the court because Thomas, according to Judge Sebeus Maine, had seriously violated his obligations as a student and deserved corporal punishment. In his ruling, the judge clearly identified the importance of what was at stake: Thomas's refusal to read the Protestant version of the Ten Commandments threatened the stability of the public school, "the granite foundation on which our republican form of government rests."[31] Contrary to appearances, there had been no violation of freedom of conscience: the Bible readings were free of any dogmatism; it was all done objectively, with no inappropriate comment. The lawyer for the defense was more openly anti-Catholic: he denounced the "foreign priests" who influenced the pupils in an attempt to subvert the country's laws. The daily reading of excerpts from the Protestant Bible was, according to him, the firmest guarantee that "America can never be Catholic."

Giving up recitation of the Ten Commandments "in the usual form," said a prominent Boston businessman, could only destroy "our public educational system ... convert[ing] the schools of the Puritans into heathen temples."[32] All these denunciations of a foreign, authoritarian, and antirepublican Catholicism echoed the famous manifesto of the American Society to Promote the Principles of the Protestant Reformation, which declared in its preamble that "the principles of the Roman court are totally incompatible with the Gospel of Christ, freedom of conscience, human rights, and the Constitution and laws of the United States of America."[33] It would be hard to find a clearer articulation of the view of the country's Protestant elites: Protestantism was republican in its very essence, whereas Catholicism, a religion defended by a "false prophet," was by nature antidemocratic and even un-American.[34]

The Whall case might leave the impression that the Catholic Church was defenseless against the blows of the nativist majority. Nothing could be further from the truth: there would have been no Whall case were it not for the provocation of a dynamic immigrant, Father Bernardine Wiget, who had been trained at the Jesuit seminary in Fribourg before being expelled from his country at the time of the Swiss civil war of 1847. Father Wiget's great ambition was to shield new Irish immigrants from the nefarious influence of the public schools, those republican-Protestant dens of iniquity.

Father Wiget had developed the habit of denouncing from the pulpit all the manifestations of "infidelity and heresy" that were proliferating in the public schools: in particular the recitation of Protestant hymns and prayers. By threatening to reveal in church the names of children who had been caught reciting in class the Protestant version of the Ten Commandments, Father Wiget had been able to touch the impressionable mind of Thomas Whall so that he persisted in his refusal to do what his teacher demanded, leading to the exemplary punishment publicly inflicted on the recalcitrant boy. From a Catholic perspective, there was no doubt about it: Thomas Whall was a modern-day Catholic martyr. He had demonstrated "heroic faith under torture," according to the author of an inflammatory article published in the *Irish Illustrated Nation* on April 30, 1859.[35] The "martyr" was exhibited around the United States and received as a reward an impressive collection of crosses and medals. He was thereby serving a cause beyond his understanding: the promotion of Catholic parochial schools, which his mentors saw as the only means of preventing too rapid an assimilation that would pave the way for Protestant proselytism and the dangers of an excessively secularized society.

Religion and the Public School

The creation of a modern school system—a school common to all the people—that would replace most existing religious schools, raised two important questions. How to make the student into a moral subject, given the extreme religious diversity of the country? And how to make him or her the enlightened citizen of a republic?

The mission of the public school, as it was first discussed by Massachusetts educators in 1837, was to teach reasonable, informed, and intelligent citizens and make them understand that civic morality and the public good transcended their own selfish interest. But this civic morality had no independent existence; it derived from a more general morality, inspired by Christianity and based on two assumptions: individual autonomy and self-discipline. Autonomy because man is a free agent who must choose for himself the political party or political opinion best suited to his sensibility, just as he exercises his freedom of conscience by choosing his form of worship free of pressure from family or state. Self-discipline because the man of the people, left to his natural inclinations—ignorance, superstition, and vice—would be in danger of becoming a rebel, an enemy of society, if not even a "Goth and Vandal at home," more dangerous than a foreign enemy.[36]

There is "no security for a Republic but in morality and intelligence," declared Horace Mann, the great advocate of the public school system in America and the first secretary of the Massachusetts School Board.[37] What did he mean by intelligence? Not innate intelligence and individual talent, but the fruit of lengthy work in the public school whose principal function was to create social bonds. The public school, according to Horace Mann, is "indispensable" to republican government, because it gives everyone, rich or poor, the same education and hence the same possibility for social mobility. It is also, most importantly, the best way of controlling the "unexampled energies" unleashed among the masses by universal suffrage.[38] The quintessential site for the "culture of our moral affections and religious susceptibilities," the public school is the best way of controlling the "passions ... which might ... lacerate [our] soul[s] and bring down upon [them] an appropriate catastrophe," making us worse than savage beasts.[39] But how are morality and religion to be united without proselytism? It was clear to Mann and the supporters of the common school that the teaching of religion was legitimate only if it was itself secularized, that is, free from any article of faith and any religious dogma. Its only purpose was to disseminate the elements of a universal morality enabling the student to judge for himself, "according to the light of his reason and conscience."[40] The teaching of morality understood in this way did not exclude the reading of the Bible; quite the contrary. The practice was normal, matching the wishes of the majority of the parents. But the teacher was to avoid any comment that might serve the interests of a particular sect or denomination. If that were to occur, it was legitimate to ban the use of the Bible: some schools did so in response to the express wishes of parents. Nothing would be worse, wrote Horace Mann, than to teach in school an official dogma sanctioned by law and intended to influence young children and "predetermine" their religious opinions.

The public education system, although not excluding religion, avoided any interpretation liable to inflame divisions or sectarian disputes among families or within particular school districts. This was the price of American secularism: acquaintance with the Scriptures was tolerated, even encouraged, but it was emptied of any doctrinal substance. Religion was thereby used to further a noble cause: the ideal of a republican commonwealth based on the "intelligence of the citizens," that is, their free will and their sense of justice and responsibility.[41]

From the Catholic point of view, this noble program was still biased and sectarian: it was fundamentally Protestant, in light of the weight given to free

will, and it was antireligious because it placed all religions on an equal footing by adopting a supposedly neutral or secularized reading of the Bible. The
Catholic clergy found this last point particularly unacceptable; they refused
to consider any separation between dogma and teaching practices. For the
vicar general of the diocese of New York, John Power, the reading of the Bible
could not be detached from the wise predication of an enlightened Catholic
clergy: "The Catholic church tells her children that they must be taught their
religion by AUTHORITY—the Sects say, read the Bible, judge for your-
selves. The Bible is read in the public schools, the children are allowed to
judge for themselves. The Protestant principle is therefore acted upon, slyly
inculcated, and the schools are Sectarian."[42]

In the same vein, John Hughes, the militant bishop of New York, denounced the illusion of an educational system that claimed to have secularized the religious question: "To make an infidel what is it necessary to do?
Cage him up in a room, give him a secular education from the age of five
years to twenty-one, and I ask you what will he come out if not an infidel? . . .
They say that their education is not sectarianism; but it is; and of what kind?
The sectarianism of infidelity in its every feature."[43]

Given such intransigence, which went so far as to refuse to agree to the
publication of an ecumenical Bible acceptable to all Christians,[44] it is not
hard to understand why the Catholic authorities were so insistent on remov-
ing Catholic children from the public schools.

BUT WHEN THEY CREATED CATHOLIC SCHOOLS modeled on the common
schools that Protestant elites had established, Catholics demanded equal
treatment. They too wanted to benefit from state aid. This was what Governor William Seward of New York proposed in 1839. Badly received by the
school authorities of New York City, the proposal was abandoned, and then
brought up again before the state legislature. A law passed in 1842 permitted
the authorities of the city's school districts to determine the curricula and to
include if they wished readings from the Bible of their choice. This law had
little effect, because the nativists, who were politically well organized, succeeded in gaining control over most school boards and in imposing only one
Bible: the King James Version.

The New York debate did, however, have a decisive impact on a similar
debate among educators in Philadelphia. Like Bishop Hughes, Bishop Francis
Kenrick of Philadelphia demanded that Catholic students in the city's schools

have access to the right Bible: the (Catholic) Douai Bible. The school authorities refused and this uncompromising decision led a few school principals from Kensington—an industrial suburb of Philadelphia populated by Irish immigrants— to ban all readings from the King James Version.[45] This decision was enough to provoke the anger of the leaders of a new nativist party, the American Republicans. Its members organized a large protest march in Kensington to express their indignation: banning the Protestant Bible, they thought, evidenced an antirepublican spirit and posed an intolerable threat to "any man who loves his country, his Bible, and his God."[46] This first demonstration by nativists in the heart of Irish neighborhoods provoked violence and the death of a marcher at the hands of an Irishman. Other protest marches followed to vindicate the honor of native-born Americans and of the American flag that had allegedly been abused by the new immigrants. Outraged nativists paraded the unfurled flag in the streets of Philadelphia bearing the legend: "This is the flag that was trampled under foot by the Irish papists."[47]

Nativist anger reached its apogee in early May 1844 with a new protest march in Kensington, which degenerated into three days of rioting and resulted in the destruction of two Catholic churches and about thirty houses. The Protestants had been afraid of a new Saint Bartholomew's Day massacre, but they were the ones who terrorized the Irish neighborhoods in the Philadelphia suburbs. More rioting erupted two months later in Southwark, another Philadelphia suburb, when a cache of weapons was found in a Catholic church. The state militia had to intervene to restore order after three days of violence that caused the death of thirteen demonstrators. Carnage was barely avoided in New York thanks to protective measures put in place by Bishop Hughes: two thousand armed Irishmen stood guard outside the Catholic churches of Manhattan. Warned by the bishop that "if a single Catholic Church were burned in New York, the city would become a second Moscow,"[48] the municipal authorities took the precaution of banning a planned nativist march in Central Park.

The Catholics had had their martyr, Thomas Whall, who was beaten for refusing to read the King James Version of the Bible; the Protestants now had theirs, George Shiffler, the first man who died in the Kensington riots. Each camp commemorated its dead and wounded in large mourning ceremonies. These events strengthened the political influence of the nativists who established—first in New York in 1844 with the Order of United Americans, and then in Philadelphia in 1845 with the United Sons of America (USA)—

ethnic and cultural defense associations, organized in secret, like Masonic lodges, and anticipating the Know Nothing Party by ten years.[49]

DESPITE APPEARANCES, THE WAR BETWEEN the two Americas was not only religious; it was also cultural, economic, and political. Irish workers who accepted low wages threatened the jobs of "native" Americans. And most important was the looming danger of a massive withdrawal of Catholic students from all public schools, which would compromise the secular ideal of the educational elites. Why should "the school for all" be rejected as long as it satisfied the great majority of American families, regardless of religious affiliation? The proliferation of Catholic schools,[50] coupled with insistent demands for public funding equal to that given to the common schools, struck a blow at the nation's fundamental values.

The American *Kulturkampf* reached its peak with the proposed Blaine Amendment, supported by the leaders of the Republican Party, one year before the presidential election of 1876. This amendment intended to prohibit any public assistance to denominational schools, both at the federal and local levels, thus instituting a real separation between church and state. Then-President Ulysses Grant supported the proposal in terms that strongly recalled the arguments of the great advocate for the American public school, Horace Mann. It is essential, said Grant, that all citizens have sufficient education and intelligence to cast informed votes. "In a republic whereof one man is as good as another before the law, the education of the masses becomes of the first necessity for the preservation of our institutions."[51] And only the public school had the capacity to foster the development of a true civic intelligence. The Blaine Amendment did not win the required two-thirds majority in the Senate because of opposition from Democratic senators who denounced the anti-Catholic aims of its sponsors. But the latter succeeded in imposing their "secular" views at the local level: over the next fourteen years, twenty-nine states passed laws prohibiting any public funding to religious (primarily Catholic) schools.

As in France, the debate about the separation between church and state was inseparable from the question of education. There was, however, one notable difference: the secular school in France excluded any religious teaching, whereas in the United States it retained the requirement of nonsectarian religious instruction, and, despite numerous Catholic protests, this requirement did not exclude the use of the Protestant Bible. Any other approach, the Protestant elites asserted, would inevitably lead to "immorality": "Not to give us any religion, or morality radicated [i.e., rooted] in religious sanctions, is to give us immorality and irreligion. Here neutrality is impossible."[52]

IN THE SECOND VOLUME OF *Democracy in America*, Tocqueville considers the "progress of Catholicism" in the United States. In modern times, he concedes, people are "by nature not particularly inclined to believe," but if they do have a religious sensibility, Catholicism is the religion they will adopt: "If Catholicism were ultimately to escape from the political animosities it has stirred up, I have virtually no doubt that the spirit of the age, which now seems so hostile to it, would become quite favorable, and that it would suddenly make great conquests."[53] This apparent paradox requires explanation. First of all, at the time Tocqueville was writing he could not have anticipated that the political antagonisms between Protestants and Catholics would be lasting and that nativist elites would soon be claiming that democracy is incompatible with the Roman religion. Nor could he have foreseen the effects produced by the great waves of Irish immigration (1845–1853) or the violence of the school battles and the rioting they unleashed. The Catholicism Tocqueville described was a minority religion still dominated by priests and bishops of French origin.[54] It was a tolerant and Americanized Catholicism that provoked little fear and still took pride in its good relations with the Founding Fathers. After all, Catholics had fought alongside Washington in the War of Independence and he had made it a point to publicly praise their eminent contribution to the building of the new federal republic.[55]

But Tocqueville's prophecy, sometimes cited with approval by the advocates of a liberal and modernized Catholicism, sometimes denounced as deceptive and dangerous by Ultramontane clergy,[56] is only comprehensible in the light of its author's moderate cast of thought. In Tocqueville's view, Protestantism was not the religion best suited to democracy, because it was unstable, lacking in dogma, and structurally weakened by its internal divisions. He described the lower classes as naturally emotive and impassioned; they needed a religion that would calm them down and rein in their emotions, and that religion was Catholicism.

Empirical to some degree, Tocqueville's argument seems primarily prudential and utilitarian: to each social class corresponded the religion best suited to its situation and temperament. Skepticism was perfectly fitting for the "upper classes," but it would be troubling for the people and would risk provoking the "deviations of the spirit of innovation." Evangelicalism, he believed, gave the people the emotions they called for, but it risked overexciting spirits with excessive exaltation, as Tocqueville and Beaumont had observed at Niskayuna. There remained Catholicism, which moderated passions while allowing for the expression of controlled emotions, seizing "the senses and the soul deeply."[57]

But the liberal Catholicism Tocqueville imagined, tolerant of other religions and respectful of republican forms of government, was not the one historians of nineteenth-century America describe. The Bible wars, the intolerance of the nativists, and the combativeness of the Irish clergy established a lasting distance between American Catholicism and the ideal democracy the French visitor dreamed of. Real democracy was in fact excessively "Protestantized" by xenophobic elites who could not imagine the liberal evolution that Tocqueville anticipated.

This slow evolution, marked by the collapse of nativist movements and the gradual assimilation of the Irish, German, and later Italian Catholics into the American mainstream, facilitated the rising power of the Catholic vote in the Democratic Party. In 1928, Governor Al Smith of New York, a Catholic, won the Democratic nomination for president. He lost to Herbert Hoover, but did receive 15,016,443 votes, compared to 21,391,381 for his rival. A man of the people, a resolute opponent of prohibition, and a descendant of Irish immigrants, born and raised on the Lower East Side in Manhattan, Al Smith was denounced as the Antichrist by a coalition of conservative Southern Democrats and prohibitionist Republicans from the North and the Midwest. Even in New York, a well-known Episcopalian lawyer and member of the WASP elite did not hesitate to claim, once again and as though nothing had changed since 1850, that there was complete incompatibility between the rights enshrined in the United States Constitution and the conceptions of authority upheld by American Catholics. The spirit of submission to Rome was considered contrary to the very principle of representative government.[58] A Baptist newspaper in Dallas asserted that Smith's victory would lead to the shameful spectacle of the stripping of the Goddess of Liberty, whose resplendent robe would soon be cut into pieces by liberty-hating nuns and made into "dish rags for a Catholic convent."[59]

Al Smith confronted all these calumnies with composure. He demonstrated, despite his defeat, that a Catholic could be a credible candidate for the presidency and even secure the enthusiastic support of a majority of Catholic *and Protestant* voters in the large industrial centers of North America. But it took thirty-two years before another Catholic, John F. Kennedy, made his entry into the White House, after brilliantly demonstrating that he was not, after all, the Vatican's man.

5

Religion, Race, and National Identity

As the last two chapters have shown, for nineteenth-century political elites the national identity of the United States was rooted in the myth of a Puritan past rehabilitated by eminent historians. This conception of a fundamentally Anglo-Protestant nation was still alive in the early twentieth century, and even came back into favor in the twenty-first century among some intellectuals, the most prominent of whom was the late political scientist Samuel P. Huntington. Huntington contended that American identity had two essential components: a set of racial, ethnic, cultural, and religious characteristics introduced by the first New England colonists, to which had been added an "American Creed"—a set of political values (liberty, equality of opportunity, representative democracy) and social values (individualism, the work ethic). The Creed was "shaped" by these characteristics,[1] the most important of which is religious in nature: "Almost all the central ideas of the Creed," according to Huntington, "have their origins in dissenting Protestantism," Calvinist at first and now almost exclusively evangelical.[2]

But the Creed and the values that have underpinned it for three centuries are, in Huntington's view, now threatened by the new Hispanic immigration.

Immigrants from Mexico and the rest of Latin America do not, in fact, conduct themselves like their predecessors. They do not, Huntington explained in a very controversial article published in 2004, seek to integrate into the dominant culture. They choose to preserve their ethnic identity and their own traditions, thereby rejecting "the distinct Anglo-American culture of the founding settlers," the very foundation of the American Creed.[3] In this view, if Hispanic immigration is not stopped or slowed, the nation will eventually be in grave danger. America, "as we have known it for more than three centuries," will be in danger of disappearing forever, to be replaced by a fractured society, irremediably divided between two populations with different languages and cultures, two peoples that have stopped sharing the American dream.[4]

What is striking in this argument, as American immigration scholars were quick to note, is the sense of *déjà vu*.[5] Already in the early twentieth century, congressmen, sociologists, and biologists were denouncing the same danger in almost identical terms: Anglo-Protestant America was threatened by an uncontrollable wave of new immigrants, who resisted all forms of racial, cultural, religious, and political assimilation. The only difference between the positions of the "nativists" of the early 1900s and that of Huntington concerns the groups that were deemed to be incapable of assimilating: before it was Celts and Germans, then Southern Europeans, Slavs, Russians, and Poles, and finally Asians; today, it is Hispanics and Latinos. If one merely substitutes one set for the other, one finds a century later the same argument, the same fears, and the same dread of an irremediable loss of American identity.

This persistent concern with identity is inseparable from a romantic view of the nation, conceived as an organic whole, layered by religious beliefs, a long-standing language and culture, and most important an ethnic or racial substratum identified variously as German, Saxon, Northern, Yankee, or Anglo-Saxon. New immigrants, according to the once fashionable arguments of Social Darwinism,[6] did not belong to the "proper" race. It was appropriate to limit their numbers, which Congress did by adopting the quota laws in the 1920s. These very restrictive laws were aimed at slowing if not simply prohibiting immigration from the countries of Asia and Central and Mediterranean Europe.

Now, a century later, new nativists, inspired by the arguments of Samuel Huntington, among others, also wish to limit immigration by advocating harsh regulations intended to put an end to the wave of undocumented immigrants from Mexico. Their motives are not necessarily racist, but their worries remain the same: the first priority is to defend American identity, whose essential values are said now and forever to be "Anglo-Saxon" and "Protestant."

In Search of the Anglo-Saxons

There is nothing particularly American about this determinist and culturalist approach. It corresponds to a historic tradition, very much in fashion among certain French writers who were obviously influenced by the German variant of the Romantic movement.[7] These writers shared a preoccupation: finding the distant origins of the political liberty of the Moderns; demonstrating that Protestant values were, in fact, inseparable from the primordial values of the ancient Saxon tribes. They sought—and found—the elements that founded Anglo-Saxonism in their reading of Tacitus.

Guizot, for example, in his course of lectures in 1828, evoked the "motives, inclinations, and impulses" of the barbarians who conquered the Roman Empire. These barbarians, according to him, "with the exception of a few Slavonian tribes . . . were all of the same German origin."[8] And Guizot detected among them an exceptional freedom of thought and an irrepressible need for individual independence that, he explained, was soon to spread its blessings throughout European civilization. Other freedoms manifested themselves later, beginning with freedom of conscience, resulting from the Reformation, which would in turn engender an "explosion of the human mind," presaging the philosophical revolution of the eighteenth century: "Wherever the Reformation penetrated, wherever it acted an important part, whether conqueror or conquered, its general, leading, and constant result was an immense progress in mental activity and freedom; an immense step toward the emancipation of the human mind."[9]

Other historians, less cautious than Guizot, attributed exceptional weight to the influence of race in the construction of a narrative that was intended to be perfectly linear. For instance, Édouard Laboulaye, a liberal critic of the Second Empire and a great admirer of Tocqueville and Bancroft, offered a singular reading of the "point of departure" of American democracy, which he located, as they did, with the arrival of the Puritans. It all started in New England with the "pure democracy," symbolized by the Mayflower Pact. Ignoring all distinctions of rank, origin, and fortune, the Pilgrims demonstrated that "democracy escaped from feudal society and that political liberty triumphed alongside religious liberty."[10] Who were these early settlers, so attached to reason and political liberties? Religion alone was not enough to explain their indomitable passion for individual liberty. Other motives were necessary, and Laboulaye found the explanation in the race of the immigrants. He explained (without demonstrating) that they "did not belong to the conquerors of the Norman race, but to the Saxons." They brought with them a "special genius," admirably described by Tacitus: individual liberty. In short, "the *character of the race* impelled them toward independence."[11] Laboulaye, a professor of comparative legislation at the Collège de France and a member of the Institut, an indefatigable promoter of the ambitious project of financing the "gift of France" to the United States—a huge statue of Liberty—was the first renowned historian to establish an explicit link between "Germanic race," religion, and political liberty.[12] From this perspective, the liberty of the Moderns was merely the end point of the very ancient liberty of the Barbarians, discovered by Tacitus in the depths of the German forests and idealized beyond measure by the German Romantics, beginning with Herder.

THIS TYPE OF INTERPRETATION, based on the permanence of the genius of the Saxons, became less common in France, for obvious reasons, after the defeat of the French in the Franco-Prussian war of 1870. From then on, it was preferable to speak of the innate virtues of the English, the *Anglo*-Saxons, or the *Yankees*, "that republican race with ineradicable originality" whose qualities Laboulaye had already pointed out: a "grim and adventurous" character that was at the same time "religious and moral."[13] Michel Chevalier provided the best, most original, and most Romantic definition of *Yankee*. An authentic descendant of the Puritan colonists of new England, the "Yankee," according to Chevalier, is the opposite of the Virginian. He is "adventurous"; he is "narrow in his ideas but practical"; he is "the laborious ant"; "industrious and sober," he can also be "crafty, sly, always calculating"; "expeditious in business," he has no equal "in acting upon things," while always managing "to lull his conscience."[14] At the time Chevalier was writing, the Yankee was the ideal pioneer, able "to build himself a log hut, six hundred miles from his father's roof, and clear away a spot for a farm in the midst of the boundless forest."[15] He has an inexhaustible supply of energy that he uses in a constant struggle with nature:

> More unyielding than she [he] subdues her at last, obliging her ... to yield whatever he wills, and to take the shape he chooses. Like Hercules, he conquers the hydra of the pestilential morass, and chains the rivers; more daring than Hercules, he extends his dominion not only over the land, but over the sea; he is the best sailor in the world. . . . More wise than

the hero of the twelve labours, he knows no Omphale that is able to seduce, no Dejanira, whose poisoned gifts can balk his searching glance. In this respect he is rather a Ulysses, who has his Penelope, counts upon her faith, and remains steadfastly true to her. He does not even need to stop his ears, when he passes near the Syrens, for in him the tenderest passions are deadened by religious austerity and devotion to his business.[16]

The contrast is striking between the jurist, Laboulaye, who finds that the Moderns possess the liberty of the Barbarians and the economist, Chevalier, who discovers that they share the mythology of the Ancients. But the result is identical: the ancient character, whether barbarian or mythological, is always heroic; it produces the same type of man—the entrepreneur or the pioneer, enamored of political liberty and deeply marked by the religion of his ancestors; in short, the only one able to build a great nation.

The great question in the late nineteenth century was that of the survival of the supposedly superior "Anglo-Saxon race." The massive influx of new immigrants was a source of anxiety. The French geographer Élisée Reclus, a disciple of Bakunin and author of a monumental nineteen-volume *Géographie universelle* (translated into English as *The Earth and Its Inhabitants*), wondered whether it would be possible to absorb immigrants "so different in their usages, traditions and national temperament from the Anglo-American."[17] Was it necessary to take restrictive measures against European immigration, modeled on those that targeted the Chinese in 1882? Many politicians had already proposed them, Reclus remarked. But he took pains to distinguish racist xenophobia from a socioeconomic form of xenophobia:

> It is obviously a question not of racial hostility but of purely economic and political considerations. The educated classes, primarily in New England, naturally object to an administration appointed by ignorant electors exercising their right of suffrage in a blind or venal way. On the other hand the American labouring classes resent the unfair competition of an alien proletariate tending to lower the rate of wages by a third, a half or even more, thereby helping rich manufacturers achieve monopoly power.[18]

As a good demographer, Reclus noted that the "new ethnical elements"—Italians, Slavs, Slovaks, Croats, Serbs, Poles, and Czechs—were almost as numerous as English, Scottish, Irish, and Welsh immigrants and that they would soon be the *majority* of new arrivals. These projections were reinforced by a comparative analysis of the birth rates of "native" American and immigrant families. The former, the "pure Americans," or the great "families of Puritan origin," because they feared the future and no longer had the means to guarantee the economic success of their children, had considerably reduced the size of their families, which had shrunk in the course of three generations from an average of ten children per couple to only three. The birth rate had declined so much in the northeastern states—"the founding states of the Republic"— that, without the influx of immigrants, the country would soon be depopulated.

Élisée Reclus described a situation and pointed to certain tendencies; he did not judge his contemporaries and expressed no worries about the future of America, its genius, or its fundamental values. He knew that, whatever the "natives" thought or said, from a demographic perspective, the new immigrants "represented a much more active element than residents settled for several generations." Because their numbers were growing and because, on average, their families were more fertile, their descendants would in the long run be dominant. Consequently, he concluded, they would make up the "future nation." Reclus's logic is assimilationist and he frequently alludes to the building of a melting pot, sometimes described as a mixture of "races" gradually melding into a new human type, sometimes as "metals of various qualities," brought together by chance and ready to fuse "in a single furnace."[19] Echoing Crèvecœur's tone in referring to the emergence of the "American," Reclus in turn presents a memorable portrait of the racial mix of the "man of the New World." "He seems, *under the influence of the milieu,* to have come closer physically to the Indian: one sees more often Americans with the reddish tinge, the long straight hair, the cold and piercing gaze, the rugged face, the arched nose, and the haughty attitude characteristic of the aborigines. One might say that the dying Redskin has reappeared in his destroyer."[20]

Élisée Reclus was neither a racist nor a eugenicist. His description of the melting pot—metals in a furnace—is coupled with an ironic blend of Modern and Barbarian, Yankee and Amerindian, which owes more to Montesquieu's theory of climates than to the influence of the sciences of race, although they were very fashionable at the time he was writing. His view of the demographic situation was lucid, merely based on the observation of current tendencies that he projected into the future.

BUT THE FALLING BIRTH RATE AMONG Anglo-Saxons was a central concern for the advocates of restrictions on immigration, who were deter-

mined to maintain insofar as possible the presumed advantages of the Founders' race. Starting from the same assumptions as the American demographers
who influenced Élisée Reclus, one of the major prophets of the superiority of
the "Nordics," Madison Grant, deplored the low birth rate of the descendants
of the "natives" of the colonial period. Grant considered them to be the bear-
ers of all the racial characteristics appropriate for the "desirable classes." And
yet these eminently positive racial traits of "the superior classes, which are of
superior type physically, intellectually and morally," were in his view endangered by the uncontrolled influx of "undesirable" classes that had recently
come from Central and Mediterranean Europe.[21] Hence there was a risk, denounced by all the supporters of the Immigration Restriction League, of an
uncontrollable mixture of races fostering the upsurge of primitive characteristics buried in the heredity of the inferior races. In the face of the real danger of
a growth in the number of "moral perverts, mental defectives, and hereditary
cripples,"[22] Madison Grant—a lawyer by profession, the founder and president
of the New York Zoological Society, and a director of the Museum of Natural
History—argued for a vigorous eugenic policy of sterilization of adults considered "undesirable" by the rest of the national community. But he acknowledged that this policy would not be enough to guarantee the perpetuation of
the Founders' race. A great danger loomed for the future of America: the "race
suicide"[23] of the best Anglo-Saxons, unable or reluctant to produce as many
children as the hordes of immigrants who were daily landing at Ellis Island.

The only valid solution for Grant and the majority of the restrictionists
required a radical redefinition of immigration policies: the institution of quo-
tas that were expansive enough to favor the growth of the superior race of
the "Nordics" (including Anglo-Saxons, Teutonics, and Scandinavians), but
restrictive enough to put an end to the influx of immigrants of inferior races,
defined sometimes as "Alpine" (including the Slavs and Jews of Central Europe), sometimes as "Mediterranean" (Italians, Greeks, Spaniards, and Southern French). The ideal race, in Grant's view, was not purely Anglo-Saxon but
an alloy limited to the Nordic peoples in general. In the eyes of the advocates
of a regenerated America, the great melting pot made popular by the English
writer Israel Zangwill was an abomination that had to be eliminated as soon
as possible, before it was too late; that is, before the dominant traits of the inferior races crushed or dispersed the splendid characteristics of the great race
of the first colonists.[24]

We Americans must realize that the altruistic ideals which have controlled our social development during the past century, and the maudlin

sentimentalism that has made America "an asylum for the oppressed," are sweeping the nation toward a racial abyss. If the Melting Pot is allowed to boil without control, and we continue to follow our national motto and deliberately blind ourselves to all "distinctions of race, creed, or color," the type of native American of Colonial descent will become as extinct as the Athenian of the age of Pericles, and the Viking of the days of Rollo.[25]

The advocates of an America turned in on itself, protected from the new Barbarian invasion, justified their xenophobic project in the name of a new historiography that had mobilized all the advanced disciplines of the time—demography, phrenology, Darwinism, Mendelianism, eugenics, and linguistics. In the view of the eugenicists, the mixture of the Anglo-Nordic races, vigorously encouraged by Congress with the passage of the quota laws in the 1920s, guaranteed the perpetuation of a group reputed for its intellectual and moral superiority.[26] The "improvement of the race" therefore implied strict control over immigrant influxes: ever more northern Europeans, fewer Slavs, Jews, and Latins, and the complete prohibition of immigration from Asia.

Immigration Policies Seen from France

How were these arguments, already very controversial in the United States, understood, referred to, and discussed by French social scientists? The works of Emile Boutmy and André Siegfried illustrate the French position. Boutmy (1835–1906), a historian by training, was the founder of the École Libre des Science Politiques, and Siegfried (1875–1959), a political geographer and sociologist, taught for a long time in the same École, before becoming the director of an institution that is now known as Sciences Po. These two social scientists, with very different sensibilities, devoted a good deal of time to the study of American society and shared a certain idea of the American character that surprisingly anticipates the later work of Samuel P. Huntington.

In *Éléments d'une psychologie politique du peuple américain* (1902), Boutmy attempted to define, in his speculative fashion, the essence of the American spirit, which he saw as simultaneously patriotic, ethnic, and religious. The ethnic element is central in the model proposed by Boutmy. There is at the outset a homogeneous "human type," that of the first colonists, "the invariable characteristics of which were indomitable energy [and] strength of conviction."[27] Boutmy acknowledges the existence of a certain ethnic pluralism from the beginning of the conquest of North America, since English colonists rubbed shoulders with French and Dutch colonists. But this diversity, in his view, was quite transitory; the "ethnic pockets," clearly identifiable in the early seventeenth century, had gradually disappeared: they had "slowly dissolved in the mass of Anglo-Saxons."[28] The first waves of immigration after the independence of the United States and during the first part of the nineteenth century did not alter the dominant characteristics of the Anglo-Saxons: the new immigrants came from England and Scotland and were thus made up of elements identical to the great mass of colonists already present. Their assimilation was easy and racial and national homogeneity "was therefore quickly reconstructed after each infusion of new substance."

Everything changed, according to Boutmy, beginning with the great wave of Irish immigration in the 1840s, followed by other waves from Germany, Italy, Czechoslovakia, Poland, and Russia, bringing about the inevitable result of a slow decline in the "Anglo-Saxon element" in the population and the rise to power of "Celtic, Germanic, Latin, and Slavic elements that were very disparate and more or less refractory." Was there immediate danger? One might fear as much, Boutmy observed, since these new immigrants had a tendency to live in the same places, to "stick together and apart from others," to "confirm their ethnic sympathies," and to marry only women of their own race. In addition, they remained loyal to the country of their ancestors and, like the Irish, did not hesitate to provide financial support to the revolutionaries of their country of origin. The racial heterogeneity of the United States consequently risked affecting the very nature of American patriotism, weakened by the multiple allegiances of the new arrivals. "Our patriotism can be represented by a circle that has only one center, theirs by an ellipse with two foci."[29]

Did it then necessarily follow that America would face disunity, that there was a risk of the implosion of a society threatened from within by a clash of races and civilizations? Despite these preliminary considerations, Boutmy was not a pessimist; he was convinced that the heterogeneity of American society nevertheless created social bonds thanks to the triumph of a value unknown in Europe: Yankee individualism. This individualism, to which, like Michel Chevalier, he attached a good deal of importance, was the individualism of a man of action, always ready to overcome the obstacles posed by untamed nature, asserting control over his own fate, convinced that each could become whatever he wanted to be and that each was "worth what he had made of himself."[30] The American dream, so clearly pictured by Boutmy, was not only the product of selfish private passions. It was also a source of altruism and public spirit: "Individuals have a fund of energy that their private affairs do not manage to exhaust; some of it remains that they apply to countless enterprises of social interest and, when necessary, to the highest enterprise of all, the interest of the state."[31] That was the nature of "bourgeois patriotism," which was down to earth and utilitarian, but capable of grandeur once politicians, like the earlier pioneers who set out to conquer the West, felt themselves invested with a civilizing mission.

Boutmy's analysis was excessively optimistic. All elements of conflict in the history of the United States were overlooked in favor of an argument that gave pride of place to consensus, the shared acceptance of individualist and liberal norms, the questionable assertion that everyone could choose his path and easily overcome the obstacles of life and nature. Two major conclusions of the book illustrate the special place it holds in the context of French scholarly work devoted to America at the time. The first concerns the Puritan spirit: it did not shape once and for all American ways of thinking. The second touches on the question of immigration: the huge size of the country and its economic dynamism favored the continuation of an open immigration policy. Boutmy did not express the slightest sympathy for nativist policies. He suggested that the poorest and least assimilated of the immigrants would sooner or later become good Americans, once they adopted the great American dream, that is, "to be free to choose your path, to see victory before you, with no artificial barrier blocking its approaches, to move forward with the certainty of reaching it . . . to sense that your will is stronger than fortune."[32]

Unlike Tocqueville, Boutmy granted little place to religion in his analysis of the psychology of the American people. Or rather he attributed to it a declining influence—adopting an argument akin to Weber's thesis of the disenchantment of the world. The faith of the Pilgrim Fathers and their "vigorous spiritual unity," based on an austere "government of souls," could not survive the system of tolerance that was gradually established in the New England colonies. Of the Puritan past, Boutmy writes, there subsisted only habits detached from former beliefs, that is, a "practical sense" and an "indefatigable energy." Belief in an absolute and intransigent dogma was gradually replaced by the habits of consumers subject to competition and to the "huge and shifting mass of hundreds of sects . . . which each individual joins as unthinkingly as he will leave it, out of liking for the personality of the pastor or for a particular aspect of the ritual, rather than out of deep faith in the superiority of its doctrine." This explains the superficiality of American Christianity that offered only "moral hygiene" or a kind of positivism. "There remains of Christianity," Boutmy concludes, "only a sort of residue, half pressed and strained dregs, which still taste like bitter and comforting wine, but lacking in depth and bouquet."[33]

Denouncing the proliferation of sects, the gradual abandonment of the major Calvinist principles, the dismissal of the "somber and threatening" aspects of dogma, and the triumph of the "ignorant missionaries" recruited in the new Methodist and Baptist Churches, Boutmy believed that these were the deplorable consequences of the growing secularization of American society. To the heroic age of the Puritans, based on a "metaphysics steeped in legend," had succeeded the age of evangelical improvisation, the theology of which was "non-existent or worse than non-existent, dry and pedestrian beyond imagining." In short, there had been a veritable "collapse of dogma and theology," foretelling a radical secularization of American society. The most forward looking sects, such as the Unitarianism so fashionable in New England, had radically transformed the reading of the Scriptures by eliminating the divine and drawing from the Bible "either a Confucian morality, or a natural religion derived from Rousseau."[34]

What is interesting in Boutmy's argument is that he does not presuppose that there was an American Creed conceived by the Puritans, revived by the Founding Fathers, and preserved down to the early twentieth century by the masses who were still largely Anglo-Saxon. The Puritan spirit was no longer the order of the day; the dominant force, in his view, was a certain bourgeois patriotism that was at bottom nothing but a barely disguised reformulation of Tocqueville's thesis concerning enlightened self-interest. As Boutmy himself acknowledged from a methodological perspective, the traditional hierarchy of relations between history, politics, and economics were reversed so as to give a preeminent place to economics and a secondary role to historical and political factors. If he saw a point of departure for the American character, it was outside any religious or ideological phenomenon; it was the product of the encounter between humans and their milieu, "the totality of the physical and geographical conditions surrounding the new arrival."[35] Everything else followed from this initial shock:

> The source of any impulse felt by the will, the matrix of any imprint received by the character, is here obvious necessity, the *summons*, so to speak, to recognize, occupy, and develop this huge territory. This necessity somehow gives the mind its notion of the supreme good; all other motives give way before this one or are imbued with it. In a word, the

United States is above all an economic society; it is only secondarily a historical and political society.[36]

So if there is an ideal type of "good American," it is the pioneer, the clearer of forests, the hero winning the West. There thus reappears in this French search for a psychology of the American people the image of the backwoodsman, simultaneously hunter, clearer of land, and warrior, popularized by Theodore Roosevelt in his epic history of the "American race," *The Winning of the West.*[37]

In a chapter on "method," Boutmy criticizes Tocqueville for his indulgence in generalized deductions and his ignorance of particular facts, without which, he claims, it is impossible to grasp the behavior of a "race" or a nation. Among other things, he criticizes Tocqueville for not having studied the geographical and physical milieu and therefore failing to substantiate his "admirable psychological study" with examples.[38] In doing so, he ignored the persuasive power of some posthumous works of Tocqueville, the most impressive of which is probably "Two Weeks in the Wilderness," written in 1832 and published by Gustave de Beaumont in 1860 in the *Revue des Deux Mondes.*[39] In this account of a journey "to the furthest limits" of civilization in the midst of impenetrable forests a few miles from Detroit in the new territory of Michigan, Tocqueville and Beaumont discover a new "clearing," in the center of which sits a pioneer's log house. The appearance of the master of the house is austere; his "well-defined muscles" and "slender limbs" indicate his ethnic origin: he is clearly a Yankee. The principal characteristic of the pioneer is his persistent energy, "his willpower which has thrust him into the labors of the wilderness for which he seems little suited." At first sight, the pioneer seems cold and insensitive, with a face marked by "stoic solidity." In reality, he is a passionate being, restless and adventurous, who "deals in everything, including religion and morality." It is with men of such mettle, Tocqueville concludes, that a "nation of conquerors" is built, that is, "a people which, like all great peoples, have only one thought and which step out to acquire wealth as the sole aim of their efforts, with a persistence and a scorn for life which we might call heroic, if this term were suitable for anything else besides the efforts due to virtue."[40]

Tocqueville's pioneer is not simply the plaything of economic necessity. Any clash between man and nature is voluntary and directed toward a single aim: to transform a "wilderness" into land suitable for cultivation and, in the end, to make his fortune. Tocqueville's portrait of the settler is identical to the backwoodsman that Theodore Roosevelt so highly praised. But sixty years separate the works of the two writers. Tocqueville was describing a present in the process of formation, the activity of an "unknown man" who is in reality "the representative of a race to which the future of the New World belongs."[41] Roosevelt deplored the exhaustion of the race: the lack of courage, the comfort, the opulence, and the effeminate and overly Europeanized manners of his contemporaries. He therefore vaunted the virtues of war and hunting and, more broadly, a return to the heroic values of the mythic pioneers who had conquered the West. Going back even further in time, Roosevelt did not hesitate to claim that those pioneers were the direct descendants of the early Germans who subjugated the Celtic and English tribes of the British Isles.

In a striking summary, Roosevelt connects the great myth of winning the West to another myth fashionable among ethnographers of the time: the ancestral superiority of the Germans or Saxons. Urban industrial America of the late nineteenth century obviously no longer had much in common with the America of the clearers of forests of the early part of the century, and Roosevelt acknowledged that "blood" had been "mixed." Just as the early Saxons had joined with the Celts to become English, so the English, Dutch, French, and Germans "fused" into one American people.[42] The most important thing was to preserve the hereditary characteristics of the Anglo-Saxon peoples. Since the hereditary transmission of acquired characteristics was not absolutely certain, it was strongly recommended that the Moderns imitate the Ancients—the pioneers, the frontiersmen—to recover that primitive energy without which a great people was doomed to failure and decline.[43]

André Siegfried and the American Creed

A generation separates Émile Boutmy, the founder of the École Libre des Sciences Politiques, from André Siegfried, the future director of the school, whose father, the industrialist Jules Siegfried, and uncle, the banker Jacques Siegfried, had provided financial support for it. Boutmy's program was part of a broad nationalist movement of recovery in the face of the German challenge. Major French intellectuals, including Taine and Renan, had attributed the catastrophic defeat of Sedan in 1870 to one particular cause: the ignorance and unpreparedness of French political and military elites. Clearly influenced by the writings of the renovators of the French nation, Boutmy had in his way proposed an intellectual and moral reformation of France by launching a "Proposal for an Independent Faculty of Political Science," drafted in collaboration with his friend Ernest Vinet. His intentions were clear: to re-constitute an elite that would soon set the tone for the nation, in short to "restore a mind to the people."[44] This was the source of Boutmy's interest in the allied peoples whose minds were obviously well made. His *Essai d'une psychologie politique du peuple anglais* preceded by one year the *Éléments d'une psychologie politique du peuple américain.*[45]

As previously indicated, Boutmy, in his considerations on the American character, granted some prominence to economic factors. In his view, the Pu-ritan spirit of the seventeenth century had been diluted in the eighteenth and nineteenth centuries by progress in winning the West. The brutal clash between humans and wilderness had produced Yankee individualism, a sec-ularized appropriation of the Puritan spirit. The place granted religion in Boutmy's system was hence not central: religion was merely "moral hygiene," useful for the Yankee's colonizing enterprise.

Siegfried, bringing to mind the analyses of the geographer Élisée Reclus and the economist Pierre Leroy-Beaulieu, paid little attention to the physical surroundings. He laid the greatest stress on the influence of ideas on politi-cians' decision making. Less optimistic than his predecessors, Siegfried did not believe in the virtues of the melting pot. Like Leroy-Beaulieu, he thought that the true Americans, born in the United States of American parents, still made up a large majority (61 percent of the white population), but he did not draw the same conclusions from this observation.[46] For Leroy-Beaulieu, a large influx of new immigrants did not fundamentally change the character of a people, which had already been formed and defined by the great waves of nineteenth century immigration. The Americans not only had solid institu-tions, but most importantly they demonstrated a singular "spirit," so strong and persuasive that it literally imbued the new arrivals.[47]

Siegfried, whose account came later, had doubts about the moral and polit-ical unity of the American people, about its racial homogeneity and the solid-ity of the ancestral values embodied in the Protestant tradition of the pioneers of the independence era. He saw an imminent danger: it was not immigration as such that threatened "the moral and political character of the country," but its makeup, which was so exotic and multifarious that it raised questions about the future: The American people "are dismayed by the heterogeneous germs which they feel growing up within their body politic—Catholic, Jew, and Oriental, all of whom they feel to be out of sympathy with their tradi-tions. They have a vague uneasy fear of being overwhelmed from within, and of suddenly finding one day that they are no longer themselves." And the diffuse but very real fear of "an insidious subjugation by foreign blood" touched the very fiber of modern America, its "center of gravity," which had until then resided "in the Anglo-Saxon and Puritan stock."[48]

Siegfried's whole argument turns on this hypothesis: America is unhinged, its fundamental values threatened, and it is on the verge of losing confidence in itself. "Is it possible to contemplate a United States that is neither Protestant nor Anglo-Saxon?" Siegfried wondered, making it clear that this was not his question but that of the advocates of a defensive nationalism for whom the real America belonged, as a matter of principle, to shareholders of a new kind: "the privileged few who can claim founders' shares."[49]

To that old America, devoted to the cult of the Founders, proud of its race and of its Anglo-republican-Protestant creed, Siegfried contrasted the America of the Moderns, made up of recent immigrants, unselfconsciously affirming their own traditions and thereby rejecting the judgment of "inferiority" imposed on them by members of the Nordic races. Natives of Central and Mediterranean Europe, mostly Italians, Slavs, Latins, and Eastern Jews: "Like uncut jewels, they had come from Europe with their traditions of brilliant civilizations."[50] They had no intention of giving up their ancestral traditions to satisfy the demands of the advocates of total assimilation. Implicitly echoing the writings of the philosopher Horace Kallen, one of the first thinkers to discuss American multiculturalism,[51] Siegfried illustrated the point of view of the Moderns in this way:

> The American-Italian who writes English with a Mediterranean flourish, the American Jew with his centuries of accumulated knowledge, and even the Negro whose singing and dancing have added to the artistic patrimony of the whole human race, have all contributed to American civilization; and when they enroll themselves in the movement they insist that they should be received just as they are and with all the honors of war.[52]

Siegfried had not failed to observe the growth of the Ku Klux Klan, one year after the passage of one of the most restrictive immigration laws in United States history, the Johnson Reed Act of 1924. He saw it as a possible turning point in the history of the United States, a confrontation between two rival conceptions of "Americanism." The first, consistent with the arguments of the Social Darwinists, fostered the cult of ancestors and the reproduction of the same people. The national future, for the supporters of this conception, presupposed complete assimilation of the newcomers. It was up to the Italians, the Russians, the Germans, and so on, to demonstrate that they had indeed become like Americans of Anglo-Saxon stock. If, unhappily, they showed a "delay in assimilation," if they did not become "100 percenters," if they resisted Americanization programs—in short, if they did not "adopt Anglo-Saxon moral, social, and religious principles,"[53]—the future was irrevocably closed to them and new exclusionary laws were therefore fully justified to put an end to the influx of their compatriots.

Even worse, they were barred from the very possibility of successful assimilation if they were subjected to the proto-fascist racial logic advocated by the most fanatical of the nativists. The nation was not for sale; it could belong only to "the one race with which its religion, moral code, and exclusive traditions are associated."[54] All foreigners were suspected of being unpatriotic according to the draconian norms that the leaders of the Ku Klux Klan promulgated. There was even talk of denying the right to vote to Catholics, suspected of owing allegiance to a foreign sovereign, and to the Jews "who work against America." As for Bible reading in public schools, it should be made obligatory and joined with a rule of conduct based on "the teaching of Christ Jesus, as given in the Holy Bible, the Word of God." Finally, proclaimed *The American Standard*, the organ of the Ku Klux Klan, there must be a "return of the negroes to their homeland in Africa."[55]

Another conception of Americanism, more in harmony with the Moderns' way of thinking, cultivated difference and, even more, the cultural richness of the new immigrants. Its advocates, who were few but active in intellectual circles, included "believers" and "mystics," such as Israel Zangwill, author of a successful play, *The Melting Pot* (1908), and Waldo Frank, author of a virulent social critique of the America of the pioneers, *Our America* (1919). These intellectuals rejected any fixed notion of America mired in the distant Puritan past; they envisioned a nearly millenarian radiant future: a new nation in the process of defining itself, whose future would remain open and whose creed would be that of "a land which could revive the weary by the breath of its independence."

Which of the two conceptions would win out? Siegfried cautiously refrained from a definite conclusion: "The final destiny of the country is still in suspense," he wrote, "and it is unable to foretell what tomorrow will be its soul."[56] But this caution was nonetheless belied by the abundance of arguments and examples supporting the nativists' position. Everything is presented in such a way as to make the reader share the terror of the old America in the face of the "tidal wave," the "inundation of Latin-Slav Catholics and

Oriental Jews" coming off the boats from Europe. The use of watery and medical metaphors was not accidental. The "fantastic medley of peoples," a "bewildered and amorphous crew," the presence in the great cities of "indigestible blocks" of people, and the intrinsic inferiority of the "heterogeneous germs" who did not offer the "moral character" requisite for assimilation all rightly worried Protestant America.[57] It therefore reacted by mobilizing all the resources made available by the new science of eugenics to erect the protective ramparts of a new "restorative nationalism," whose necessity Siegfried understood, even though he pretended to deplore its lack of finesse: "It has already had its Bulldog Drummond. It now needs to learn from the intellectual depth of Maurice Barrès."[58]

Characterizing them collectively as the "pseudo-American [who] ferments at the bottom of the Melting Pot, unassimilated to the end," Siegfried presented a particularly unflattering portrait of the most recent immigration of "Russian Jews," whom he viewed as "irreconcilables, who attempted to become a part of Western civilization only to repudiate it in the end"; their intelligence was undeniable but dangerous, because it could be neither domesticated nor disciplined.[59] In a particularly harsh observation regarding the patriotic zeal of new immigrants, Siegfried even expressed suspicion of the sincerity of children waving the American flag: "If the Stars and Stripes is waved at a jingo demonstration in New York, you may be sure that it is a Jew who holds the standard, while the 100 per cent American whose great-great-grandfather was a friend of Washington stands aside disgusted."[60]

There should be no mistake: the Jews, apparently forgetful of their traditions, eager to Anglicize their names the better to blend in with the Christians, like blacks with light skin passing for white, were no more Christian than blacks were white. They remained Jews once and for all, "pseudo-Americans."[61] In Siegfried's view, as a result, a certain form of anti-Semitism was largely excusable, because Protestant America was acting like an "organism defending itself."[62]

Was Siegfried a racist and an anti-Semite? It is a vexed question and it raises the risk of writing history retrospectively, applying a modern point of view marked by the knowledge of the devastating effects of racism and anti-Semitism in the second quarter of the twentieth century. Siegfried certainly believed in the existence of races, despite the lack of rigor in his definitions. The French, for example, constituted a "race," in the same way as the Italians did. In addition, while not believing in the racial superiority of the Anglo-Saxons, he easily saw Westerners taken as a whole as "superior" to Africans,

Asians, and Middle Easterners, and he shared most of the racial prejudices of the political and intellectual elites of his time. His digressions on "the Wall Street Jew" and "the synagogue Jew," "those Jews whose religion has become bitter and dry," and "the bearded Jew from a far-off European ghetto," all of whom are equally unable to assimilate because "the temperature at which fusion takes place [in the melting pot] is too low" and "an insoluble residue is liable to remain," reproduce the most hackneyed prejudices of the time.[63] One may smile at the clichés of the "Italian macaroni eater" or the incorrigibly individualistic French, but it is impossible not to be surprised and dismayed by the litany of purportedly accurate images of "some Alsatian Jew, a 'kike' from Breslau, a 'sheeny' from Lemberg or Salonika, or even—and I do not exaggerate—some Hebrew from Asia, with goat eyes and patriarchal beard."[64]

As early as 1927, an American reader of *America Comes of Age* expressed the "very painful impression" she had experienced in reading those passages, more characteristic of an anti-Semitic pamphleteer such as Édouard Drumont than of a university-trained scholar.

> Yes, I know, you will say that you are concerned with the "facts." But you use these facts, which prove nothing against Jews in general, to incriminate all of them. This is the age-old injustice from which they suffer! No one knows or wants to know the Jewish soul. What is seen as a quality in others is considered a vice in them: ambition becomes "cupidity" in a Jew; joy in living, in breathing free air is condemned as "revolutionary." The most noble aspirations, love of work and study, provoke reprobation or jealousy.[65]

Siegfried's answer to this letter is unknown, but there were no changes made in the many reprints of this successful book to attenuate the painful impression produced by these caricatures.[66]

Siegfried should nonetheless be credited with the fact that he did not hesitate to criticize the most striking excesses of the nativist camp, beginning with the neo-Malthusian eugenics whose arguments he summarized with scathing irony. He came out against the "new code of racial ethics," that advocated the sterilization of the degenerate and against the imposition of birth control on the poor and immigrants in order to preserve the superiority of the Nordics, the "Anglo-Saxon stock" whose birth rate was unfortunately declining.[67]

The new code of racial ethics was not religious in the strict sense of the term, but it lent support to a certain Protestant moralism centered on hygiene, discipline, and racial purity. This accounts for the copious advice Siegfried offered to foreign visitors wishing to attain a better understanding of American ways of thinking: "If you visit the United States you must not forget your Bible, but you must also take a treatise on eugenics. Armed with these two talismans, you will never get beyond your depth."[68]

ANDRÉ SIEGFRIED WAS FULLY AWARE OF American religious diversity, the "confusion of sects," the excesses of fundamentalism, and the missionary zeal of the advocates of Prohibition. But he accepted one of the key tenets of nativist circles of the time, namely, that "Protestantism is the only national religion, and to ignore that fact is to view the country from a false angle."[69]

What did he mean by Protestantism? Certainly not Lutheranism, although it was practiced by many German and Scandinavian immigrants, nor Anglicanism, which was dominant in Virginia and some mid-Atlantic states, but Anglo-Saxon Puritanism. In his view, there was no doubt that American democratic culture expresses a "Calvinist point of view" that had never stopped affecting American ways of thinking. In its most visible and most questionable manifestations, the Puritan spirit, the eternal righter of wrongs, dealt with everything, from the battle against alcohol to the fight against slums, tobacco, feminism, pacifism, and so on. All of this worked "to purify the life of the community and to uplift the state." Nothing eluded the inquisitorial gaze of Americans of Anglo-Saxon stock, which explained the enduring contempt of Protestant elites for the newest immigrants who shared neither the same origins nor the same values.[70] Religion, for Siegfried, involved ethnic issues, leading Protestant elites to treat the insufficiently assimilated immigrants who did not belong to the dominant "race" as unrepentant sinners.

"It is impossible to understand the United States unless one fully appreciates the Puritan spirit" he asserted at the beginning of *America Comes of Age*. But it is not clear that Siegfried understood the Puritan spirit. In fact, Siegfried confused the Calvinism of the Pilgrims with a watered-down version of Calvinism later popularized by the evangelists of the Second Great Awakening. He also confused the troubled faith of the Puritans with the certainty of salvation readily affirmed by the born-again Christians who were so influential in the nineteenth century.

Siegfried's analysis certainly recalls Max Weber's argument in *The Protestant Ethic and the Spirit of Capitalism*. But Weber's wealth of detail, precise sources, and historical rigor are clearly lacking.[71] In a chapter on "the religious aspect," Siegfried asserts that unlike the Catholic, "the Puritan . . . regards his wealth as an honour, and when he hoards up his profits, he says smugly that

Providence has been kind."[72] The formulation is striking: the Puritan "hoards up his profits"; but it compresses four centuries of history and fails to take into account the successive reinterpretations of Calvin's thought. Weber's treatment of the subject was unquestionably subtler, although his own thought has often been simplified and watered down by his interpreters.

Weber presents first Calvin's thesis of predestination and raises the fundamental question that his disciples all had to confront: "Am I one of the elect? . . . And how can I be sure of this state of grace?"[73] Calvin provides no clear answer to the question. He rejected on principle any attempt to understand the divine mysteries. Nothing visible on earth makes it possible to distinguish the elect from the damned. And this is why the community of the elect are "God's invisible Church."[74] However, in order to perpetuate the master's thinking, Calvin's disciples sought to overcome this unbearable uncertainty by providing means of "dispersing [the] religious doubts" of believers by proposing that they recognize visible signs of their election in their daily life.[75] For example, an "effectual calling," which is a successful and disciplined professional career lasting a lifetime. "The God of Calvinism demanded of his believers not single good works, but a life of good works combined into a unified system."[76] The professional asceticism envisioned by Calvin's disciples was thus a comforting arrangement, intended to calm the anxiety inherent in the master's doctrine by producing a new notion: "the idea of proving one's faith in worldly activity."[77] For Weber, the price paid for the modernization of Calvinism was an oversimplification of Calvin's theology, centered on visible socioeconomic success. Unlike Luther, Calvin did not promise grace to sinners who repented. But the rigor of his doctrine produced in reaction "those self-confident saints whom we can rediscover in the hard Puritan merchants of the heroic age of capitalism." Calvinism, modified by a new intense work ethic "disperses religious doubts and gives the certainty of grace."[78]

This Protestant ethic, cut off from the theological foundations of true Calvinism was the one Siegfried believed he was observing in the United States. But, less rigorous than Weber, he did not attempt to distinguish original Calvinism from its later metamorphoses. His history of Protestantism seems oddly simplistic and linear. It was in fact evangelicalism, much more than the early forms of Calvinism, that the French visitor found distasteful.

> Every American is at heart an evangelist, be he a Wilson, a Bryan, or a Rockefeller. He cannot leave people alone, and he constantly feels the urge to preach. His good faith may be incontestable and his efforts often magnificent, but one is always aware of a certain moral superiority, which

is the most unsympathetic of Anglo-Saxon traits. His self-satisfaction as a member of God's elect is almost insufferable, and so is the idea that his duty toward his neighbour is to convert, purify, and raise him to his own moral heights.[79]

Echoing Tocqueville's notions about the compatibility of modern Catholicism with democracy, Siegfried deplored the racism and "the ethnic beliefs of these American Pharisees," the Protestants. In his view, the Catholic Church had the advantage of being open to all, to the poor, the humble, the foreigners, whatever their race or national origin, thereby seeking to establish itself as fundamentally egalitarian and democratic. Contrary to what Huntington later asserted, Siegfried did not see the Catholic Church as an obstacle to immigrant assimilation, but rather a magnificent "trump card in a country where the poor immigrants are looked upon as second-class citizens." Moreover, Catholicism acted as an antidote against the Puritan fanaticism of the "zealots for national morality,"[80] against whom Siegfried launched ironic attacks for their excesses over Prohibition and the celebrated 1925 "monkey trial," in which the state of Tennessee successfully prosecuted a high-school science teacher for teaching Darwin's theory of evolution, in direct violation of a creationist law backed by fundamentalist pastors.[81] Siegfried thus did not see Catholicism as a counterculture endangering Anglo-Saxon supremacy, but as a useful way of facilitating the assimilation of the poor and those who could not bring themselves "to look upon beer-drinking as a crime."[82]

SIEGFRIED'S FEARS ABOUT AN ANGLO-PROTESTANT America on the verge of losing its soul—an America fundamentally changed by the massive arrival of "exotic" immigrants, giving rise, as in an organism defending itself, to a reinvigorated nationalism—seem retrograde and racist today, although they were accepted in a period that was deeply marked by Social Darwinism and fantasies of the racial superiority of the Nordics. Siegfried's opinion probably reflected the dominant view of the elites of his time. He did not ignore the opposite viewpoint of those who were beginning to imagine a more open, diverse, ethnic America escaping from the straitjacket of Anglo-Protestant ideology. But he minimized the impact of this new national narrative, a precursor of the multiculturalism of the 1980s.

Eighty years later, Samuel P. Huntington made an almost identical argument in his attempt to denounce the modern "multiculturalists" who, in his view, were bent on "deconstructing America."[83] Was the America of the

Founders as Protestant and Anglo-Saxon as Huntington asserts?[84] To support his position, Huntington uses multiple sources and quotes in random profusion drawn from the commentaries of the most famous European visitors—Tocqueville, Michel Chevalier, Philip Schaff, F.J. Grund—while neglecting the impact on those visitors of a neo-Romantic historiography that overemphasized the influence of Pilgrims, Yankees, and other Anglo-Saxon ancestors. Any historical event that contradicts the thesis of an Anglo Protestant America is either minimized or brushed aside, as though nothing had changed for three hundred years. The violent internal conflicts of American Protestantism are barely mentioned; the fanatical anti-Catholicism of the nineteenth century Protestant elites is acknowledged but dismissed with the surprising claim that American Catholics have all been "Protestantized." Even the influence of Enlightenment philosophy on the Founding Fathers, most of whom were deists or agnostics, is oddly minimized, on the ground that Enlightenment philosophy was merely the secularized continuation of an old Puritan tradition. Like Guizot or Georg Jellinek (in a famous debate with Boutmy), Huntington is convinced that "America is the child of [the Protestant] Reform,"[85] and that until the late 1950s, "immigrants were in various ways compelled, induced, and persuaded to adhere to the central elements of the Anglo-Protestant culture."[86]

Huntington deplores the damage done to this ancient culture by new Hispanic immigrants, unwilling to assimilate, with the result that America is being transformed into a "bilingual, bicultural society," that could be soon deprived of the "core Anglo-Protestant culture . . . it has had for three centuries."[87] Huntington bases his argument essentially on the question of language and the impression that Spanish will gradually become a dominant language if nothing is done to stem the tide of immigrants. But the recent field work of American sociologists shows something entirely different: American multilingualism, as it exists today, in fact seems to be as ephemeral as the multilingualism prevalent in the early twentieth century.[88] The Spanish spoken by new immigrants is merely a transitional language, whose use is inseparable from long-standing strategies of integration. The language of success and social mobility, in New York as in Los Angeles and Miami, is still English, since immigrant families, following a generational logic clearly demonstrated by the sociology of immigration, encourage their children to join the dominant culture. The linguistic shift—that is, the movement from a monolingual Hispanic culture to an almost exclusively Anglo-American culture (stripped, to be sure, of its Protestant aspect)—shows up in the third generation, as it had one hundred years ago for the descendants of German, Italian, Russian, and Polish immigrants.[89]

It is important to recognize that when American demographers declare that in 2100 more than half of all Americans will claim partial Hispanic origin, there are no grounds for concluding that Spanish will become a real rival of English and that "if the trend continues, the cultural division between Hispanics and Anglos will replace the racial division between blacks and whites as the most serious cleavage in American society."[90] The Hispanics or Latinos of the next century, assuming those identities still have any meaning, will in fact be mostly Americans who have been assimilated for three generations, will be married to non-Hispanics, and will almost certainly have an Anglo-American culture. This is the American paradox: a multicultural, multilingual society, relatively tolerant toward foreign languages, but one that ensures—through its conception of the American dream, its educational system, and its modern media—the predominance of the English language. In this sense, the future of Spanish in the United States is the same as the future of Occitan in France. The monolingualism of the market, allied with the official or unofficial monolingualism of the state, always wins out in the end, despite the open-mindedness of political elites and the survival of linguistic ghettos or barrios.

In denouncing the dissolving influence of "multiculturalists" and other "deconstructionists" of the American identity and in expressing his fear of a Hispanic *reconquista*, Huntington strangely echoes Siegfried's call for a "reinvigorated nationalism" centered on time-honored Anglo-Protestant values. Americans, according to Huntington, should "attempt to reinvigorate their core culture" and engage in a "recommitment to America as a deeply religious and primarily Christian country ... adhering to Anglo-Protestant values, speaking English, maintaining its European heritage."[91] Huntington's views are not racist in the strict sense of the term, but they are Hispanophobic and his work is nothing but the modern revival of a nativist tradition, vigorously defended by Madison Grant in the 1920s and well represented in France by André Siegfried's writings on North America.[92]

6

A Godless America

BETWEEN 1927 AND 1932 A NUMBER OF influential novelists, historians, philosophers, political scientists, and journalists were seemingly in agreement that God was dead and nowhere was his absence more obvious than in America. Or, more precisely, a new pagan divinity had taken the place of the Christian God: "the almighty dollar," technology, mechanization, or mass production. These new gods were the emanation of an industrial society that was displaying all the failings of hyper-mechanization: gigantism, standardized assembly-line work (Taylorism), industrial paternalism encouraging consumption (Fordism), and cheap consumer goods. Production was a nonstop process and the slogan of the age was "produce to produce, and consume to produce even more." What a worker acquired with his high wages had to be spent immediately in a vicious circle of production and consumption, organized work and planned leisure. Old-fashioned production, based on the skills of a master and his apprentice, had been replaced by automated production. The artisan concerned with aesthetics and quality and the producer of rare objects that were difficult to replace had been supplanted by the assembly-line worker, a mere cog in the enormous factory named the United States of America.

Most surprising in reconsidering the literature of the 1930s is the convergence of opinions, the coordination of anxieties, the similarities in vocabulary, and the shared nostalgia for a golden age that gave pride of place to the peasant and the craftsman and valued quality over quantity. Solutions diverged from one writer to the next depending on political sensibilities, but a distant utopia emerged from the profusion of opinions: whatever the cost, the "Spirit" of old Europe had to be rediscovered or reinvented; a spurt of creativity and originality would restore the continent to its grandeur in stark opposition to the steamroller of American uniformity—a uniformity that paradoxically mirrored the uniformity of the Soviet Union. If the period had an "axis of evil," it was the American-Soviet axis, clearly identified and denounced by all the writers surveyed in this chapter.

The Historiography of Decadence

In the 1930s a small group of young French intellectuals deplored the "decadence" brought about by the growing prevalence of modern machinery and new modes of production. These intellectuals are sometimes referred to as the "nonconformists of the 1930s,"[1] because they did not accept what they saw as a dangerous attempt—widely encouraged by French businessmen and bankers—to imitate the United States. In fact, they were nonconformist in the sense that they were "antimodern": they did not accept as inevitable the adoption of production methods perfected by Frederick Taylor and Henry Ford.[2] Their anti-Americanism was overt and vigorous and built on an argument that had already been expressed by André Siegfried (see chapter 5). In the final chapter of *America Comes of Age*, Siegfried draws a sharp contrast between two types of civilization: "European vs. American civilization." While agreeing that great economic progress has been made in the United States, the author deplores the consequences for individuals who have lost their "status." Indeed, what is appreciated in Europe—luxury, aesthetics, craftsmanship, work well done—has been replaced in the United States by mass-produced objects intended for immediate consumption.[3] The American system of production belittles humanity in the name of an ideal as yet unknown in Europe: "All social forces, including idealism and perhaps even religion, converge toward the single goal of production: we are faced with a society of output, *almost a theocracy of output*, that is directed toward the production of things rather than men."[4]

The heightened rhetoric—"a theocracy of output"—dramatically evokes the death of God and of humanity as traditionally conceived in Europe. Of course, the use of the adverb "almost" attenuates the sense of outrage, but the rest of the argument clearly confirms the seriousness of the development.

New American modes of production had irrevocably destroyed what makes an individual more than a statistic: a unique person capable of inventing and shaping his own personality. For it had to be recognized that "comfort for the greatest number of people ... a house, a bath, and a car for every workman can only be obtained at a tragic price, no less than the transformation of millions of workmen into automatons." Mass production was a scandal because it was antihumanist. A craftsman was able to create with his entire personality; he left his mark on the object, he even demonstrated a certain "refinement," inseparable from an aristocratic conception of work. A worker, in contrast, is only a tool serving an end over which he has absolutely no control: "mass production."[5]

In his preface to André Philip's *Le Problème ouvrier aux États-Unis*, Siegfried takes the analysis a step further. He asks whether, all things considered, the French do not have "a more religious view of life than [the] descendants of the Puritans." Assembly-line work, Taylorism, and Fordism, according to him, had disastrous consequences: passivity, monotony, and the standardization of the individual himself revealed the triumph of materialist values that were radically opposed to the values of the French. At bottom, Siegfried argues, "in the United States, *production is the supreme religion.*"[6]

The theme of the superiority of quality over quantity, which was still novel in 1927, became a commonplace in the writings of the 1930s. The manifesto of *Ordre nouveau*, the group of intellectuals assembled around Arnaud Dandieu, Robert Aron, Denis de Rougemont, Henri Daniel-Rops, and Alexandre Marc, for example, defended "qualitative work that creates new values" against "quantitative, fragmented, and undifferentiated work" produced by another kind of civilization that, by fostering a mindless mode of production, crushes the "superior values of the human personality."[7] The defense of the craftsman anticipated the theory of "personalism," which was constructed on the basis of a simple proposition: the machine must exist for the person, not the person for the machine. In short, this meant devaluing the collective workforce and asserting forcefully "the primacy of man over society."[8]

QUANTITY VERSUS QUALITY, comfort versus freedom of the spirit, conformity versus intelligence, craftsmanship versus the assembly line: the gap between American and European civilization was obviously vast; it was indeed a difference in nature. From this perspective, the European experience was situated in what could be called a *modernity of the Ancients*, which sought to preserve ancient ideals in the modern world in order to give a prominent place to humans as an agent of production. At the same time another modernity had appeared in America—the modernity of *Machines*—which, according to Siegfried "absorbed" the individual in an act of "material conquest." The fear was that a dehumanizing American conception of modernity would soon spread over Europe to the detriment of its traditions.[9]

The conclusion of *America Comes of Age* clearly set forth the terms of a debate that troubled the intelligentsia in the 1930s. But the book offered no solution to the inevitable decline of old Europe, whose artisan model of production, in Siegfried's view, was doomed sooner or later to disappear. The political program of a new generation of intellectuals active in movements or journals with revealing titles—*Ordre nouveau, Esprit, Plans, Troisième Force*—was different in nature. These intellectuals were no longer content merely to express nostalgia for the modernity of the Ancients, but rather determined to resist a development that they did not see as inevitable. For them, it was necessary to consider the causes of the decadence of Europe in order to reverse the course of excessive mechanization. New solutions were needed, radical if not revolutionary, to extract Europe from the vice that was crushing it between American mass production and Bolshevik materialism.[10]

The proposed way out of the dilemma—Personalism, New Order, Third Force—seemed credible only if the charges against American capitalism were credible. In this context, the religious question assumed great importance. To impose their ideas more successfully, the nonconformists of the 1930s did not hesitate to cast a spotlight on the hideous spectacle of the "death of God" in the United States. They were brilliantly assisted in this task by novelists whose eyewitness testimony seemed to bolster the propositions of the advocates of a renaissance of European spiritualism.

FOR THE MOST VIRULENT OF THE NONCONFORMISTS, the First World War, the crash of 1929, and the "great capitalist anxiety" that resulted from them were not the primary causes of the new world disorder: they were the consequences, or rather the symptoms, of a much older disease that could be traced back to the foundation of the United States.[11] This insidious disease had already reached Europe, and it would spread around the world if urgent measures were not taken. Far from being a mere fever brought on by an external pathogen that was easily curable, the disease was structural. It was a "cancer" of the social body, which created not only "physical and economic decline" but also and most importantly an "aberration in spiritual life." Its manifestations were easily identifiable: the construction of an abstract and artificial world, ignoring, by definition, all "physical and emotional phenomena," and driving all true passion out of human life—in short, a world marked by the "suppression of desire."[12] Calvin, according to Aron and Dandieu, was the guilty party; his Protestant ethos, thanks to the Puritans, had conquered North America before spreading to the modern centers of power: Wall Street and the White House. It was on the verge of conquering the world.[13]

But although the evil had to be attacked at the root, Calvin and the Puritans were not the only ones responsible. According to the founders of *Ordre nouveau*, the principal villain was Descartes.[14] For these writers who were obviously influenced by the antirationalist movements of the 1930s—Bergson and Sorel in France, Husserl, Scheler, and Heidegger in Germany—Descartes was the source of all the ills of the modern world. The philosopher was reproached for his taste for abstraction, his cult of reason, his desire to measure objects precisely (consider Cartesian coordinates), his excessive individualism, and his methodical attempt to cut himself off from the world of passions and emotion. Descartes was presented as the inventor of American modernity, and this produced the pithy formulations that peppered the polemic: "Taylor and Ford are the spiritual heirs of Descartes"; there is an obvious and strong "kinship" between Descartes' method and "Detroit's standard method"; "America . . . is Descartes in the streets."[15]

This was, to be sure, a caricature of Descartes' philosophy, which led Aron and Dandieu to draw an improbable link between the great French thinker and Henry Ford: "From Descartes to Ford means: from the isolated individual passionately forging a rational tool for understanding to regimented individuals in rationalized factories repeating identical mechanical gestures beyond their grasp. It means that Descartes lies at the origin of a human epic whose gigantic but degraded end point we are now witnessing."[16]

In these circumstances, the religious sentiment had almost disappeared in the United States. Descartes and his American offspring had indeed launched a "process of leaving religion behind"[17] with an atheist dogma, abstract gods devoid of any substance, and especially a civil religion very different from religion in the usual sense. A single dogma existed in the United States: the primacy of the economy; a single cult: blind reason; a single mystique: production. And the object of adoration was not the God of Abraham but a new industrial paganism based on the "abstract gods" of credit and production, "rational, implacable, and inhuman categories." The new faith in the virtues of capitalism was inseparable from fierce discipline akin to that of a police state. Everything was subjected to minute surveillance at all times, following strictly applied Cartesian principles. The result was surveillance over the slightest words and deeds of workers and employees, countless production controls, the imposition of strict business standards, defined according to the principles of "scientific management," the collection of statistics, and so on. All of this was made possible by the institution of a huge apparatus of espionage in which managers and employees behaved, without even realizing it, like policemen.[18]

The same iron discipline was imposed on primary school students, whose mental performance was measured by the "monstrous application of the principles of Binet and the behaviorists." The move from education to mass production was easily made since intelligence had been reduced to an "activity as automatic and controllable as possible, under the aegis of benevolence and apparent freedom." This was how the American school prepared students for "the unbearable hardships of high productivity and high wage labor as it had been organized by the Taylors and the Fords."[19]

If there is a religion in the United States then it is the "religion of success" that reduces individuals to identical elements whose creative activities amount to a multitude of petty controls, with the deplorable result of creating disgust at any spiritual effort and, implicitly, a rejection of any transcendental value and any reference to the divine. This kind of argument leads to the Nietzschean conclusion of the death of God. Then what remains of religion? Nothing, because a pseudo-religion—the religion of success—has taken the place of true religion. "Confronting it," Aron and Dandieu write, "the other religion, the old one, discreetly and smilingly fades into the background. Reduced to a kind of fairy tale that one rereads in sad times of life, it still seems too emotional, too individual, and in the end too irrational to provide adequate support for the myth of production."[20]

THE *ESPRIT* GROUP, CENTERED AROUND the strong personality of Emmanuel Mounier, a prominent Catholic intellectual, and his associates

(George Izard, Nikolai Berdyaev, André Déléage, Jean Lacroix), was no longer concerned with providing scientific explanations for the American disease. The case was closed; America was being eaten away by a "cancer" already observed by numerous French visitors. As Mounier explained in a polemical article intended to introduce the ideas of the *Esprit* movement,[21] it was now acceptable to demonize American capitalism as pure materialism, a sort of "poison that is sterilizing our souls" and is transforming men into living robots "marching in step, in a technological revolt toward a new inhumanity." In his private correspondence, Mounier denounced the "terrifying rise of money and the machine,"[22]—a denunciation repeated even more dramatically in a prospectus published that year to announce the launching of the journal *Esprit:* "Capitalism is reducing a growing mass of people, through poverty or well-being, to a state of servitude incompatible with human dignity; it has oriented all social classes and the entire personality of individuals toward the possession of money; this is the desire that has possessed the modern soul."[23] Devoid of a soul, or a soul obsessed with money, the individual in capitalist society has ceased being a man; he is totally subjected to the tyranny of matter, and the only faith remaining to him is "faith in matter." Capitalism is as materialistic as Marxism, "capitalism's rebel offspring."[24] God no longer exists because he has been replaced by a usurper, *money*, which "has made itself into a god and imposed its worship." This new cult has had fearsome effects: it has dissolved the social bond and transformed men into "interchangeable numbers who can therefore be bought." But money, this deified accounting device, is a false god and perhaps even the Antichrist who has succeeded in installing in man's heart "the ancient divine dream of *the beast*, the savage, irresistible, and unpunished possession of a slavish matter infinitely expandable by the force of desire."[25]

The explanation is based on a series of binary oppositions: avarice–the gift of the self; matter–spirit; capitalism–materialism; individualism–collectivism; Christ–Antichrist; and, implicitly, the United States–the Soviet Union. At first sight, these oppositions are based on contrary and equally hateful values. In reality, the reader of these founding documents detects a hierarchy of contraries, made more explicit in Mounier's private correspondence. Stripped of its excesses, Marxism in its pre-Bolshevik phase embodies a certain idea of justice and a "sense of communion" that are not incompatible with the principles of primitive Christianity. What is at stake, then, is an attempt to "realize in the name of God and Christ the truth that the Communists are realizing in the name of an atheist collectivity."[26]

In other words, the secularization of the public and private spheres had advanced too far in capitalist countries to serve as a model for France (and Europe). There remained the other model, "collectivist materialism." Once purged of its most shocking excesses and of its state-sponsored atheism, the communist model did offer the hope of a possible solution: an authentic communitarianism based on the gift of the self to others and the desire to serve the collectivity. At this point, like a *deus ex machina,* the thesis of "Personalism," so cherished by the young adherents to the *Esprit* movement, intervenes. In contrast to the atomized individual of capitalist societies, doomed to the eternal search for profit—never satisfied because the cycles of the capitalist economy generate crisis after crisis (as the stock market crash of 1929 had recently reminded everyone)—stood the figure of the *Person.* What is needed, Mounier writes, is "the crushing of the individual" to precipitate the advent of a second Renaissance, based on the flowering of the person.[27] The word "crushing" is not innocent, because the one being crushed, in Catholic theology, is always Satan, and as Mounier makes clear in an article written for an American Catholic magazine, "individualism is at the root of the evil."[28]

The description of modern capitalism proposed by Mounier and his friends is thus poles apart from Max Weber's argument. The German sociologist had claimed to discover behind the capitalist's frenetic search for profit a genuine Protestant ethic, inseparable from the fulfillment of a "vocation" which bore within itself the sign of a likely salvation.[29] The solution proposed by Mounier, the "Personalist revolution," rejected almost all the values that had come out of the Reformation. All that counted were the transcendence of the individual, the gift of the self, and the denunciation of every form of bourgeois egotism.

The Millenarian Temptation

Faced with the tragedy of occupied France, at a time when an Allied victory over the Axis powers seemed uncertain, Mounier despaired and imagined an unexpected return of the religious impulse. What could be called his "millenarian temptation" is a frequent phenomenon in the history of religions, but is usually associated with Protestant fundamentalism, and rarely observed in Catholic countries.

In his "Entretiens" of May 1941, Mounier states that he does not wish to "exclude the apocalyptic outcome."[30] For this purpose, Mounier presents three symbolic figures already familiar to the reader: the Ancients, the Moderns, and the Barbarians.[31] Each term in the triad is intertwined with the two others, following a complex play of analogies and historical shortcuts. For Mounier, the Ancients evoke the inhabitants of the decadent Roman Empire, including those Christians who naïvely believed that the Empire would endure. The Moderns were his contemporaries, Christians or not, who also imagine that the capitalist regime and its parliamentary pseudo-democracy is built to last. For both the Ancients and the Moderns, "the Barbarians were absolute evil." Nonetheless, other Ancients and other Moderns, free and adventurous spirits, realized that the arrival of the Barbarians might represent an opportunity, the sign of a renaissance or a millenarian "Advent." In Rome, some bold spirits understood that the Barbarians were coming to "crush pagan man so that the new grace could find its path."[32] In Paris—as in Berlin—other bold spirits were asking themselves whether they were not seeing the accomplishment of an earlier prediction: "Weren't we saying a few years ago that we would escape from bourgeois man, from the bourgeois Church, only through fire and the sword? Have those times not come? Could that be the meaning of a totalitarian victory?"[33]

In another interview given a few days later, Mounier goes into more explicit detail about his eschatological vision, even though he realizes the risk of being misunderstood. He thus proceeds to ask the shocking question *par excellence*: "Why shouldn't it be fascism that gives birth to the new Europe?" The adoption a reasonable historical perspective cannot exclude ambiguities: "[History] manifests a perpetual tactic of generating good through evil, moderation through aberration."[34] While rejecting the very idea of collaboration with the invader, Mounier acknowledges that there is in the German victory a dynamism, an energy, an "impressive expansive force" that is impossible not to admire. This, in turn, leads to an unbearable paradox: the ideals of the new Barbarians contain "a deeper kinship" with our ideals than with those of "certain allies."[35]

The revolution envisaged by Mounier was nonetheless designed to defeat Nazism; there can be no doubt about that. The question that tormented the founder of *Esprit* concerned the post-Nazi period. Would it be necessary to adopt and channel certain values developed on the other side of the Rhine? The answer was affirmative: "It is beyond question that the Western world must undergo a profound revolution and that certain values that are exaggerated or distorted in Nazism must play their role in that revolution."[36] Readjusting the values advocated by the Nazis? This dangerous idea led Mounier to draw a very questionable analogy with the fall of the Roman Empire: it was up to the new rulers of Vichy to mimic the conduct of the new Christians in the fifth century A.D. It was up to them to seize, like the Christians, "the intact force . . . of Barbarian hearts."[37]

The same apocalyptic logic was expressed a year later, after the Battle of Stalingrad, by Mounier's friends. But its meaning had radically changed, according to the testimony of a frequent contributor to *Esprit*, the poet Pierre Emmanuel. At this time, with the Barbarians on the verge of defeat, the Soviet Union played the role of the angel of the apocalypse, opening the way to a pro-Communist reading of European history:

> [Our] mystical folly went along with the feeling that the old world, unable to find any reason for surviving, was doomed to disappear in the nihilistic crisis of neo-Nazi Europe. When souls are shaken by the very idea of the millennium—that exalting and terrible earthquake that brings out the spirit of prophecy—they no longer think according to reasons but through visions. That moment came for me—it was I think at the time of Stalingrad—when Russia ceased to be an object of reason and became an object of vision. With that, I made my exit from history and entered into eschatology.[38]

LIKE FRENCH ESSAYISTS AND PHILOSOPHERS, French novelists who traveled to the United States in the 1930s repeated the same arguments, with more stylistic flourishes and a comparable sense of awe regarding the ravages of mechanization. Duhamel's best seller, *Scènes de la vie future*, vividly illustrates the theme of a clash of civilizations opposing old Europe to young America. European civilization, according to him, was still trying to define an ethics capable of making people more human, despite the traumatic experience of the Great War, whereas American civilization was "predominantly mechanical."[39] America was built on four principal industries: "the mine, the iron-works, the paper factory, the abattoir"—four masterpieces of successful standardization, carried out according to the principles of Ford and Taylor, of which Duhamel presents a nightmarish picture.[40] If there was a God in Duhamel's America, that God was, as Philippe Roger has pointed out, the "mechanistic Moloch."[41] Nothing escaped from its grasp, and all human energy was devoted to feeding the Moloch in an economy of desire that was constantly creating new needs. Far from freeing man from labor, machines, even the most useful among them, made him a slave condemned to produce

ever more in order to consume ever more in a vicious circle of wants provoking new desires. What place could there be for man and for religion in this
"industrial dictatorship"?[42] A limited place, to be sure, because men now had
only a single desire: to succeed at any cost and above all to get rich in order
to buy useless or superfluous objects. Everything, in the end, was a question
of money:

> The beings who today people the American ant-hills ... demand pal-
> pable, incontestable wealth, recommended, or, preferably, *prescribed by
> the national divinities.* They yearn desperately for phonographs, radios,
> illustrated magazines, movies, elevators, electric refrigerators, and auto-
> mobiles, automobiles, and, once again, automobiles. They want to own
> at the earliest possible moment all the articles mentioned, which are so
> wonderfully convenient, and of which, by an odd reversal of things, they
> immediately become the anxious slaves. They have not enough money;
> not enough money even now? No matter! The principal thing is to keep
> selling, even on credit, above all on credit! American commerce knows
> how unceasingly to push back the limits of the market, unceasingly to put
> off till the morrow the threatening saturation-point.[43]

Who are these "national divinities" with such great influence? Another
chapter of the book gives the answer. They are the huge billboards and other
"pachyderms of publicity" which, "with the serene persistence of machines,"
at night, "resume their work of propaganda and intimidation."[44] One is in the
presence of a "new religion" imposing on men a "burlesque visual masturba-
tion" whose effects approach madness with "these hateful noises, these inso-
lent lights, these shameless proposals, these cynical injunctions, this lack of
consideration, these intrusions, these obsessions, these lapses from delicacy,
these importunities, and these insults."[45]

And although there are still churches in the United States, they are not
located where they appear to be. The only true places of worship are either
those devoted to work or to leisure. In the "cathedral of commerce" harsh
rites are performed to accomplish "prodigies" inseparable from the "niggardly
counting of every minute" that makes work on the assembly line so melancholy and so repetitive.[46] As for the religion of leisure, it is practiced primarily in the "new temples" scattered throughout the territory of the United
States: the great football stadiums—the only meeting places enabling crowds

to express fervor, to commune in the mass experience, and "taste the mysterious pleasures of the herd, the hive, and the ant-hill."[47]

The mystery of faith in the United States is thus entomological in nature, which no doubt explains the countless references to ants, termites, and bees in Duhamel's book. The author's wild imagination leads him to propose a new experiment in natural selection: "Breed . . . the human tool, as you have bred the working ox, the milch cow, the laying hen, and the fat hog."[48] This is indeed the direction taken by a the American science of eugenics, and its effects are already being felt in the Old World.[49]

The future seemed dark to Duhamel, particularly because he saw no credible way out of Europe's crisis. But the nonconformists of the 1930s were even more pessimistic. Duhamel, according to Robert Aron and Arnaud Dandieu, had not grasped the "deeply morbid" nature of the American malady. Too archaic, too attached to the values of rural France—to the wine grower, the cheese maker, the craftsman—Dr. Duhamel had misdiagnosed the disease. He had not understood that *Americanism* was a serious illness that, through excessive mechanization and artificiality, had undermined the "vital balance" of human societies and heralded the coming catastrophe: the probable death of the "vital instinct" in whose absence no human society could survive. But the editors of *Ordre nouveau* did not believe the outcome was preordained, provided Europeans rejected blind technology and rediscovered, in all its splendor, "the aggressive and creative force" of the *Spirit.*[50]

The critic Maurice Blanchot waxed ironic about the good doctor's tall tales that were intended to defend man but forgot to mention him. An enemy of the machine, Duhamel had not hesitated to indict it. By exaggerating its predominance, he had made it "an idol of unprecedented power," capable of destroying everything, and was unable to imagine how to promote effective resistance.[51]

In another review of *Scènes de la vie future,* published the same year, Emmanuel Mounier was equally harsh. Duhamel had been right to denounce American Barbarism and to christen it as "Americanism." But he had not drawn the necessary conclusions. In the face of the "idolatrous growth of mechanization," it was imperative to rediscover what was specifically human: life, initiative, spontaneity.[52] Like the founders of *Ordre nouveau,* Mounier sounded the alarm against the false gods of mechanization; he called for a return to the true God, to real spiritual values, and, as noted earlier, to the *person,* finally restored to its fullness. Only an unprecedented act of resistance—a new order, a personalism, a second Renaissance—could finally deliver old Europe from barbaric American mechanization.

WITH THE DEFEAT OF THE AXIS POWERS, one might have expected French intellectuals to show at least some appreciation for the virtues of American mass production and the impressive logistical effort deployed by Allied troops to liberate Europe from the Nazi yoke. But many of the most respected intellectuals, untainted by collaboration, continued to repeat *ad nauseam* their fear of American mechanization, as though nothing had changed since the 1930s. The "technological Moloch" was still American, and it threatened the very future of humanity.[53]

Bernanos, Sartre, and the Robots

Georges Bernanos—a supporter of the Resistance from the outset, who conducted a press campaign against Vichy France from Rio de Janeiro where he had settled—was inexhaustible on the subject. France, and this was its great weakness, was threatened by "the invasion of Machinery."[54] The origin of this system lay in the cotton-weaving machine invented in Manchester, England, and perfected thereafter in other forms and for other uses in the United States. This had produced a new categorical imperative forged in the United States: "Technology first! Technology everywhere!"[55] Old French civilization, the most refined of all, was more than ever confronted by the civilization of machines, whose principal and unstoppable effect was "the liquidation of all values of the spirit."[56] A close look at machine civilization suggests that it is the first materialist civilization in the world. It claims to be civilized, but is in fact a form of Barbarism, even more cruel than that of the Savages, because it "ignores or rejects the high intellectual disciplines that make a man worthy of being called man."[57] Consequently, it leads man toward nihilism; it drives him into the most abject of surrenders, as though he were possessed by another in a world devoid of hope and abandoned by God: "Man has made the machine, and the machine has become human, through a kind of demonic reversal of the mystery of the Incarnation."[58]

Written chiefly between 1944 and 1948, these comments by the Catholic writer obviously echo and even surpass the antitechnological fantasies of the nonconformists of the 1930s. They foreshadow the most virulent forms of the anti-Americanism of the 1970s and 1980s, when the formulation, "Capitalism and totalitarianism are merely two aspects of the primacy of the economic sphere" was asserted as an unquestionable equation.[59] And for Bernanos, the primacy of the economy and technology is a defining characteristic of inhumanity:

> [The world of technology] does not build itself; it gives the illusion of self-construction because in it one truncates, mutilates, removes everything that once belonged to free man, everything that had been made for his use and that could in the future remind the *totalitarian robot* of the dignity he had lost and that he would never recover. With more machines that demolish, perforate, and excavate, with more advanced explosives, the disguised demolition men with the name "builder" on their helmets are in the process of organizing a world for the use of a man who does not exist.[60]

This world without man and without God is not Hell, in the author's fertile imagination, but rather nothingness, the cold, the uninhabitable. What purpose will be served by the totalitarian robot, the new Leviathan of the modern age? To make the coming world as uninhabitable for Christians as the great ice ages were for mammoths.[61]

The best evidence of the ultimate perversion of American civilization—which is in fact a "counter-civilization"—is the endless production of ever more powerful nuclear weapons. And what is the atomic bomb but a super-machine that might one day destroy all existing machines and all existing civilizations? "For in the end," Bernanos concludes, "there is not one among us who has not already had the dream, or the nightmare, of a complete destruction of all the continents by an out of control atomic bomb."[62]

The only prominent writer who kept a cool head was Jean-Paul Sartre, as surprising as that may seem to anyone who remembers the notorious declaration: "America has rabies!" Sartre was still fascinated by America after his initial journey there in early 1945.[63] Setting himself apart from the radical pessimism of Christian humanists such as Mounier and Bernanos, Sartre thought he could detect in America the traces of an authentic freedom where one would least expect it, on the assembly line. Beginning with a very Hegelian analysis of the master-slave relationship. Sartre focuses on the novelty of the relations that have been established between industrialists and workers. Like André Siegfried, André Philip, and Arnaud Dandieu before him, Sartre describes all the failings of modern Taylorism: the worker repeats the same motions hundreds of times a day; he feels that he is transformed into an object and believes he is losing "inner freedom of thought." From this painful and repetitive experience, Sartre nevertheless extracts an unexpected lesson. Taylorism "provides a foretaste of concrete liberation," because it detaches the worker from his former subordination to the master's whims. The worker now no longer worries about "pleasing the master." His work is, of course, not chosen, and what he produces does not belong to him. But because he nonetheless produces things by transforming matter, he controls the "government of things," which constitutes the prelude to his real emancipation.[64]

Pushing the paradox further, Sartre claims that the possession of the ultimate machine, the nuclear weapon, contrary to appearances, is perfectly liberating. The pessimists, Sartre explains, live in a state of perpetual anxiety. They fear the improper use of the bomb will bring humanity to the edge of destruction; they predict the death of man after the death of God; everything can explode from one minute to the next. But, says Sartre, the nuclear age has provided the basis for a new hope, based on the most radical freedom: the freedom to decide one's own future: "As this war comes to an end, the circle is complete; in each one of us humanity discovers its possible death, assumes its life and its death." Man is therefore free because he can "now count only on himself," and his survival depends on a new Pascalian wager that remains to be taken up: betting on the impossibility of total war and acting in consequence.[65]

Is there still a God in America? God is dead, Sartre tells us, since humanity alone is now responsible for its own fate. God is dead in the United States, Bernanos claims: he has been replaced by the technological Moloch. God is dead for the capitalist as for the communist, Mounier asserts, because they are both desperately seeking paradise on earth. The Christian God, Aron and Dandieu suggest, has withdrawn, replaced by the abstract gods of credit and mass production. Who still pays homage to God in North America? The novelist Céline believed he had found the right answer when he described, with scathing irony, the journey of his protagonist Bardamu to New York, and especially his walk through the Wall Street area of Manhattan. First observation: "You can enter it only on foot, like a church." Second observation: everything there is miraculous, "it's a district filled with gold," and, most importantly, there one hears the delicate whisper of the wings of the Holy Spirit, "the sound of dollars [changing hands] ... more precious than blood." Bardamu enters the holy of holies and there meets the employees "who guard the cash." He discovers he is not the only communicant: "When the faithful enter their bank, don't go thinking they can help themselves as they please. Far from it. In speaking to Dollar, they mumble words through a little grill; that's their confessional. Not much sound, dim light, a tiny wicket between high arches, that's all. They don't swallow the Host, they put it on their hearts."[66]

The dollar, technology, speculation, wealth: these were the variants of the name of God in the America of the 1930s as seen by the French intelligentsia. If there was a God, if spirituality still had any meaning, if there were still nations of believers protected by Providence, they were to be found in Europe, certainly not in North America, the continent of triumphant materialism, the first definitively disenchanted world.

Sex and Puritan Morality

The debate of the 1940s about American mass production and its tragic consequence, the death of God, effectively prevented serious reflection about the place of religion in the United States. In the absence of analysis, clichés and old French stereotypes about American Puritanism continued to circulate freely. By the late 1940s, Puritanism had taken a sexual connotation which it did not have in the 1920s. The Protestant ethic was out of fashion. A new preoccupation with sex and the liberation of women centered the debate on the sexual mores of the American people. Were young Americans truly liberated from the old "Puritan" yoke? Distinguished French visitors expressed serious doubts. Their inquiries, based on gossip, chance encounters, and fleeting glimpses, remained fairly impressionistic. They obviously ignored the recently published findings of the Kinsey reports on sexual behavior.[67] Anglo-Saxon "Puritanism" remained, for French observers, the essential truth of a sexuality permanently marked by the morality of the Pilgrim Fathers. The myth of American Puritanism remained so strong that it affected even foreigners recently settled in the United States. Or so at least Sartre claimed when in 1945 he met, in the course of a trip to New York, a compatriot who timidly tried to initiate an off-color conversation with the philosopher. The French exile, whose speech had already been affected by numerous Americanisms and a nasal accent that was more American than French, thought he was acting properly by asking Sartre about his American journey: "He felt obliged, at moments, to wink suggestively as he said 'Ah, New Orleans, beautiful women!'"[68] But the unfortunate man, Sartre observes, has already been ravaged by the surrounding culture: the attempt at a libertine conversation is nothing but a façade, the automatic reflex of an exile who would still like to pass himself off as a Frenchman. By saying "beautiful women," he is "rather conforming to the American representation of the French than to the desire to create a relationship with a compatriot. 'Beautiful women,' and he laughs, but coldly, *Puritanism is not far off.* I feel chilled."[69] Puritanism, Sartre thinks he knows, also exists in the countless taboos against love outside marriage.[70]

But Sartre was aware that there may have been a substantial gap between the myth of Puritan asceticism and the real practices of libertine sexuality outside the bonds of marriage: "And then there are those carpets of used condoms in the back yards of coed colleges, those cars parked at night with their headlights off...."[71] Had Puritanism really disappeared for all that? Nothing was less certain, because the sexual act itself had paradoxically become disembodied, lacking in conscience, and therefore in real pleasure, since, Sartre calmly asserts, "so many men and women drink before making love, to sin while drunk and with no memory."[72] In the absence of conscience, love as practiced by Americans is nothing but "chaste depravity," as had been said a century earlier with the same self-assurance by the Catholic writer Paul Bourget.[73]

Continuing the inquiry a year later, on the occasion of a lecture tour, Simone de Beauvoir visited Smith and Wellesley Colleges. She examined the sexual mores of the female students and, speaking to an old French lady who seemed to her to be particularly open-minded, asked the indiscreet question already posed by Sartre: Is it true that the students are "so free and live such chaotic lives that, as I've heard, there are certain parts of the campus where you find piles of condoms?"[74] It's possible, was the answer. But is the sexual act as free and passionate as in France? "Mademoiselle T. tells me that despite the number and nature of their experiences, all these American girls remain innocent in a certain way; becoming a woman doesn't change them or mature them—it's as if it were an operation, in which they didn't participate."[75]

The American version of love is thus surprisingly chaste and disembodied. Sexual initiation, Beauvoir explains, is nothing but an illusion, at best "an extension of certain ambiguous childhood games," in short, anything but "fulfillment." The old French stereotype of the Americans, those eternal children, is reproduced here in all its splendor, as an obvious fact. Sexual relations as experienced by American students do not amount to passionate relations between real lovers. "I imagine that *the boldest of the girls remain rather puritanical* and that in their search for pleasure the boys and the girls, by mutual agreement, make every effort to ward off all the mysterious agitations of sensuality."[76]

Simone de Beauvoir, like Sartre and countless other French observers, was thus convinced that the Puritan heritage was ingrained in the American soul. The point of departure of American morality and sexuality is indeed Puritanism, the "credo to which all of America adheres."[77] It is so powerful that it transforms the private life of individuals and renders them incapable of freeing themselves from the tyranny of the past. None of the manifestations of American modernity has lightened the burden of the past, not the mysteries of capitalist finance, not even the "prodigious dangers of the industrial age." "You cannot understand Chicago, Los Angeles, or Houston if you forget that they are haunted by the troublesome, propitious, irritated, or complacent ghosts of the old Puritans."[78]

This kind of essentialism, based on a peculiar reading of the history of the United States, has not disappeared. It resurfaces in the vision of a sexual relation imagined by another noted visitor who, in 2006, was attempting to relive the experience of Tocqueville in his voyage across America. In *American Vertigo*, Bernard-Henri Lévy describes his visit to a brothel lost in the desert of Nevada, the Chicken Ranch, to talk about sex with a prostitute. He admits that he causes something of a stir when he tells her that he has "not come for *that*, but for a magazine [*The Atlantic Monthly*], Tocqueville, sex in America, and so forth."[79] Entering a bedroom "hung with makeshift drapes, which she proudly tells me is 'decorated like a harem,'" he discovers that the site of debauchery is in reality an austere cell that represents the triumph of a kind of sexual asceticism, framed by a set of hygienic standards:

> Next to the bed is a message board, like the temperature charts in hospital rooms, where every other week the results of venereal-disease and AIDS tests are written: the brothel is a sanitary place. On the bedside table, conspicuously displayed, a choice of condoms, the use of which is required at all levels of service, down to and including, she gravely explains, a mere striptease: the brothel is a place of safe sex.[80]

It is impossible on reading these impressions to escape from the old French stereotype of chaste love, rooted in a primordial and pervasive Protestant ethic: "Protestant ethic and price list for love. . . . Another face of the same *puritanism* and its obscene nether side."[81] Lévy thus joins with Sartre, Simone de Beauvoir, and especially Tocqueville, each of whom thought they had found in the Puritan ethic the very essence of America.

7

The Rise of the Religious Right

IN THE PRECEDING CHAPTER, we examined the remarkably similar worldviews of a small group of French intellectuals who—despite their differences—all proclaimed the death of God in the United States and harshly denounced the mechanization and mass production that in their view dominated American society. This critique was accompanied by a call for a spiritual revolution to combat the world of greed, financial speculation, and material comfort and to restore fundamental human values. For these intellectuals, Soviet materialism was identical to American capitalism; it was only in Europe, caught between the pincers of the two great powers, that a new spiritual age—the age of the spirit—could take root.

The Second World War put an end to the dream of a European spiritual renaissance. It did not, however, preclude the possibility of economic and social recovery. Postwar economic growth [which the French call the thirty glorious years—*Les Trente Glorieuses*] demonstrated that American technology was not as inhuman as had been suggested and that the methods of "scientific management," far from leading to the apocalyptic crises that had once been predicted, produced immense economic and social progress over time.

The French debate about America changed registers in the early 1950s. Foreign policy was the central concern and the role of the United States in the cold war divided the intelligentsia between procommunists and advocates of American-style liberalism. The debate concerned, on the one hand, the real or supposed dangers of American imperialism, and on the other, the ravages of Soviet totalitarianism. The Korean War, the Suez crisis, and the Vietnam War mobilized the anti-imperialist camp, while the publication of Khrushchev's secret speech about the crimes of Stalin, the occupation of Hungary, and then of Czechoslovakia provided new arguments for the antitotalitarian side. The question of religion in the United States or of the place of God in American political discourse did not preoccupy French intellectuals of the time.

The Watergate crisis and the resignation of Richard Nixon followed by the election of Jimmy Carter marked a turning point in French perceptions of America. The American debate on the "immorality" of Nixon's machinations surprised many French citizens, and the election of Jimmy Carter, a "self-made man with a passionate interest in both electronics and the Word of God," was even more startling. Suddenly, morality and religion no longer appeared irrelevant to an understanding of American politics. Carter's election was decisive, because it inaugurated a cycle of unprecedented presidential religiosity which culminated in the election of George W. Bush in 2000 and continues to intrigue the European intelligentsia. Since Watergate, clichés have proliferated in the French press. There has been talk of religious plots, the revenge of the Puritans, moral crusades, presidents who thought they were inspired by God himself, battles against the Evil Empire. Observations of this sort reached a peak with the election of George W. Bush. One French journalist from the Catholic weekly *La Vie* described the White House, the mythical locus of world power, as a seedy hotel "taken hostage by a fundamentalist cult." Others ventured to write that a "cult" of evangelicals, led by George W. Bush and his advisers, was preparing to "conquer the world."[1]

Stereotypes like these obviously exaggerate the influence of religion on American politics and give too much prominence to fundamentalists during the Reagan and George W. Bush administrations. But they contain a kernel of truth and implicitly raise major questions. Was the United States still a Puritan nation? Were the religious references so prized by American presidents and members of Congress truly sincere, self-interested, or hypocritical? Did they bear the stamp of a Constitutional patriotism derived from the best sources of the Protestant tradition? More generally, was the focus on religion in American politics a distinct American trait, a sign of "American exceptionalism"?

Seen from France, evangelical Protestantism appeared to have successfully invaded the American public sphere, at the same time that old Europe, swept along by powerful secularizing forces, was every day moving further away from its Christian roots.

The singular piety exhibited by the presidents elected since Nixon's fall is not in itself new: other presidents in other times also appealed to Scripture. But the intensity of that piety, its public character, and its evangelical exuberance seem unprecedented in the political history of the United States. The explanation for the emergence of this new form of presidential religiosity lies not only in the often colorful character of the individuals converted to evangelicalism. It is also and most importantly due to the influence of new political and cultural factors. Among these factors, the most significant and the least known to a French audience is the electoral strategy of American political parties, and most particularly the "Southern strategy" of the Republican Party, developed in the aftermath of the passage of the Johnson administration's civil-rights legislation. The recapture of the South by Lincoln's party came at a price: the rightward shift of Republican ideology and especially the leaders' adoption of the cultural and religious values that the majority of the white, Southern, evangelical electorate holds.

But it is essential not to lose sight of the fact that the centrality of religion in American politics, undeniable for the period under consideration here, has not erased another long-term trend: the increasing secularization of American society. That secularization will be the subject of a concluding chapter.

Varieties of Presidential Religiosity

The election of an American president never goes unnoticed in the French press. It provides an opportunity to take stock of American society, to anticipate the future, and to describe the peculiarities of a complex political system.

In the wake of the Watergate crisis, Jimmy Carter was an intriguing figure because he was a self-acknowledged born-again Christian. Evangelicalism was little understood by French commentators who chose instead to clothe Carter in the garb of a Puritan. For example, Jacques Sallebert, special correspondent for the French radio station Europe n°1 at the 1976 Democratic Party Convention, summarized the nominee's acceptance speech in these terms: "America has examined its conscience. It has reacted in a powerfully Puritan manner."[2] Sallebert did not hesitate to play with paradoxes: he discovered in

Carter both a new Puritan and a new Joan of Arc, carrying out a divine mission to restore America's "moral direction." Carter's election would be the election of a "missionary" and his program would literally take the form of a "crusade."[3]

Carter's notorious *Playboy* interview reinforced the French stereotype of the Puritan in action: "Christ set some almost impossible standards for us. The Bible says, 'Thou shalt not commit adultery.' Christ said, I tell you that anyone who looks on a woman with lust in his heart has already committed adultery. I've looked on a lot of women with lust. I've committed adultery in my heart many times. . . ."[4]

Yet Carter, contrary to a very widely shared opinion in France, was not a Calvinist. His very personal brand of moralism was that of a Southern Baptist, who prayed, according to his own testimony, up to twenty-five times a day and manifested his faith by frequently teaching Sunday School classes in a Baptist church. His easy victory demonstrated that winning over the white, Baptist, conservative Southern electorate was indispensable in order to reach the White House—a lesson that his future Republican opponents would not forget.

WHILE CARTER WAS A PURITAN IN the eyes of the French press, Clinton, another Southern Baptist, was not and could not be, given the frequency of his extramarital affairs, well documented in the American media. He was, rather, as the correspondent of *Le Figaro* wrote in the midst of the Lewinsky affair, a "victim of the Puritanism that is still deeply characteristic of America."[5] According to *L'Événement du Jeudi*, Clinton was being subjected to "the sanctimonious legacy of the Mayflower [that] was still weighing on the American soul."[6] The sacrificial victim of a monstrous "libidocracy," his impeachment by the House of Representatives revealed, according to the weekly *Figaro Magazine*, an America that was capable of following "its logic to the bitter end . . . against a backdrop of Puritanism."[7] The daily *Libération* portrayed the special prosecutor, Kenneth W. Starr, as a Grand Inquisitor who was afflicted with a "sickly, nasty, and nefarious Puritanism."[8] For those who had paid little attention to these peremptory assertions, the weekly *Marianne* dotted the *i*'s with the tantalizing headline: "Warning, Dangerous Puritans!"[9] These stereotypes greatly oversimplified the history of the United States, which was now set in the virtuous circle of an eternal return: a moral order which, despite some detours, had never stopped being Puritan since the origin of the country.

This kind of historical determinism, repeated in one article after another, obscured the existence of another America—tolerant, liberal, indulgent, refusing to confuse private and public life or to explain one by the other. This other vision of a tolerant America emerged when it became clear that Clinton, despite his impeachment by the House of Representatives would not be removed from office by the Senate.[10] French commentators were at a loss to explain this outcome. They offered a radically new explanation that directly contradicted their previously held beliefs: It was "the end of the Puritans" claimed the correspondent of *Libération* in February 1999.[11] *Le Monde* went further a few days later: the "crusade" of the neoconservatives had obviously failed. If they were no longer entitled to "rule over the morality and sexuality of Americans," this was because there had been a "profound change in American society.... A certain America [had] won out over another: humanistic common sense over fundamentalist pastors."[12] The old paradigm of Puritan America had lost its explanatory value; another reason had to be found, one that better suited the circumstances. It was suggested by *Le Nouvel Observateur* in an investigative article examining the causes of "Monicagate": The new generation of baby boomers, the weekly explained, had demonstrated remarkable maturity, a "modern" capacity to separate private conduct from public affairs. Those Americans resembled the French like brothers: they were tolerant and "sophisticated," in short, they had become "Europeanized."[13]

And yet, Clinton was less European than one might imagine. His reactions in the wake of the Lewinsky affair and his public repentance in front of hundreds of religious leaders invited to share his suffering and grant their forgiveness were still typically American. Clinton indeed said "I have sinned" at the White House prayer breakfast in September 1998: "It is important to me that everybody who has been hurt know the sorrow I feel is genuine—first and most important my family, also my friends, my staff, my Cabinet, Monica Lewinsky and her family, and the American people. I've asked all for their forgiveness."[14] A year later, in the same circumstances, Bill Clinton asserted that he had "been profoundly moved . . . by the pure power of grace" that had finally granted him—he felt it inwardly—"an unmerited forgiveness."[15]

Was he perhaps overdoing it? That is what 140 religious leaders claimed in a petition addressed to the president after the first public acknowledgement of his "sins." It was time, the signatories wrote, to put an end to these repentance sessions, too public to be sincere, that were first and foremost acts of political propaganda that "compromise[d] the integrity of religion."[16] But Clinton held fast. He had sinned and that had to be publicized. His redemption required frequently reiterated public confessions.

Clinton was not the only one expressing exaggerated religious zeal. In another context, his predecessor, the Episcopalian George H. W. Bush, thought it appropriate to display old-fashioned piety to satisfy his Southern electorate. His inaugural address contained an interminable prayer using the themes of the love of God, shared faith, and the necessity of helping the people and all those in need. The younger Bush was more inspired in the same circumstances. He simply quoted a letter from John Page to Thomas Jefferson, written at the beginning of the War of Independence: "We know," Page wrote, "the race is not to the swift nor the battle to the strong. Do you not think an angel rides in the whirlwind and directs this storm?" And Bush concluded by adopting the same terms inspired by a psalm of Nahum: "This story goes on. And an angel still rides in the whirlwind and directs this storm."[17]

Less enigmatic in his First Inaugural, Clinton had quoted Paul's Epistle to the Ephesians: "we recognize a simple but powerful truth, we need each other," and concluded with a quotation from the Epistle to the Galatians: "And let us not be weary in well-doing, for in due season, we shall reap, if we faint not."[18] As for Carter, he had showed a certain preference for the Old Testament, quoting the words of the Lord reported by the prophet Micah: "He hath showed thee, O man, what is good; and what doth the Lord require of thee, but to do justly, and to love mercy, and to walk humbly with thy God."[19]

IT SHOULD BE UNDERSTOOD THAT the advice of apostles and prophets quoted so far is not at all unusual in the American political tradition. This old religious rhetoric was inaugurated by George Washington and imitated by all his successors, including the least openly religious among them. Thomas Jefferson, the most irreligious of American presidents, took pride in his First Inaugural in 1801 in the great qualities of a republican people "enlightened by a benign religion, professed, indeed, and practiced in various forms, yet all of them inculcating honesty, truth, temperance, gratitude, and the love of man."[20] More than a century later, Franklin D. Roosevelt did not hesitate to evoke Christ driving the money changers from the temple to bring out the grandeur and the radical nature of his political message: "The money changers," he proclaimed, three years after the stock market crash, "have fled from their high seats in the temple of our civilization. We may now restore that temple to the ancient truths. The measure of the restoration lies in the extent to which we apply social values more noble than mere monetary profit."[21] Roosevelt's bold declaration pointed to the continued strength of a political tradition imbued with biblical references that had elicited Tocqueville's admiration in the 1830s.

What is the explanation for the persistence of this tradition? It is probably connected to the remnants of a system of Protestant education that used the Bible as a basic reference. It also has to do with the nature of the American Revolution, sustained by the religious fervor of dissenters and a panoply of biblical imagery denouncing the misdeeds of English tyranny and calling, often in millenarian terms, for the advent of a new social order, purified of all the excesses of a decadent monarchy.

The reader will recall that the huge success of Tom Paine's republican tract, *Common Sense*—more than 120,000 copies were printed the year of its publication in Philadelphia in 1776—was due to a skillful appeal to the Old Testament, tending to demonstrate that a monarchical regime was contrary to the will of God.[22] The agnostic Paine had understood, long before Tocqueville, that the spirit of liberty was fully compatible with the spirit of religion. The American Revolution created republican institutions with the active support of most of the churches founded by the colonists. The absence of a religiously inspired counterrevolution, the churches' acceptance of egalitarian and democratic values, and the rejection of any hereditary political authority and any religious supremacy could not but strengthen the affinities between religion and politics. Only the Anglican Church, the official church of the British monarchy, suffered a degree of ostracism until it was Americanized by cutting ties with Canterbury and adopting the name of the Episcopalian Church. Hence, the Anglican system that had been dominant in the colonies of the South was quickly replaced by an alternative model based on tolerance and religious pluralism. A new national mythology was gradually constructed on the basis of the eminently secular notions of a "representative republic" and "democracy," at a time when the Hanoverian monarchy was consolidating a British identity based on a "homogenising Anglican-aristocratic" model.[23] At the very time British society was preserving its traditions, revolutionary America, as the historian J. C. D. Clark has suggested, was striving to create what had never been seen before: a society "at once more ethical and more materialistic, more libertarian and more deferential to the sovereignty of collective opinion."[24]

BUT IT WOULD BE MISTAKEN, on the basis of the evocation of this old tradition, to conclude that there has been complete continuity in the political and religious history of the United States. The use of a religious rhetoric that all American presidents shared from George Washington on is obvious. But behind this use, there are significant variations that separate the more religious from the less religious presidents. And the extreme religiosity of figures like Jimmy Carter and George W. Bush has received no satisfactory explanation in France.

Consider the exemplary case of George Bush Junior. His openly flaunted piety clearly exceeded that of his predecessors. To a reporter who had asked him during the 2000 primaries to identify his favorite philosopher, he had replied: "Christ ... because he changed my heart."[25] And when he was still governor of Texas, he had proclaimed June 10, 2000, as "Jesus Day." He even claimed that his election to the presidency coincided with a new cycle of intense collective piety, "a Third Awakening."[26]

The fully documented, tortuous progress of his conversion makes it impossible to doubt the sincerity of his faith. Brought up as an Episcopalian by his famous Connecticut family, he set his sights on winning the Texas gubernatorial election. Bush could not have been unaware of the influence of the Evangelical Baptists and Methodists in the state. After his marriage, he found it useful to regularly attend his wife's evangelical church, the Highland Park United Methodist Church in Dallas. Converted at the age of thirty-nine by Billy Graham in his parents' vacation house in Kennebunkport in 1985, George W. Bush professed a "renewed faith," the political advantages of which had not escaped his notice: he knew how to communicate with the evangelical electorate that was a majority in the Southern states. The first thing he did was to put this skill at the service of his father's presidential ambitions.

As the political advisers of the elder Bush noticed during the 1988 presidential campaign, the younger Bush was immediately able to establish warm ties to the evangelical figures introduced to his father. He was now thoroughly versed in evangelical doctrine.[27] In putting his intimate knowledge of the world of born-again Christians at the service of his father, Bush Junior helped him to ward off the danger represented by the candidacy of Pat Robertson— the celebrated charismatic televangelist who, during the 1988 primaries, had claimed: "I have a direct call and a leading from God to run for president."[28] In the view of the Reverend Doug Wead of the Assemblies of God, the son had a certain advantage over the father: "George W. was instantly comfortable with all of the evangelical figures" he was introduced to.

> He knows their language, and it was obvious to them all that his conversion experience had been genuine and profound. He certainly understood evangelical Christian theology better than his father. ... With most other

presidential candidates, [evangelical voters] hesitated, they tested, and tried to find a common denominator so they could say "Well, he's kind of ours, he just doesn't know it"; or, "He's ours but he doesn't understand the culture." And with G. W., they knew it was real. I don't know how to explain that without defining the whole subculture itself.[29]

The Electoral Strategy of the Republican Party

A sort of golden legend grew up in the United States about the personality of President George W. Bush. He was seen as a saint, a prophet, a crusader, the man God had chosen to solve the world's problems.[30] After he was reelected governor of Texas in 1998, Bush himself had declared: "I believe that God wants me to be president." But this oft-quoted statement is almost always truncated and taken out of context. When he said it, Bush was not addressing voters or members of the Republican Party. He was speaking with a small group of co-religionists who were always fond of hearing about conversion experiences, and he hastened to add: "But if that doesn't happen, that's okay. . . . I have seen the presidency up close and personal. I know it's a sacrifice, and I don't need it for personal validation."[31] Feeling the presence of the divine in prayer, at the time of a sudden conversion, in a moment of adversity, or on the occasion of a difficult decision is not at all unusual for a born-again Christian. It is itself evidence of belonging to an evangelical milieu, the signature of a particularly exuberant form of Christian religiosity. Carter and Clinton had made similar remarks. And a political opponent like Al Gore had no hesitation, when he was campaigning against Bush in 2000, in reminding his born-again supporters that before any serious decision was made, one first had to ask "WWJD?" The acronym, understood by all evangelicals, stood for "What would Jesus do?" in the same circumstances.[32]

The very ordinariness of President Bush's evangelicalism raises a key question: What geopolitical factors are best able to explain the success of Republican evangelicalism? And by implication: Why is an evangelical candidate more likely than a non-evangelical or a non-Protestant to win a presidential election?

To understand the importance of evangelicalism in the presidential strategy of the Republican Party, it is necessary to go back to the 1960s—a time when a Republican had little chance of winning a presidential election. Between 1932 and 1964, the Republicans had elected only one president, a national hero who did not fit under the traditional partisan labels, General

Eisenhower. After the election of Kennedy in 1960 and Johnson in 1964, all indications seemed to point to the lasting supremacy of the Democratic Party. In 1964, in fact, the Republican candidate, Barry Goldwater, won only 38.5 percent of the vote against 61.1 percent for Johnson. But his defeat masked a remarkable success in the states of the Deep South, where most African-Americans still did not have the right to vote. Goldwater won in five of those states with a majority of 55 percent.[33] He thereby demonstrated that a political program focused on traditional family values, the defense of states' rights, and marked indifference to the new rights won by African-Americans made a representative of the party of Lincoln a credible candidate. This was precisely what Johnson had anticipated the day he signed the Civil Rights Act in July 1964: "I think," he said to his assistant Bill Moyers, "we just delivered the South to the Republican Party for a long time to come."[34]

The new law prohibited all discrimination in the workplace and in public transportation; it applied to private businesses with more than fifteen employees as well as to all public services. It also prohibited the use of federal funds for hospitals, schools, or colleges and universities that maintained discriminatory practices based on race or skin color. The disaffection of hitherto solidly Democratic Southern voters capitalized on by Goldwater in 1964, by George Wallace in 1968, and by Nixon in 1972 made the election of a Republican president increasingly likely. The road to Washington now went through the South, as figure 7.1 shows.

Nixon, Reagan, and the Bushes each won a majority of Southern white votes. The same effects, with some delay, affected the composition of the House of Representatives. After a gradual increase, the Republicans won most Southern districts, beginning with the 1994 elections. This success was noteworthy in a country in which more than 95 percent of incumbents are generally reelected with landslide majorities.

THE 1976 ELECTION OF JIMMY CARTER seemed to signal for the Democrats that there was a real possibility of regaining the Southern electorate. Carter did win in ten of the eleven states of the former Confederacy. But his stinging defeat by Reagan in 1980 pointed to the weakness of an electoral strategy that attempted to satisfy both black and white voters who felt threatened by the liberal order inaugurated under the Johnson administration. In 1972, Nixon had won 80 percent of the Southern white vote. After the Carter parenthesis, Reagan obtained 60 percent of the same vote in 1980 and

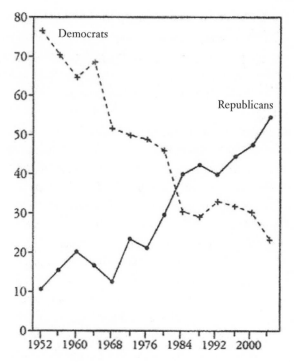

FIGURE 7.1 Party Identification of White Voters in the Southern United States from 1952 to 2004 (in percentages).

Source: Earl Black and Merle Black, *Divided America: The Ferocious Power Struggle in American Politics* (New York: Simon and Schuster, 2007), 37. Reprinted by permission of the authors.

70 percent four years later, thereby consolidating the efforts of his predecessors for years to come.[35]

What were the real and symbolic tools that Reagan used to win over voters who were so quick to change allegiances? Although the former B-movie actor was divorced and indifferent to religion in his private life, Reagan was fortunate enough to receive decisive support from the Christian conservatives of the Moral Majority, an organization for the defense of traditional family values that the fundamentalist preacher Jerry Falwell had established. The evangelical right had traditionally not been very politically active. Its principal purpose was religious: to spread the Good News and promote the conversion of adults. In 1965, Jerry Falwell could still claim: "We have few ties to this earth." A good Christian, of course, had to conduct himself as a good father and responsible citizen who paid his taxes and respected his country's laws. But "our only purpose on this earth is to know Christ and to make Him known."[36]

What led Falwell and many other evangelicals to change course in the late 1970s? First was a series of Supreme Court decisions unfavorable to the promotion of religious ideas and traditional moral values defended by the Christian right. In 1962, when one-third of American public schools authorized morning prayer, the Supreme Court, in *Engel v. Vitale*, declared the recitation of an ecumenical prayer that the school board of a local district in New York had composed unconstitutional.[37] In the court's opinion, the prayer violated the First Amendment's prohibition against the establishment of any official religion.[38] Obligatory prayer was unacceptable because it obviously exerted pressure on religious minorities by requiring them "to conform to the prevailing officially approved religion," which was not necessarily theirs. And according to the principles that the authors of the Constitution and the Bill of Rights upheld, as interpreted by Justice Black: "religion is too personal, too sacred, too holy, to permit its 'unhallowed perversion' by a civil magistrate."[39]

This decision scandalized traditionalist circles, Catholic and Protestant. According to Billy Graham, it was conclusive evidence of the rapidly increasing "secularization of the United States." James Pike, the Episcopal bishop of San Francisco, claimed that it "deconsecrated the nation." It even meant, in the view of Cardinal James McIntyre of Los Angeles, that the "American heritage of philosophy," based on an ideal of religious liberty, had been abandoned in favor of another philosophy incompatible with religion: "Soviet materialism" and "Soviet regimented liberty."[40] Supreme Court decisions prohibiting the reading of Bible verses in schools (1963) and barring the required teaching of creationism (1968)[41] provoked the anger of traditionalists, soon exacerbated by the "immorality" of other decisions concerning the private conduct of individuals. The Supreme Court invalidated state laws criminalizing the use of contraception and the practice of abortion in 1968 and 1973 respectively.[42]

But it was an apparently anodyne decision concerning the tax status of Southern evangelical religious schools that provoked the political mobilization of evangelical preachers in the Deep South. The Internal Revenue Service had traditionally granted the charitable activities of churches tax-exempt status. The exemption assumed that its beneficiaries respected federal law. But the proliferation of denominational schools in the South beginning in the 1960s was not simply a response to the progress of evangelical religiosity among students' parents. Its primary cause was the racist refusal to accept the mixture of black and white students in the public schools, in accordance with the 1964 Civil Rights Law and the decision in *Brown v. Board of Education* (1954). As a result, there was a sudden proliferation of thousands of private schools, christened for the occasion Christian Academies. Since the new schools remained segregated, the IRS, following several federal court decisions, began to revoke their tax-exempt status. For the same reasons on January 19, 1976, the IRS also revoked Bob Jones University's tax exemption. The latter decision, according to Paul Weyrich, "enraged the Christian community."[43] Carter was in no way responsible for this decision (he was elected in November 1976), but the establishment of a strong Department of Education under his administration led his adversaries to suspect the worst: "Evangelicals, in particular, saw it as an agency empowered to control or undermine Christian academies by forcing them to comply with federal civil rights and curriculum guidelines. The issue was financial as well as theological. If the federal government could take away the academies' tax exempt status, the parents would face much higher tuition fees."[44]

Reacting to these punitive measures and claiming that the Carter administration was undermining the religious liberty of children and their parents (who were paying for their education), a fundamentalist teacher named Robert Billings—close to Jerry Falwell and Paul Weyrich, the future strategist of the evangelical right—created an organization for the defense of the Christian Academies.

The Emergence of the Moral Majority

Very influential in the legislative elections of 1978, this new lobby later broadened its sphere of influence by taking up other pet causes of evangelical conservatives: the fight against abortion, the restoration of prayer in public schools, and the denunciation of the Equal Rights Amendment and the "secularizing" practices of liberal elites. This collective action gave rise to a formal organization, created by Paul Weyrich and headed by Jerry Falwell, the Moral Majority Incorporated. Its executive director was none other than Robert Billings, who had proved himself by defending the Christian Academies.[45] Racial concerns were thereby skillfully masked by the declaration of authentically religious aims, as the jurist Noah Feldman has pointed out. The creation of segregationist fortress schools coincided with "a process of court-ordered secularization in public schools."[46] By transforming ordinary private schools into Christian Academies, the white Southern elites had succeeded in changing a momentary racist reaction into a much more acceptable movement for the defense of Christendom.

During the 1980 presidential primaries, Ronald Reagan skillfully demonstrated his mastery of Southern politics. To send a clear signal that he accepted all the traditions of the South, even the most unpleasant ones, shortly after his nomination at the Republican Convention in 1980, Reagan went to Philadelphia, Mississippi—encouraged by ultraconservative Representative Trent Lott of Mississippi—to deliver a speech supporting states' rights. Philadelphia was the town where, sixteen years earlier, in the summer of 1964, three young civil-rights activists had been assassinated while investigating a church burning. The symbolic choice of this location signaled to Southern elites that the former governor of California was one of them. A few days later, Reagan went even further. He managed to appeal to the most conservative evangelicals by visiting Jerry Falwell's Christian college, Liberty Baptist College, in Lynchburg, Virginia, where he declared his unshakeable attachment to school prayer: "I have always thought that a voluntary non-sectarian prayer was perfectly proper, and I don't think we should have expelled God from the classroom."[47] Reagan had clearly realized that the most dynamic organization of the new Christian Right was Jerry Falwell's Moral Majority, with three hundred thousand members (seventy thousand of whom were ministers of religion) and fifty chapters (one for each state), led by evangelicals personally appointed by Falwell, half of whom worked for Churches sponsoring Christian Academies.[48] This organization therefore became the spearhead of the Republican party's Southern strategy.

By denouncing the "moral decline of our nation" and the perversion of traditional family values fostered by "amoral secular humanists and other liberals," the Moral Majority's fundamentalist leaders were especially successful in increasing the electoral participation of evangelical voters who had hitherto been reluctant to get involved in politics. The results were considerable. In the course of two years, more than two million new voters were registered and the turnout of Southern evangelical voters increased from 61 percent in 1976 to 77 percent in 1980.[49]

The very success of the Moral Majority precipitated its decline after eight years of Reaganism: donations were dwindling and its financial base became so fragile that Jerry Falwell decided to cease operations in the summer of 1989. As he declared in Las Vegas: "Our goal has been achieved. . . . The religious right is solidly in place." Falwell's Moral Majority was eventually replaced by another evangelical organization, the Christian Coalition, launched during the 1988 presidential primaries to support the presidential ambitions of another famous televangelist, Pat Robertson, a charismatic Southern Baptist. Thanks to the organizational genius of its director, Ralph Reed, this new organization had, by the mid-1990s, a powerful lobby in Washington, representatives distributed in nine hundred local sections, more than one million active members, and a budget of more than $20 million. To extend its influence, the Christian Coalition trained more than seven thousand activists in specialized schools to mobilize potential Republican voters and to support Republican candidates most favorable to its cause. In the 1994 elections, Christian Coalition activists managed to distribute thirty million voter guides to churches that requested them. These guides analyzed the votes of incumbents and measured the degree to which they supported the cause of the evangelical right. They had a definite impact in states in which Christian Right candidates were running against more moderate or secular candidates, and thereby contributed to the victory of the Republican Party, then led by Newt Gingrich, in the 1994 congressional elections.[50]

The Republicans now had a loyal block of voters essential for the consolidation of the party's gains. Representing between one-quarter and one-third of the total electorate, a growing majority of evangelical votes went to Republican candidates: 63 percent for Reagan in 1980, 78 percent for Reagan in 1984, and 81 percent for Bush senior in 1988. The younger Bush did almost as well as his father, winning 78 percent of white evangelical votes in 2004.[51] The results were spectacular in the South, where Reagan won ten of the eleven states of the old Confederacy in 1980 and all of them in 1984, as Bush senior did in 1988. Running against Bill Clinton, a real Southerner and a born-again Christian, George H. W. Bush lost the 1992 election, but nonetheless preserved a majority in seven Southern states: Virginia, North Carolina, South Carolina, Florida, Alabama, Mississippi, and Texas. Clinton won only his home state of Arkansas, along with Tennessee, Louisiana, and Georgia. The Deep South, with the exception of Georgia, remained under Republican domination.

The Republican Party's Southern strategy had thus fully succeeded thanks to the systematic politicization of issues as diverse as abortion, homosexuality, school prayer, the Equal Rights Amendment, the public financing of religious schools, and school desegregation. In the process, the evangelical, Baptist, and Pentecostal right quietly abandoned its old Democratic roots.[52]

The conservative evangelicalism of the younger Bush was therefore not at all unusual: it was culturally determined by the political environment in which he was operating. His conversion, so often heralded in evangelical circles, the frequency of his morning prayers, the impression that God had a direct influence on him, were all traits in complete conformity with an old evangelical tradition, first implanted in the South, and later disseminated in the Midwest and Southwest. Moreover, like Reagan before him, George W. Bush also made a "pilgrimage" to the South during the 2000 presidential primaries, in the form of a visit to Bob Jones University in South Carolina, at a time when this center of Protestant fundamentalism was still racially segregated. The university did accept students from ethnic minorities, but it prohibited any form of socialization between "students of color" and white students. This prohibition was based on a very particular reading of Genesis, according to which God, by destroying Babel and scattering the builders of the tower throughout the world, had indicated His preference for a "divided world" and not a "one-world community consisting of one religion, one economy, one government, and one race."[53] This visit, which his rival John McCain sharply criticized, helped him win the South Carolina primary and confirmed for the most conservative evangelicals that he was one of them.[54]

The *modus operandi religione* of George W. Bush, so disconcerting in French eyes, was perfectly suited to the circumstances. It also contributed to the success of a party whose Southern strategy had, over the long term, made possible the recapture of the White House after thirty years of Democratic control, except for the Eisenhower interlude. The defeat the Republican Party suffered in the 2006 midterm elections did not fundamentally challenge that success: in the states of the old Confederacy, only 36 percent of white voters voted for the Democratic Party, compared to 58 percent in the North and Northeast. Bastions of the Deep South such as Georgia, Alabama, and Mississippi, remained under the complete domination of the Republican Party.[55] More generally, the vast majority of evangelical voters (72 percent in 2006, compared to 75 percent in 2004) remained loyal to the GOP. This was where George W. Bush found his most faithful supporters.[56] In the South, where conservative Baptists belonging to the Southern Baptist Convention are the most numerous, and in certain states on the periphery of the South (Colorado, Kansas, New Mexico, and Arizona, where the Southern Baptist Convention is particularly influential), the party of Lincoln, in the disenchanted words of a Republican congressman from Connecticut, had "become a party of theocracy."[57]

The price the Republican Party had paid to make itself into a "Southern" party was its propagation of rather obscurantist values and the combination of religious aims with political considerations to secure the loyalty of an electorate of born-again Christians. From then on the national leaders of the Republican Party were recruited almost entirely in the South. They unselfconsciously used theocratic language that could not fail to embarrass more moderate Republicans. Tom DeLay, the then Republican House majority leader, made so bold as to define his political mission in these terms: "God is using me all the time, everywhere, to stand up for a biblical world view in everything that I do and everywhere I am. He is training me."[58]

DOES THIS MEAN, AS SOME HAVE THOUGHT, that the Republican Party succeeded in turning America into a "baptized nation" ruled by the worshipers of the Lord Jesus Christ?[59] Is it right to assert that the ruling regime is a veritable "American theocracy"? These claims are obviously excessive, and the Bush administration's defeat in the 2006 midterm elections clearly showed that the danger represented by the evangelical right, itself a minority in the Republican Party, has been greatly exaggerated. It is true that evangelical voters were Bush's most unconditional supporters and the ones most prepared to support the war in Iraq.[60] But they were not alone in defining the ideology of a party that, outside the Southern states, was more successful in persuading voters when it showed moderation on issues such as euthanasia, abortion, and acceptance of gay rights (marriage excepted). The easy reelection of Arnold Schwarzenegger as governor of California was vivid proof of that. The moderates also had a place in the Republican Party and the ideological polarization fostered by party leaders was an inaccurate reflection of a centrist Republican majority that remained hostile to the extremes.[61] The evangelical right was dominant only in the states of the old Confederacy. That is where it most successfully mobilized conservative voters, with an effectiveness that recalled that of the trade unions when they were "the organizational engine" for the Democratic Party in the industrial states of the North and the Northeast.[62] One of the reasons why McCain lost the 2008 presidential election is that he forfeited the chance to recapture the centrist Republican majority when he chose Sarah Palin as his running mate. In doing so he appeared to be the captive of the far right and lost the appeal he initially had among moderate Republican and independent voters.

The battle between conservatives and progressives, believers and nonbelievers, evangelicals and moderate Protestants, is not just a political battle, it is also a legal one. It was in the federal courts that the "wall of separation" between church and state was articulated and subsequently subjected to countless interpretations and reinterpretations. And it was against this wall, first conceived by Thomas Jefferson in the early nineteenth century, that the conservative leaders of the Republican Party mobilized with the greatest intensity in order to restore religion to its proper place in the political sphere. Their relative failure, as the next chapter will show, clearly demonstrates that the Christian right has not yet defeated the American secular tradition, despite numerous attempts to breach the wall of separation between church and state.

8

The Wall of Separation Between
Church and State

THROUGHOUT THIS BOOK, we have seen that religion in the United States is both familiar to the French and very hard for them to understand. Familiar because it has been the object of numerous investigations, scholarly commentaries, and often peremptory assertions. Hard to understand because it is situated in a complex and contradictory historical world, punctuated by advances and retreats, secular periods and religious moments. This world, which is stratified like geological sediments, bears many visible traces—songs, mottos, oaths, commemorations—whose use has sometimes disconcerted French and indeed American observers. At first sight, religion dominates the social and political landscape. It is impossible, for example, to buy anything without using a dollar bill bearing the famous motto "In God We Trust." In school, it is hard to avoid the recitation of the Pledge of Allegiance, which places the United States under the aegis of a benevolent deity: "one nation under God." It would be inconceivable for the average American, regardless of his or her origin, not to partake in the most important family meal of the year, Thanksgiving, which thanks God for the favor granted once to the Pilgrim Fathers. And it is hard to ignore the newly elected office holders, who swear to defend the Constitution with their hand on the Bible. And who has not heard at the end of a political speech the ritual phrases: "So help me God," "God bless you," or "God bless America"? It is not unusual for a president to refer to the Old Testament in his inaugural address or to describe his country as a New Jerusalem. War speeches, from Wilson to Bush, have a crusading tone, and ministers of religion go to the White House with such frequency that an ill-informed visitor might think there is no real separation between church and state in this country.

"In God We Trust"

French attempts to explain the multiple references to religion usually involve exaggerating the differences between the two countries to such an extent that American culture becomes unrecognizable. The often rudimentary comparisons strengthen old prejudices: France is supposed to be secular and republican; America, in contrast, has remained subject to the moral rule of evangelical preachers. In France, an influential author has written, "we believe in the Enlightenment"; in the United States people are constantly affirming their belief in God. In France, "the churches have to give way before the state"; in America, "the state has to give way before the churches."[1] There are innumerable examples of this kind. When French observers draw up an inventory of the references to God in American political discourse, they suggest that the best formula for grasping the essence of America would indeed be "In God We Trust."[2] This is supposed to be a foundational motto, a semantic shortcut explaining everything else, the politics of the Founding Fathers, as well as those of the presidents of the twentieth and twenty-first centuries. But an essentialist interpretation of this kind is possible only if one ignores the history of this motto.

Its origin, relatively late in American history, lies in the darkest hours of the Civil War, when the outcome was still uncertain. The unprecedented violence of the conflict had particularly moved a group of Protestant preachers who favored the abolition of slavery. It was necessary, they believed, to propitiate an angry God by Christianizing the symbols of a republic that was, in its very foundations, too divorced from the truths of revealed religion. The worship of a pagan divinity, the goddess Liberty that appeared on coins, could not fail to stir God's wrath. Under the circumstances, would it not be a good idea to change the motto on the currency? Petitions were sent to the secretary of the Treasury, Salmon Chase. Receptive to the argument, Chase instructed James Pollock, the director of the National Mint, to change the motto, because "the trust of our people in God should be declared on our national coins."[3] Pollock was all the more willing to comply because he himself defended the idea of Christianizing the Constitution. In 1864, Congress authorized the minting of new two-cent coins with the motto "In God We Trust."[4] But the printing of the motto on paper currency was authorized only in 1957, one year after the eighty-fourth Congress had made the motto on the currency into the national motto.[5]

It is a widely held opinion in France that other references to the divine, such as "one nation under God" in the Pledge of Allegiance, signal the religious character of American democracy. The idea is not mistaken, but it also needs to be placed in historical context. The Pledge of Allegiance, recited every morning in most public schools since 1892, was originally impeccably secular: "I pledge allegiance to the Flag of the United States of America and to the Republic for which it stands, one nation, indivisible, with liberty and justice for all (1924 revision)."[6]

The 1954 revision read: "... one nation *under God*, indivisible, with liberty and justice for all."[7] This God was neither the God of the Pilgrims nor the God of the Founding Fathers, but a God, cobbled together in the 1950s to point to the true nature of the quasi-eschatological battle between Christian America and the communist and atheistic Evil Empire. "From this day forward," President Eisenhower proudly declared on the day Congress passed the law changing the wording of the Pledge, "the millions of our schoolchildren will daily proclaim in every city and town, every village and rural schoolhouse, the dedication of our nation and our people to the Almighty."[8]

It is thus possible to date precisely the symbolic intrusions of religion into the political sphere: 1776, the "Creator" in the Declaration of Independence; 1862, the motto "In God We Trust" on coins; 1954, the addition of "under God" to the Pledge of Allegiance; 1956, transformation of the motto on coins into a national motto. And it was major events—the War of Independence, the Civil War, and the Cold War—that precipitated the adoption of these symbolic measures, by reviving faith among political elites. The formulas chosen, it should be noted, are more deist than Christian in nature. The divinity invoked is always an abstract and disembodied God. Jesus Christ, despite the dominance of Protestantism in the United States, is never officially referred to. And the oath on the Bible, which is so valued by presidents (although nothing in the Constitution requires it), is almost always sworn on a closed Bible, barring any theological or sectarian interpretation.

It is interesting to note that "God bless America"—one of the most popular patriotic songs, particularly in the wake of September 11, 2001—has secular origins far removed from any evangelical concerns. The song was composed in 1918 by a Jewish immigrant, Irving Berlin, the brilliant composer of hundreds of popular songs and Broadway musicals. Now considered quintessentially patriotic, the song had been intended for dancers in an irreverent musical revue titled *Yip Yip Yaphank*.

THE FREQUENCY OF REFERENCES TO God is deceptive in many respects. It masks a more ambiguous reality that escapes superficial observers of United States history. It is not so well known that the American political tradition has gone through periods in which the divine was completely absent. For example, the Federal Constitution drafted by the delegates to the Philadelphia Convention in 1787, and ratified in the following year, omits any reference to God, the Creator, or any kind of supreme being. It is literally "godless," and the few references to religion that can be found in it are all negative.[9] This omission did not go unnoticed. It was immediately denounced in very vigorous terms, as a disgrace that endangered the very future of American democracy, an impious way of encouraging "deists, Jews, pagans, Mahometans, and even the pope himself" to accede to high federal office.[10] A godless Constitution, warned Amos Singletary, not only opened the gates of power to papists and infidels, but would probably lead to the restoration of the monstrous cult of the god Baal.[11] Similarly, a delegate to the North Carolina ratifying convention expressed his fear that, in the absence of a religious qualification, "a Turk, a Jew, a Roman Catholic, and what is worse than all a Universalist, may be president of the United States."[12] An article in the antifederalist newspaper, the *New York Daily Advertiser*, went so far as to fear the outbreak of a civil war if a Jewish president were elected. Once he was sworn in as commander-in-chief of the armed forces, "our dear posterity [might] be ordered to rebuild Jerusalem."[13]

The response of the advocates of the new Constitution was not at all reassuring to the zealots who favored a Christian nation. The author of articles published in Connecticut and Massachusetts newspapers over the signature of "Elihu" delighted in the abandonment of the old fable that human laws are derived from the precepts of divine law. The new Constitution, in his view, was well adapted to the new age when "the light of philosophy has arisen ... miracles have ceased, oracles are silenced, monkish darkness is dissipated. . . . Mankind are no longer to be deluded with fable."[14] Thoroughly satisfied with Article 6 of the federal Constitution, which prohibits any religious test, William Van Murray predicted in a 1787 essay that America would soon become "the great philosophical theater of the world," because it was open to all religious opinions, "Christian, Mohamentan, Jew, or Gentile." A modern government, he explained, could not fail to conform to the laws of nature. The drafters of the Constitution had therefore been right to abolish religious tests, the religious oaths formerly required of candidates for high office, because they obviously violated the laws of nature.[15] John Adams, the most moderate of the Founders, argued for the same position when he asserted, as early as 1786, that the thirteen states provided the first example of governments "founded on the natural authority of the people alone, without a pretense of miracle or mystery."[16]

REJECTING THE EVIDENCE, many conservative politicians have at different times tried to Christianize the Constitution by adding a clause favorable to religion. Early in the Civil War, for example, representatives of ten Protestant denominations, who saw the omission of the name of God as one of the probable causes of the war, presented a petition to Congress proposing to change the wording of the preamble to the Constitution to read: "We, the people of the United States, humbly acknowledging almighty God as the source of all authority and power in civil government, the Lord Jesus Christ as the ruler among nations, his revealed will as the supreme law of the land, in order to constitute a Christian government and in order to form a more perfect union. . . ."[17]

The proposed amendment was not adopted, but zealous believers brought it up again on many occasions in almost identical terms until the late 1960s. They also attempted, with equal lack of success, to change the preamble.[18] They had no doubt failed to recognize that, though lacking any reference to God, the Constitution is a sacred, almost untouchable, document that can be amended only on rare occasions and with the support of a supermajority.[19]

"In God We Trust," as I have pointed out, was neither the first nor the most significant American motto, and certainly not the "innermost" motto of the United States. The true founding mottos—*E Pluribus Unum*, *Annuit Cœptis*, *Novus Ordo Seclorum*—featured on the Great Seal of the United States, adopted in 1782 and printed on the dollar bill, lie outside the realm of Christian symbolism. Taken from Virgil, these cryptic formulas reveal the prevalence of a different political tradition, derived from the Enlightenment and bolstered by references to ancient republican Rome.

E Pluribus Unum ("Out of many, one") is taken from a poem by Virgil titled *Moretum*, about making a delicious herb-and-cheese dish.[20] *Novus Ordo Seclorum* ("A new order of the ages") is taken from Virgil's Fourth Eclogue, where it evokes the beginning of a new historical cycle, coming after the "age of iron," in the prophecy delivered by the Cumæan Sibyl: *Magnus ab integro sæcolorum nascitur ordo* ("The great order of the ages is born anew"). *Annuit Cœptis* ("[He] approves our enterprise") is taken from Book I of the *Georgics*, where Virgil describes the long sequence of the gods of antiquity (Pan, Neptune, Ceres, Minerva, Sylvaner) and, addressing Caesar, implores him: *Audacibus adnue cœptis* ("Bless our bold enterprise").[21]

That leaves the "Creator" of the Declaration of Independence, so frequently invoked by the Christian right to bolster the claim of the religious origins of American republicanism. But this creator was a pure creature of the Enlightenment, a great architect of the universe, quite foreign to the Biblical tradition, as Walter Berns demonstrates in his analysis of the cultural sources of American patriotism. The Declaration of Independence, whose principal author was Thomas Jefferson, does indeed mention a Creator and a God of nature. This has nothing to do, Berns explains, with "the God whom, today, 43 percent of Americans . . . claim regularly to worship on the Sabbath."[22] Nature's God is not in the declaration to blame or punish men, since he has given them no orders or commandments. He promises them nothing and remains indifferent to their state of grace or sin. In contrast to the God of the Old Testament, he is not a jealous God: he grants men fundamental rights—"life, liberty, and the pursuit of happiness." According to other sources often quoted at the time, he also grants them freedom of conscience. This freedom, which Jefferson, Madison, Washington, and others fiercely defended, means in essence a fundamental and unalienable right to worship different gods or to ignore all of them. "The legitimate powers of government," Jefferson wrote in *Notes on the State of Virginia,* "extend to such acts only as are injurious to others. But it does me no injury for my neighbour to say there are twenty gods, or no god. It neither picks my pocket nor breaks my leg."[23] Men may have a religion—all are permitted—but they must obey the law, whatever the nature of their belief.

NATURE'S GOD INVOKED BY JEFFERSON is all the less demanding because he has surrendered all his powers to men, as the Declaration of

Independence asserts: it is up to men, who are alone sovereign, to choose the form of government best suited to the defense of their unalienable rights. The American Revolution had not created a theo-democracy. It haughtily ignored the work of the Puritans, considered anachronistic in the eighteenth century, and it tolerated only the republican form of government.[24]

The Founders frequently stated that American democracy was not Christian. The best evidence of this is one of the first treaties, unanimously ratified by the U.S. Senate during the Adams administration, the Treaty of Tripoli, signed by the president on June 10, 1797. Article 11 of the treaty provided:

> As the government of the United States of America *is not in any sense founded on the Christian Religion*—as it has in itself no character of enmity against the laws, religion or tranquility of Musselmen—and as the said States never have entered into any war or act of hostility against any Mehomitan nation, it is declared by the parties that no pretext arising from religious opinions shall ever produce an interruption of the harmony existing between the two countries.[25]

It would be difficult to be clearer on the subject, regardless of what the leaders of the Christian right continue to claim today. Another indication that is also little known is *The Life and Morals of Jesus of Nazareth*, which Jefferson composed while holding the office of president by putting together judiciously chosen excerpts of the four Gospels. What became known as the *Jefferson Bible* was particularly noteworthy in that it omitted any reference to the divinity of Christ, to his miracles, and to the Resurrection. It ended abruptly with this truncated quotation from the Gospel of Matthew: "And he [Joseph of Arimathea] rolled a great stone to the door of the sepulchre, and departed."[26] In rewriting the New Testament, Jefferson explained that he sought to separate "diamonds" from the "dung," that is, what was truly authentic from what was not. The latter included the miracles and the Resurrection.[27]

On this basis, is it legitimate to conclude that America is a secular state like France? The question is problematic because the French notion of *laïcité* has no exact equivalent in English. But there are analogous terms, such as "secular," "secularism," and "secularization." Born-again Christians typically denounce atheists or agnostics as secular humanists. This pejorative expression means not only the lack of religion but the adoption of the hedonistic values of 1960s culture. For a fundamentalist like Jerry Falwell, "secularizers" are the quintessential enemies who must be fought and whom a vengeful God will not fail to punish. From this perspective, all human or natural disasters, all important events since the creation of the world, express a divine plan. It was therefore not an accident that the most serious attack on September 11, 2001, was aimed at the city of New York, the metropolitan center of vice, impiety, and wealth, in short, the living symbol of a modern Sodom and Gomorrah. Falwell thus had an explanation for the tragedy that hardly conformed to the standards of secularized patriotism: "I really believe that the pagans, and the abortionists, and the feminists, and the gays, and the lesbians who are actively trying to make that an alternative lifestyle, the ACLU, People for the American Way—all of them who have tried to secularize America—I point the finger in their face and say 'you helped this happen.'"[28]

These iconoclastic remarks were obviously ill received by the press and the leaders of the Republican Party. But Falwell refused to apologize, explaining that he had been misinterpreted, because what he had said was not political but theological in nature.

The Emergence of an American Secular Tradition

By "secularism," I do not simply mean the absence of religious belief, which is fairly rare in America.[29] I refer to a larger phenomenon, a gradual "disenchantment of the world" in Weber's sense—that is, a gradual rationalization of public life, accompanied by a noticeable disentanglement of religious and lay matters. In that respect, American secularism preceded the French process of laicization and served as a model for it.

The first American argument in favor of the principle of the separation of church and state was made by the dissident Baptist Roger Williams, founder of Rhode Island.[30] Williams, who had settled in the Massachusetts Bay colony in 1631, was driven out by the civil authorities in 1636 for having denounced the intolerance of the Puritans, and especially for his opposition to the proposal, which he considered blasphemous, to create a Christian commonwealth. According to Williams, the civil authorities had no messianic role; a good government might exist "in nations, cities, kingdoms . . . which never heard of the true God, nor His holy son."[31] The civil magistrate had no business concerning himself with the beliefs of his subjects nor imposing any kind of religious uniformity. His principal task consisted of guaranteeing civil peace and assuring some degree of prosperity. "The civil magistrate," Williams asserts, "will be satisfied with the assurance that men completely lacking in religion may possess a civic morality that makes them honest and useful members of the commonwealth."[32] The freedom of conscience that Williams envisaged was complete; it applied to everyone, to atheists as well as the greatest enemies and persecutors of the Protestant religion, the Catholics.

The separation of church and state, as Williams advocated it in his celebrated *Bloudy Tenent of Persecution* of 1644, was inseparable from a fundamental theological debate about the relationship between the Old and New Testaments. Proposing the creation of a new Jerusalem or a Christian commonwealth led to an overinterpretation of the Old Testament contrary to the truth of the Gospels. For Williams, in opposition to the more orthodox Puritans, the break between the Old and New Testaments was almost total: "The Church of the Jews under the Old Testament [was] in the type and the Church of the Christians under the New Testament in the Antitype."[33] The kingdom of Israel in the Old Testament was indeed a privileged regime, chosen and blessed by God, which had to operate under Jewish law in order to survive. The kings of Israel were therefore required to enforce obedience to divine law. In contrast, the ruler of a Christian commonwealth had no religious obligation to enforce, not even the Ten Commandments: no passage in the New Testament endowed civil magistrates with the slightest religious authority, and the punishments provided for violations of the old law (blasphemy, for example) were now outside the jurisdiction of the civil authorities.[34]

The doctrine of the "free grace" of God that Williams and the most radical separatists adopted barred the very possibility of a theocracy or of a state church, because no leader could be certain of his salvation. This doctrine, in fact, gave a new meaning to Calvinist predestination by stating that a sinner could be saved by God despite his imperfection. Since God's grace was freely granted, no political leader had the obligation to punish violators of the divine law for their own good or to serve as an example. In addition, because a sinner could be a "Saint," it was impossible to know a priori who was the good leader chosen by God. The doctrine of the "free grace" of God thus had strongly democratic implications, as David Wootton has clearly shown: political power no longer had a divine origin; it could only be the result of human choice, a pure product of natural reason.[35]

As for the church, whatever its doctrine, it was necessarily dissociated from political power. It was, after all, only a "society of worshipers," comparable to a commercial association or a college of doctors whose internal disputes in no way affected the well-being of the commonwealth. By refusing to separate themselves from their still insufficiently reformed churches, by prohibiting all religious dissent and all freedom of conscience, the New England Puritans, according to Williams, had committed an irreparable act: they welcomed into their communities "the *uncleane* and the *cleane*, of the *flock* of *Christ* and the *Herds* of the *World* together," creating an unacceptable confusion in which "the *Garden* and the *Wildernesse*, the *Church* and the *World* are all one."[36] By agreeing to open "a breach in . . . the Wall of separation between the garden of the Church and the wilderness of the world," they had violated a fundamental principle. Their conduct must therefore provoke the divine punishment foretold in Isaiah 5.5-6, namely, "the total destruction of the wall . . . and the transformation of the garden into a wilderness." Williams the separatist wished to completely isolate the garden of *his* church from the disorder of the world.[37]

Accused of religious anarchism, denounced for his antinomianism, banished from his Salem parish, and having sought refuge on the shores of Narragansett Bay, Williams secured a royal charter in 1644 to establish the colony of Rhode Island, of which he was governor from 1654 to 1656. Matching his actions to his words, in Rhode Island he created an embryonic secular state, with no established church, no Test Act, and no tithes to pay for the clergy or the construction of religious buildings. His tolerant regime, open to all faiths, was indeed at the opposite pole from a new Jerusalem.[38] Williams remained in his own way a convinced Calvinist; the idea of establishing a Christian nation, including indiscriminately the "cleane" and the "uncleane," according to the terms of an alliance with God, was repugnant to him because he thought that true Christians would always represent a tiny minority in North America. To claim otherwise was to demonstrate unbearable arrogance contrary to the spirit of the New Testament.

HISTORIANS ARE STILL DEBATING about the influence of Roger Williams. While he was indeed the first to apply the metaphor of the "wall of separation" to the New World, it is not very likely that his successors, beginning with Jefferson, had any direct knowledge of his writings, all of which were published in London and were considered rather archaic in the late eighteenth century. The interest his work holds for us is twofold: it is the first American presentation of a systematic defense of a regime based on tolerance of universal application; it is also one of the key sources for John Locke's considerations on tolerance, which in turn had a decisive and well-documented influence on the writings of the Founding Fathers. In his *Letter Concerning Toleration*, Locke sought to "distinguish exactly the business of civil government from that of religion, and to settle the just bounds that lie between the one and the other." He asserted that the "boundaries" were "fixed and immoveable," and that any attempt to cross those boundaries would be as absurd as wishing to "jumble heaven and earth together."[39] And like Williams, Locke excluded the possibility of an official church imposed on the subjects of a monarchy, even by popular consent. The church could only be a voluntary association, freely chosen by autonomous subjects, exempt from any public interference. For true religion was a purely individual affair, the mark of an "inward persuasion of the mind." The state had but one purpose, to protect the temporal goods of its citizens, their possessions, their liberty, their life, and their health. Following this logic, "all the power of civil government relates only to men's civil interests; is confined to the care of the things of this world, and hath noting to do with the world to come."[40]

Locke's theory of the separation between church and state had a definite influence on the British Radical Whigs, who in turn influenced the Founders of American democracy. James Burgh, for example, the author of a utopian novel addressed to the English of the twentieth century, attacked the monstrous "mixed-mungrel-spiritual-temporal-secular-ecclesiastical establishment." Burgh hoped that compensation for clergy and educators would finally be privatized and placed "in the hands of the people," according to its sovereign will. And above all, he proposed to abolish the Test Acts in anything involving the most sought after public offices that were most likely to guarantee upward social mobility—beginning with the military career, which had until then been closed to Catholics, Jews, and Dissenters. He concluded emphatically:

> Build an impenetrable wall of *separation* between things *sacred* and *civil.* Do not send a *graceless* officer, reeking from the arms of his *trull,* to the performance of a *holy* rite of *religion,* as a test for his holding the command of a regiment. To *profane,* in such a manner, a religion, which you pretend to *reverence,* is an impiety sufficient to bring down upon your heads, the roof of the sacred building you thus defile.[41]

Plainly stated, the scandalous practices engendered by the Test Act were in essence corrupting and contrary to the virtuous aim sought by the establishmentarians.[42] It would be better to put an end to such follies by building a *wall of separation* between church and state. The formula had been launched and Jefferson later adopted it in a letter to the Baptist community of Danbury.[43]

IF THE INITIAL QUESTION WERE formulated in terms more familiar to the French cast of mind, it would be: "What is *laïcité?*" The best definition of the word was given by Ferdinand Buisson, a former collaborator of Jules Ferry, in his *Nouveau Dictionnaire de pédagogie et d'instruction primaire* (1911). It is a new word, he says, but necessary to describe the gradual secularization of French society, based on a growing differentiation between the roles of the clergy and the state. This differentiation reached its peak with the French Revolution, which succeeded in imposing, "with complete clarity the idea of the secular state, a state neutral with regard to all forms of worship, independent of all clergies, free from any theological views." But, Buisson, goes on, it took another century of political battles before French society could finally establish a "deep separation between the temporal and the spiritual."[44]

Beginning with this definition, it is easy to demonstrate once again American precedence with regard to the principle of secularism. This principle was probably given its best formulation in "A Bill for Establishing Religious Freedom," drafted by Jefferson in 1777, presented to the Virginia General Assembly in June 1779, and adopted on January 16, 1786, thanks to the decisive support of James Madison and his celebrated petition against religious tithes, that had gathered more than ten thousand signatures.[45] The law innovated in many areas: it upheld freedom of conscience and the neutrality of the state, and it abolished the tithes collected by the Anglican clergy. It also opened access to public employment, because it prohibited all oaths of allegiance. This exceptionally ambitious law offered a veritable catalogue of the natural rights of the human race. It provided:

> That to compel a man to furnish contributions of money for the propagation of opinions which he disbelieves and abhors, is ... tyrannical ... that our civil rights have no dependance on our religious opinions, any more than our opinions in physics or geometry; that therefore the proscribing of any citizen as unworthy the public confidence by laying upon him an incapacity of being called to offices of trust and emolument, unless he profess or renounce this or that religious opinion, is depriving him injuriously of those privileges and advantages to which, in common with his fellow citizens, he has a natural right. ... that no man shall be compelled to frequent or support any religious worship, place, or ministry whatsoever, nor shall be enforced, restrained, molested, or burthened in his body or goods, nor shall otherwise suffer, on account of his religious opinions or belief.[46]

The bold tone and the universal application of Jefferson's bill did not go unnoticed in prerevolutionary France. It was almost immediately translated and presented in a detailed article in the second volume of Démeunier's *Encyclopédie méthodique*. Rather than waiting—which would have been the logical thing to do—for the article "Virginie" planned for the last volume of the *Encyclopédie* (1788), Démeunier hurried things along and disturbed the orderly presentation of material. He inserted the text of the new Virginia law following the article "États-Unis," insuring its immediate publication in 1786. By doing so, he was paying homage to Jefferson who had just been named ambassador of the United States to the Court of Versailles.

Madison did not forget Virginia's experience when, three years later, he proposed that Congress complete the federal Constitution by adding an amendment prohibiting the establishment of religion while at the same time guaranteeing religious freedom. This was at the time a response to critics of the Constitution who feared intrusion by the federal government in the religious realm. To bar the risk of a hypothetical religious tyranny, the First Amendment provided: "Congress shall make no law respecting an establishment of religion, or prohibiting the free exercise thereof."[47] But the amendment was silent on the role of the individual state legislatures. It was therefore legitimate to think that they would preserve the religious privileges acquired by the established Churches. But the growing influence of the Evangelical Baptist and Methodist churches, along with pressure from the Quaker movement and the Catholic Church, impelled most states to abolish those privileges. The Virginia model gradually spread to all of them. After 1833, there was no official church with exceptional privileges anywhere in the United States.

THE VIRGINIA BAPTISTS HAD WON a victory. But when Jefferson entered the White House in 1801, the question had still not been settled in Massachusetts and Connecticut.[48] The Baptists were in the vanguard of the battle against the privileges that had been acquired by the Congregationalist churches. It was therefore quite natural that Jefferson agreed to correspond with the members of the Baptist community of Danbury, Connecticut, to explain to them the meaning and scope of the First Amendment. The president's opinion had all the more weight because the Supreme Court had at the time not yet imposed itself as the final interpreter of the Constitution. Jefferson interpreted the First Amendment to mean that by prohibiting Congress from passing laws favorable to the establishment of a religion, the sovereign people had not hesitated to build "a *wall of separation* between church and State."[49] The message was clear: the Danbury Baptists were perfectly right to pursue their struggle against the Congregationalists in the name of true religious liberty. The secular model, first adopted by Virginia, then brought into the federal government through the First Amendment, was therefore valid for all.

The Secular Credo of Justice Hugo Black

The initial debates on the separation of church and state in Virginia and Connecticut may now appear outdated. And yet, they had a decisive impact on a major Supreme Court decision that fully established the principle of secularism. In the *Everson* decision of 1947, the court considered the relation between church and state in the context of the school. At issue was the validity of a New Jersey law authorizing the reimbursement of school transportation costs incurred by the parents of students of private schools, most of which were Catholic. Did the law favor one religion to the detriment of others, thereby violating the Establishment Clause of the First Amendment? Since the clause, theoretically, applied only to laws passed by the U.S. Congress, it was necessary to justify its application to the individual states, which the court did by invoking the complicated doctrine of "incorporation." The important point here is to understand how a distant past was called upon by a Supreme Court justice to explain a new situation that had arisen after the Second World War.

The opinion of the court, written by Justice Black, provides an excellent example of critical historiography, based on the best sources available at the time. Paraphrasing the old canonical text of the bill for establishing religious freedom in Virginia, Black declared that no government, state or federal, could aid a church or force an individual to profess any particular belief or disbelief. No tax could be levied to finance religious institutions or activities, including educational activities. Quoting an earlier Supreme Court decision, Black gave a central place to the specific content of Jefferson's letter to the Danbury Baptists, and concluded forcefully: "The First Amendment has erected a wall between church and state. *That wall must be kept high and impregnable.* We could not approve the slightest breach."[50]

Justice Black had two good reasons for his interest in the metaphor of the wall of separation. First was his Baptist background. Hugo Black was at the time the only Southern Baptist on the Court; it was therefore natural that he be interested in the religious thought of Roger Williams, the most famous

American Baptist, as well as that of Jefferson and Madison who had taken up the defense of the Baptist minority in Virginia, a minority that felt persecuted by a ubiquitous Anglican Church. The second reason was jurisprudential. Hugo Black, like any self-respecting judge in a country with a common law tradition, based his decision on the only Supreme Court precedent dealing with religious freedom, the *Reynolds* decision of 1879. This decision dealt with a crucial question for the future of the Utah Territory that had been settled by Mormons: Did the United States Congress have the right to pass laws concerning marriage and prohibiting polygamy? From the point of view of the representatives of the Church of Jesus Christ of the Latter-Day Saints, polygamy was not only a social obligation but also a sacred article of dogma. In these circumstances, could the Supreme Court conceive of an exemption for the particular case of the Mormons based on the free exercise clause of the First Amendment? Chief Justice Waite, who wrote the opinion for the Court, answered in the negative. "To permit this would be to make the professed doctrines of religious belief superior to the law of the land, and in effect to permit every citizen to become a law unto himself."[51] By ending, after ten years of resistance and civil disobedience, a practice that Justice Waite considered "odious," the Mormons made it possible for their state to join the Union. In 1894, Utah was admitted as a state, with the same political rights as any other.

It is now known that Justice Waite, like his distant successor Justice Black, had conducted thorough historiographical research on the circumstances in which the First Amendment was adopted. In the *Reynolds* decision, he granted an important place to the debates on religious freedom in Virginia and to the role played in them by its two champions, Jefferson and Madison. Nothing was left out: the most obscure writings by Jefferson and Madison were called upon to explain the intentions of the drafters of the amendment. Quoting Jefferson's letter to the Danbury Baptists, Justice Waite asserted that "it may be accepted almost as an authoritative declaration of the scope and effect of the amendment."[52] What was the source of this interest in a seventy-seven-year-old document written by a president who had participated neither in the Philadelphia Convention nor in the preparatory work for the Bill of Rights? The answer has to do with the vagaries of Washington life. Justice Waite's neighbor was the great historian George Bancroft, cited earlier in this book, who willingly helped him to understand the political climate of the time with the help of documentary sources. These sources included Jefferson's bill for religious freedom, Madison's petition against religious assessments, and, most probably, Jefferson's letter to the Danbury Baptists. Once the decision had been written, moreover, Justice Waite thanked his illustrious neighbor for his help and the transmission of historical "facts" that justified his decision.[53]

In this way, an incidental document, a simple letter to a small religious community in Connecticut, became the source of a jurisprudence whose meaning and scope are still under debate in the United States. It should be noted that Justice Black's position in *Everson* was in the end a nuanced one, because he upheld the New Jersey law authorizing reimbursement of travel costs for students in private schools.

In his dissent, Justice Jackson expressed surprise that the conclusion was "discordant" with the eloquent evocation of the Jeffersonian principle of secularism. The metaphor of the wall of separation, Jackson wrote, masked a weak conviction, comparable to that of "Julia who, according to Byron's reports, 'whispering 'I will ne'er consent,'—consented.'"[54] But Black and the court majority were able to answer the objection: The law on school transportation had universal scope; it applied to all students in every school, public as well as private. Because the law was neutral and had no effect on the content of teaching, it could not be construed as contrary to the establishment clause. Black pointed out that the amendment had not been conceived as a means of fighting against religion: It "requires the state to be neutral in its relations with groups of religious believers and nonbelievers; it does not require the state to be their adversary. State power is no more to be used so as to handicap religions, than it is to favor them."[55]

THERE HAVE BEEN COUNTLESS American criticisms of the metaphor of the wall of separation. They reflect the diversity of currents of thought, some of which are Catholic in origin, others close to radical evangelicalism, and still others connected to writers and jurists who advocate a "literalist" or an "originalist" reading of the Constitution. For some Catholic circles particularly devoted to the support of parochial education, the metaphor is dangerous, because, if improperly interpreted, it poses the danger of turning the wall into an "iron curtain." In their view, the survival of Catholicism and of religion in general requires a "free circulation" between the political and religious spheres.[56] A comparable point of view has recently been eloquently presented by a well known professor of law. For Stephen Carter, the very idea of a separation between church and state is no longer adapted to the needs of modern society, just as it was not adapted to the great abolitionist movement of the nineteenth century or the civil rights movement of the 1960s. The political emancipation of African-Americans was inseparable from the political mobilization of the churches. Today as in the past, "the wall has to have a few doors in it" if you want, as Carter does, to reintroduce the religious question into a public discourse that has been overly secularized.[57]

The fiercest criticism of Jefferson's metaphor comes from William Rehnquist, the former chief justice of the Supreme Court, whose approach is based both on a literal interpretation of the Constitution and an extensive consideration of the original intentions of the Founders. If, he writes, one considers only the literal language of the First Amendment, nothing in it refers directly to the notion of a separation between church and state. The prohibition of an established church is one thing; developing ties between religious and political spheres is quite another, which is not prohibited even though the jurisprudence on the question is still confused. Only a retrospective reading of Jefferson's letter to the Danbury Baptists could induce belief in a strict interpretation of the establishment clause. As for the analysis of the original intentions of the authors of the Bill of Rights, it reveals, according to Rehnquist, a real concern to not separate the religious and political spheres within the individual states of the Union. The drafters could not have been influenced by Jefferson, because he was then ambassador to France. Rehnquist concludes that the standard argument is a historical deception: "The 'wall of separation between church and State' is a metaphor based on bad history, a metaphor which has proved useless as a guide to judging. It should be frankly and explicitly abandoned."[58]

But Rehnquist was in fact a rather mediocre historian. First, because he seems to have been unaware that the debate on the separation of church and state is an old one that goes back to the era of the Puritans and their critics. Second, because he fails to mention the close ties between Madison and Jefferson in the political battle for religious freedom in Virginia. Madison, the principal drafter of the First Amendment, was merely transposing this old battle to the federal level. Virginia had opened the path of political innovation: there should be no established church in a federal America. Moreover, Jefferson maintained a regular correspondence with Madison to keep him informed of the progress of debates on the Rights of Man in the very first weeks of the French Revolution. The French, thanks notably to Jefferson and his agents, were discussing religious freedom in the United States at the very moment when the United States Congress was developing a Bill of Rights dealing with the same question.

Separatists Versus Antiseparatists

Without going into the details of a complex and contradictory jurisprudence, what is at stake in the debate on the separation of church and state can be summarized very simply. Two camps are in contention: partisans of a strict separation between church and state, influenced by an old Jeffersonian tradition, derived from the philosophy of the Enlightment; and opponents of a strict separation, often conservatives, strongly attached to the notion of an American Creed based on the preservation of "founding" Anglo-Protestant values. For ease of discussion, I will call the former "separatists" and the latter "antiseparatists" (often referred to as "separationists" and "accommodationists" by American legal scholars).

From the perspective of the separatists, the metaphor of the wall of separation is to be understood literally. It is a general principle that implies that public authorities, whether federal or local, cannot in any way support, aid, or favor one religion in favor of another. The wall must remain high and impregnable: that is the meaning of the Establishment Clause. The Supreme Court appeared, for a period of time, to be leaning toward this strict position in prohibiting all forms of organized prayer in public places, schools, and universities. The court, for example, barred the voluntary recitation of an ecumenical prayer in school, the reading of Bible verses, a moment of silence allowing for prayer or meditation, the opening of a graduation ceremony with a homily by a minister, priest, or rabbi, and so on.[59] All these practices were invalidated because they were considered contrary to the Establishment Clause. In the same vein, the court barred the public display of a Nativity scene on the stairway of a county courthouse[60] as well as the posting of the Ten Commandments in public school classrooms and in a courthouse in the Midwest.[61]

More recent decisions, however, have been more accommodating of religious interests, and seem to favor the antiseparatist camp, particularly with regard to a previously taboo subject: the public financing of parochial schools. Rather than demanding the direct financing of religious schools—which would violate the Establishment Clause—the advocates of state aid to private schools chose an indirect and individualized approach: allowing students' parents to use school vouchers as they wished, to supplement inadequate teaching in public schools with tutoring, or to cover the cost of private education, considered more effective. This reasoning was adopted by a recent Supreme Court decision holding that state aid is acceptable as long as it is indirect, applies to all school systems, public and private, and the final choice is left to private individuals—the students' parents. This amounts to a new formulation of the principle of neutrality. According to Chief Justice Rehnquist's opinion in *Zelman v. Simmons-Harris*, a voucher program is valid if it is "entirely neutral with respect to religion," if it provides "benefits directly to a wide spectrum of individuals, defined only by financial need and residence in a particular school district" without reference to religion, and if "it permits such individuals to exercise genuine choice among options public and private, secular and religious."[62]

The Supreme Court's jurisprudence is therefore in a certain sense contradictory. On the one hand, it excludes religion from the public arena by prohibiting prayer and some public displays of religiosity confined to a single religion. On the other hand, it authorizes indirect aid to parochial schools. Adding a further level of complexity to this apparent contradiction, a few decisions point to a different accommodating logic which favors ethno-religious diversity and allows certain religions to violate otherwise valid laws. In this case the principle of diversity—by which I mean the respect of certain minority religious practices—trumps the principle of neutrality. For example, the court has agreed that Amish parents could take their children out of school at the end of the eighth grade so they could go to work in the fields or become artisans in clear violation of existing laws on compulsory education.[63] In another case, the court authorized the members of an Afro-Cuban Santeria Church to conduct animal sacrifices that local authorities considered cruel and in violation of existing health codes.[64] The court determined that, in principle at least, all religions had equal value and that it would be arbitrary and unjust to prohibit the sacrifices conducted by the worshipers of the Church of the Lukumi Babalu Aye, while other religious communities, such as the Jewish community, were legally entitled to carry out kosher butchering.[65] And when the court refused to tolerate "dangerous" traditions requiring, for example, that the members of a Native American religion smoke peyote for certain meditation rituals,[66] Congress intervened to restore the custom in the name of the principle of the equal dignity of religions.[67]

Of course, not everything is permitted—sexual mutilation or collective suicide for religious reasons remain illegal—and it will be recalled that the Supreme Court did not invalidate a federal law criminalizing polygamy among the Mormons. But the result is nonetheless clear: present-day American secularism is based on the overarching principle of state neutrality. In the court's view, every attempt must be made to prevent the return of intolerance and the wars of religion that have been so frequent in the history of Europe and the United States. It is therefore necessary to avoid taking measures favoring any particular religion or imposing a preference for religion over atheism or no religion at all. Any contrary attitude would be deeply unjust:

> By showing a purpose to favor religion, the government "sends the ... message to ... nonadherents 'that they are outsiders, not full members of the political community, and an accompanying message to adherents that they are insiders, favored members. ...' "[68]

Looked at historically, and considering the Supreme Court's jurisprudence as a whole, the principle has been firmly established that minority religions have been placed on the same footing as mainstream religions. The justices no longer consider Christianity as the central element in some hypothetical American Creed; it is simply one religion among others, gradually stripped of the "privileges, advantages, and social customs that it had enjoyed because of its status as the majority religion."[69]

The best evidence of this equivalence is provided by the evolution of an old patriotic ritual, the oath to defend the Constitution required of elected officials and high federal office holders. Traditionally, the president and new members of Congress have sworn the oath with their hand on the Bible. Nothing in the Constitution requires the presence of the Scriptures, but this old practice, a survival of the British parliamentary tradition, persists today.

In 2006, for the first time in the history of the United States, a Sunni Muslim of African-American origin was elected as a Democratic representative to Congress from a district in Minneapolis. How would this new congressman, Keith Ellison, take his oath when he was sworn in on January 4, 2007? Would he merely take a civil oath by raising his right hand? Would he use a Bible or a Qur'an?

He chose to swear on the Qur'an, despite a virulent press campaign denouncing Muslim intolerance around the world and proclaiming the incompatibility of Islam with republican institutions. Wishing to attenuate the effects of an unprecedented event, Ellison was intelligent enough to appeal to the history of the founding of the American Republic to foil his critics. To take his oath, he borrowed a copy of the Qur'an that had belonged to Thomas Jefferson. With this gesture, he reconciled the two contrary traditions I have been analyzing. By insisting on using this version of the Qur'an, he implicitly honored a separatist tradition inaugurated by Jefferson. But did he know that Jefferson's Qur'an had been translated in 1734 by the English Orientalist

George Sale—himself an active member of the Society for Promoting Christian Knowledge?[70] Jefferson probably had no more respect for the Qur'an than he did for the Bible, as I have noted earlier. But for Keith Ellison the reference was respectable enough: Jefferson was, after all, along with Washington and Madison one of the Founding Fathers of the republic.

IN THE UNITED STATES, it is not easy to maintain a balance between contradictory positions. Political divergences between separatists and anti-separatists remain deep, and a foreign observer is not always in a position to distinguish between what is permitted and what is forbidden in matters of religion. The wall of separation is sometimes unbreachable, sometimes full of doors, depending on the circumstances and the requirements of a multi-ethnic and multireligious culture. Historical narratives of identity formation are particularly unstable and contradictory. Some leading historians, legal scholars, and political scientists are convinced that the American national identity has primarily been shaped by an Enlightenment narrative, based on a rational philosophy which excludes religion from the public sphere and which would purge the public arena of the most sacred icons of the Christian religion. Other leading historians, influenced by the romantic rediscovery of America's great ancestors—the Puritans—are convinced that the nation is at its core religious and that government should support the free exercise of religion as far as possible, to the point of aiding denominational schools or faith-based organizations with public funding. These rival traditions are difficult to reconcile and the evolution of the Supreme Court jurisprudence remains ambiguous.[71] It is possible that in the future a new type of secularism will evolve: *a faith-friendly secularism.*

⌣

Obama's Faith-Friendly Secularism

WHAT IS THE PLACE BARACK OBAMA has accorded to religion in the public sphere? Initially it was considerable. From his speech at the Democratic Convention in 2004, when he was a junior senator from Illinois, to his election as president in 2008, he constantly emphasized the importance of religion in his personal life and in the political life of the country. With the new priorities of 2009 and 2010—the economic crisis and the attempt at comprehensive reform of the healthcare system—the president's religious concerns faded into the background, and indeed were not even mentioned in his State of the Union address of January 2010.

Barack Obama first made his religious philosophy explicit in his address at the "Call to Renewal" Conference organized in June 2006 by Jim Wallis, the founder and editor-in-chief of *Sojourners* magazine. Speaking to an audience of about one hundred representatives of Protestant churches, Obama pointed out that

> Americans are a religious people. Ninety percent of us believe in God, 70 percent affiliate themselves with an organized religion, 38 percent call

themselves committed Christians, and substantially more people believe in angels than do those who believe in evolution.... Each day ... thousands of Americans are ... coming to the realization that something is missing. They are deciding that their work, their possessions, their diversions, their sheer busyness, is not enough. They want a sense of purpose, a narrative arc to their lives.[1]

This is why faith is important "to feed the hungry and clothe the naked and challenge powers and principalities," as the leaders of African-American churches have consistently asserted. According to Obama, "secularists" are therefore wrong when they "ask believers to leave their religion at the door before entering the public square. Frederick Douglass, Abraham Lincoln, William Jennings Bryan, Dorothy Day, Martin Luther King—indeed the majority of great reformers in American history—were not only motivated by faith but repeatedly used religious language to argue for their cause."[2] Always in search of a compromise that would satisfy the most and least religious of Americans, Obama adopted a middle way, a delicate balancing act: "We progressives ... might recognize the overlapping values that both religious and secular people share when it comes to the moral and material direction of our country."[3] The very personal faith adopted by Obama does not exclude political considerations, recalling—at another time and in different circumstances—the religiously infused political rhetoric of Abraham Lincoln.[4] By his own admission, Obama did not have the sudden conversion experience typical of evangelicals. His faith is more reasoned, a calculated decision to share the religious experience of the residents of the South Side of Chicago where he was working as a community organizer. His conversion, he says, "came about as a choice, and not an epiphany," and while there is no reason to doubt the sincerity of his beliefs, his faith is inseparable from the use of religious rhetoric as a technique of political persuasion: "Some of the problem here is rhetorical—if we scrub language of all religious content, we forfeit the imagery and terminology through which millions of Americans understand both their personal morality and social justice. Imagine Lincoln's Second Inaugural Address without reference to 'the judgment of the Lord,' or King's 'I Have a Dream' speech without reference to 'all God's children.'"[5]

The reference to Lincoln is particularly revealing. Lincoln was personally not very religious and doubted the divinity of Christ, but like Tom Paine earlier, he knew the scriptures intimately and had an unmatched ability to

marshal powerful religious images to persuade t
the abolitionist cause.[6]

And yet Obama's political language is never p
Unlike George W. Bush, Obama is fully aware of th
tangling religion and politics in the United States.
limits a statesman must impose on the sphere of spir
a scrupulous respect for the jurisprudence of the Su[
serted in his Inaugural Address that the communit
and extends to all, including nonbelievers: "We are a   _. Christians and
Muslims, Jews and Hindus, and non-believers."[7]

Obama was expressing his adherence to a conception of the American
nation as not strictly speaking Christian, but pluralist, open to all religions,
whether or not monotheistic. Above all, it is inclusive enough to accept without restriction those who, because of atheism or indifference, reject any religion. Barack Obama is thus the first president in the history of the United
States to acknowledge in an Inaugural Address that there are Americans who
do not believe in God. In doing so, he "puts nonbelievers on the same footing
as religious Americans."[8] He also paid a remarkable homage to the religious
indifference of his parents: to his father who was born and brought up as a
Muslim but became an atheist as an adult; and to his mother, "who was skeptical of organized religion, even though she was the most spiritual person [he
had] ever known."[9]

There are many references to the political past of the United Sates in
Obama's speeches, but it is a selective past that gives a preeminent place to
the Founding Fathers and to Lincoln, their great successor. He neglects the
role of the Puritans and their political and religious utopia, the City on the
Hill that Ronald Reagan, for one, was so fond of recalling. Between the two rival narratives of American identity discussed in this book, Obama has clearly
chosen the one that is rooted in the age and the philosophy of the Enlightenment. Despite their defects (most of them were slave-owners), the Founders devised the great principles of American democracy: equality, liberty, the
sovereignty of the people, the possibility of earthly happiness open to all. And
it was the Founders who presented the first fully articulated argument for a
system of separation between church and state.

But Obama's political speeches are also full of references to religion, to the
charitable work of faith-based organizations, and to his very personal quest
for religious faith. What is the explanation for this apparent contradiction

professor of constitutional law who acknowledges the impor-
separation of church and state, and the political candidate who so
discusses his religious experience in public?[10]

The answer lies in the increasing importance given to religious issues in
presidential election campaigns since the early 1980s. I have already explained
in chapter 6 the political, geographical, and cultural reasons for the emergence of the religious right and its influence in the Republican Party. In 2008,
both Republican and Democratic candidates shared a retrospective illusion
based on an erroneous reading of the results of the 2004 presidential election. The accepted wisdom on both sides was that to win in 2008, a candidate
had to avoid Kerry's mistakes. Kerry had lost in this view because he hadn't
paid enough attention to the religious concerns of the average American: he
had neglected the "values voters." Too discreet about his own faith, Kerry had
abandoned the field to George W. Bush, who managed to win over a majority
of Catholic voters, traditionally inclined to vote Democratic. It is true that
Bush had taken risks a Catholic candidate never could have taken. Bush was
the first American presidential candidate to visit the Pope, in the Vatican,
while the primaries were in progress. It was an unprecedented gesture and
the rewards were appreciable: 52 percent of Catholics voted for Bush. Even
more remarkable, 78 percent of white evangelicals voted for the sitting president. Bush was thus the preferred candidate of evangelicals, of Catholics, and
especially of voters who attended religious services frequently (once a week
or more), regardless of religion. The Republicans were the party of the pious,
the Democrats the party of the tepid, the indifferent, and the agnostics.

Was this religious gap reversible? Could Democrats hope to recapture
some religious voters? They thought they could, provided they gave a prominent place to religious questions in the coming elections. In any event, this is
what party leaders declared in the wake of the 2004 defeat.[11]

But Obama had two other reasons for giving religion a prominent place.
First, he had to counter the persistent rumor that he was a Muslim, which
explains the frequency with which he referred to his quest for "God's spirit,"[12]
and to the religious experience that led to his baptism in the Trinity United
Church of Christ in Chicago. Second, he had to react to the excessive and
apparently antipatriotic remarks made by the pastor of his adopted church,
Reverend Jeremiah Wright. Among other things, Wright had exclaimed "God
damn America" in a sermon, clips of which were endlessly recycled on You-
Tube and many television networks by Obama's political opponents. In his
celebrated speech in Philadelphia on March 18, 2008, Barack Obama saved his

presidential campaign by presenting the best possible response to his critics. Reverend Wright's anger, he explained, was understandable for an African-American who "came of age in the late fifties and early sixties, a time when segregation was still the law of the land and opportunity was systematically constricted." But it was inexcusable at a time when the United States could finally demonstrate that it was possible to overcome the racial antagonisms and resentments of the past: "The profound mistake of Reverend Wright's sermons is not that he spoke about racism in our society. It's that he spoke as if our society was static ... still irrevocably bound to a tragic past."[13] Obama turned the page, while soberly and persuasively demonstrating that he was indeed a "post-racial candidate," whose only ambition was to represent all Americans, whoever they might be, "white and black, Latino and Asian, rich and poor, young and old."[14] This diverse and inclusive citizenship, explained Obama, fulfilled the promise of a "More Perfect Union," first evoked by the Framers in 1787.

Convinced that "values voters" were crucial if his candidacy was to succeed in 2008, Obama and his political advisers devoted significant resources to communicating with the most religious voters of the swing states, particularly white and Latino evangelical Christians. To accomplish this, Obama established a sophisticated outreach program aimed at targeting blocs of voters who had until then been reluctant to vote for the Democratic Party. He demonstrated thoroughgoing ethnic and religious ecumenicalism in appointing the leaders of his faith outreach campaign. It was headed by a young African-American Pentecostal pastor, Joshua DuBois, seconded by two Latino coordinators, the Catholic Miguel Diaz of St. John's University, and the Protestant Wilfredo De Jesús, senior pastor of New Life Covenant, an Assemblies of God Church in Chicago. His outreach campaign included frequent private meetings with religious figures of every denomination and every political stripe— among them the progressive public theologian Jim Wallis; the evangelical pastor Franklin Graham (son of Billy Graham); David Neff, editor-in-chief of *Christianity Today*; Rich Cizik, vice president for governmental affairs of the National Association of Evangelicals;[15] and Rick Warren, the evangelical pastor of one of the largest megachurches in southern California, Saddleback Church.[16] Obama also frequently visited poor neighborhoods in cities where religious organizations were particularly active and spoke before many religious groups. A good example of this combination of political and religious activity was the July 2008 visit organized by Joshua DuBois to Zanesville, in the economically distressed Appalachian region of Ohio. Obama met with the local organizers of an antipoverty program led by the Eastside Community Ministry. He seized the occasion to propose a renewal of the faith-based initiatives initially launched by George W. Bush, with the future creation of a Council of Faith-Based and Neighborhood Partnerships. And he specified that, if elected, he would devote $500 million annually to philanthropic activities organized by local religious communities. To justify this unexpected proposal, in a region where the majority of born-again Christians favored McCain, Obama stated: "I believe that change comes not from the top down but from the bottom up, and few are closer to the people than our churches, synagogues, temples, and mosques."[17]

Even if it was not decisive in producing his electoral victory in 2008, Obama's religious outreach program did have results. According to the NEP 2008 national exit polls, Obama's largest margins over McCain were among Catholic voters (54 percent for Obama, 45 percent for McCain). But McCain did better than Obama among Protestant voters (53 percent, compared to 46 percent for Obama). Comparing 2004 and 2008 exit polls, Obama did much better than Kerry among Catholics (7 percentage points higher), as well as among Protestants (5 percentage points). Obama's gains among white evangelical and born-again Christians were also significant: 26 percent of the white evangelical constituency voted for Obama in 2008, compared to 21 percent for Kerry in 2004. Conversely, McCain did not perform as well as Bush among these voters, although he did preserve Republican dominance. He won 73 percent of the white born-again vote, compared to 79 percent for Bush in 2004.[18] But these small electoral shifts do not alone explain the Democrats' victory in 2008. Other key factors include the high turnout of African-American and Latino voters (respectively 95 and 66 percent of whom voted for Obama); an exceptional mobilization of young voters (66 percent of eighteen- to twenty-nine-year-olds voted for Obama); and a plurality of white middle-class suburban voters in battleground states (50 percent for Obama). All these categories of voters were more concerned about the economy, the war in Iraq, and healthcare, education, and immigration reforms than traditional moral values.

LESS IDEOLOGICAL THAN the liberal base of the Democratic Party had anticipated, Barack Obama is a pragmatic politician who frequently looks for compromise solutions to the problems he confronts to satisfy both the left and the right of his party and, with less success, a majority of Democrats and

Republicans in Congress. This "middle way" politics is particularly visible in the economic and healthcare reform proposals Obama has set forth. It is also present in foreign policy (on the one hand, the demand that Guantánamo be closed, on the other, an increased military presence in Afghanistan). Even more clearly, it characterizes Obama's approach to religion. The search for compromise and the declared ideal of a faith-friendly secularism have met opposition from believers and nonbelievers alike.

In his "Call to Renewal" Address in June 2006, Obama made a clear distinction between two opposed camps, "secularists" and "believers." He admonished the former because they tend to "dismiss religion in the public square as inherently irrational or intolerant," and the latter because they believe they alone are able to define the great moral values of the nation. In reality, Obama explained, it is time to identify the common values that are essential to the nation's well-being, values on which "religious and secular people" can agree.[19] This search for common goals, given concrete form in the proposed development of "partnerships between the religious and secular worlds,"[20] is, of course, difficult to implement, and the first measures taken by the Obama administration have not met with unanimity.

To satisfy his party's secularists, shortly after his election, Obama reversed two decisions made by his predecessor in the White House. On March 6, 2009, he signed an executive order ending funding restrictions on embryonic stem cell research, and he removed the prohibition on federal financing of international family planning groups providing information on contraception and abortion. His pro-choice positions were in step with those of his party.

To satisfy the believers, and especially the most conservative among them, Obama declared his opposition to same-sex marriage, going so far as to declare in a public forum, organized by Rick Warren in Saddleback Church, in answer to a question on his definition of marriage: "It's a union between a man and a woman. . . . For me as a Christian, it is a sacred union. You know, God's in the mix."[21] But to strike a happy medium and not completely alienate the vote of California liberal Democrats, Obama declared his opposition to Proposition 8, the ballot measure that sought to amend the California Constitution to prohibit same-sex marriage. This measure, according to Obama, was too "divisive and discriminatory."[22] Then, in 2010, he announced the abolition of the "Don't Ask, Don't Tell" policy prohibiting openly gay men and lesbians from serving in the military.

In foreign policy, Obama's speech in Cairo satisfied both the most and the least religious of his compatriots. His explicit reference to Article II of the

Treaty of Tripoli of 1796 was particularly clever. The article declares that the
United States had not a religious but a purely political foundation, which by
implication bars any crusading spirit: "The United States has in itself no character of enmity against the laws, religion or tranquility of Muslims."[23] Progressive liberals and secularists could only applaud Obama's refusal to think
in terms of a "clash of civilizations" opposing Christian and Islamic nations.
But to satisfy the more religious among his listeners, Obama was lavish in
positive references to Islam, the "Holy Qur'an," and its Prophet, not forgetting
the other "children of Abraham"—Jews, Copts, Maronites, and other Christians in the Middle East. Everyone had a place in a world of tolerance where
"freedom of religion is central to the ability of peoples to live together."[24]
Islam was now placed on an equal footing with Judaism and Christianity, and
the image of the United States was distinctly improved, as suggested by this
spontaneous comment by the Syrian political scientist Marwan Kabalan: "It
was the most tolerant speech I have ever heard by an American President
concerning Islam and Muslims."[25] For secularists, this peaceful view of Islam
and religion in general was excessive. It minimized the existence of religious
conflicts, although they are real and particularly violent in the Middle East,
including within Islam. It was also too reductionist in terms of identity, as
though Islam were "the sole reference point for the populations of the region," whereas other elements—economic, ethnic, social, and political—are
just as fundamental.[26]

The key element of the ideal of a faith-friendly secularism, and the one
that is probably most questionable, is Obama's decision to adopt the faith-
based initiatives of George W. Bush by establishing, as promised, a White
House Office of Faith-Based and Neighborhood Partnerships and appointing
at its head a new "faith czar," the former director of his religious outreach
campaign, Reverend Joshua DuBois. The social effects of these initiatives are
theoretically perfectly neutral. No particular religion is favored and public
funds are distributed equally between secular and faith-based organizations.
But in reality, if one considers the practices developed by the Bush administration, faith-based organizations, most of them evangelical, are more numerous than their secular counterparts in benefiting from federal largesse, and
the recipients of social service programs are often encouraged to participate
in "social" activities that have more to do with religious proselytizing than
with simple humanitarian action.[27]

As recently observed by prominent legal scholars, faith-based initiatives
or voucher programs do blur the wall of separation between church and state

and too often discriminate against minority religions or purely secular activities.[28] But there is no reason why religion should not have a place in the
public realm, particularly if it respects the diversity of religious faiths and
denominations. What is the harm in celebrating Christmas in a country which
is still predominantly Christian or in displaying a crèche with other religious
symbols like a Star of David or nonreligious elements like a reindeer or a
snow-covered pine tree? But non-Christian minority religions should also be
acknowledged and provided with their own public space. This could be done
with special holidays, recognizing the symbolic importance of the Muslim
Eid, for instance. The key point is religious inclusiveness.[29] An atheist could
feel uncomfortable when asked to recite the Pledge of Allegiance, but should
everyone else be obliged to omit the words "one nation under God" to satisfy a minority viewpoint? As Obama himself admitted, "Not every mention
of God in public is a breach of the wall of separation— context matters. It
is doubtful that children reciting the Pledge of Allegiance feel oppressed or
brainwashed as a consequence of muttering the phrase 'Under God'; I certainly didn't."[30] Public manifestations of the religious spirit do not violate the
Establishment Clause if they celebrate a settled American tradition or express
strong communitarian values that can only strengthen the search for national
unity and cohesion. But once the question of using public funds for religious
or parareligious activities arises, the answer of a "faith-friendly" government
should be negative, because the risk of not being able to maintain neutrality
is too great. Perhaps the best way to envision the wall of separation between
church and state today is to see it as a porous partition that allows old customs
or symbolic manifestations of religiosity to seep through, but—in the finest
tradition of Jefferson and Madison—acts as an unbreachable wall to prevent
the improper or biased use of public funds for religious purposes.

Introduction

1. John Murrin, "Religion and Politics in America from the First Settlements to the Civil War," in *Religion and American Politics*, ed. Mark Noll (New York: Oxford University Press, 1990).

1. America, the Land of Religious Utopias

1. Voltaire, "First Letter: On the Quakers," in *Philosophical Letters*, trans. Prudence L. Steiner (Indianapolis: Hackett, 2007), 1–2. Among the prominent Quakers met by Voltaire was Edward Higginson of Wandsworth (England), the author of an *Account of a Conversation with Voltaire*. See Peter Gay, *Voltaire's Politics: The Poet as Realist* (New York: Vintage Books, 1965), 60–61.

2. Voltaire, "First Letter: On the Quakers," 1.

3. Ibid., 3.

4. Voltaire, "Second and Third Letters: On the Quakers," in *Philosophical Letters*, 5 and 7.

5. Ibid., 13.

6. In book 4 of *L'Esprit des Lois*, Montesquieu ventured on a parallel between the two great men: whether man of peace or man of war, the two legislators shared the same goal, to create people free of any prejudice who were masters of their passions. *De l'Esprit des Lois* (1748), book 4, chap. 6, in *Œuvres complètes* (Paris: Gallimard, Bibliothèque de la Pléiade, 1958), vol. 2:268.

7. Article "Quaker" in Diderot and d'Alembert, ed., *Encyclopédie ou Dictionnaire raisonné des sciences, des arts et des métiers* (1765), vol. 13:648. (Electronic edition: http://portail.atilf.fr/encyclopedie). Jaucourt's article was strongly influenced by the works of Montesquieu and Voltaire.

8. Guillaume-Thomas Raynal, *Histoire philosophique et politique des établissements et du commerce des Européens dans les deux Indes* (Geneva, 1781), vol. 9:18, 9.

9. Raynal, *A History of the Two Indies: A Translated Selection of Writings from Raynal's Histoire philosophique*, trans. Peter Jimack (Burlington, VT: Ashgate, 2006), 252.

10. Raynal, *Histoire philosophique*, 39.

11. Raynal, *A History of the Two Indies*, 252.

12. J. Hector St. John de Crèvecœur, *Letters from an American Farmer* [1782] and *Sketches of Eighteenth-Century America* (New York: Penguin, 1981), 198.

13. "Description abrégée de la secte des Quakers ou Amis" in Crèvecœur, *Lettres d'un cultivateur américain*, (1785; Geneva: Slatkine Reprints, 1979), vol. 1:175–76. This description is not included in the English edition of the *Letters*.

14. Étienne Clavière and Jacques-Pierre Brissot de Warville, *De la France et des États-Unis ou De l'importance de la révolution de l'Amérique pour le bonheur de la France* (London, 1787; facsimile edition, Paris: Éditions du CTHS, 1996), 324–25.

15. I take the expression from Marcel Gauchet, *La Révolution des droits de l'homme* (Paris: Gallimard, 1989), 212, n. 1.

16. Rabaut Saint-Étienne, *Chronique de Paris*, January 27, 1973, quoted in Gauchet, *La Révolution*, 212.

17. C.-F. Volney, Préface, *Tableau du climat et du sol des États-Unis d'Amérique* (Paris: Courcier, 1803), v, xii.

18. Ibid., 378, n. 1. As Edith Philips has shown, the infatuation with Quakerism was widespread until 1794. See Edith Philips, *The Good Quaker in French Legend* (Philadelphia: University of Pennsylvania Press, 1932), 148–61.

19. Other writers, including La Rochefoucauld-Liancourt, speak of Dunkers. They were in fact Mennonites.

20. "Pennsylvanie," in Démeunier, ed., *Encyclopédie méthodique: Économie politique et diplomatique* (Paris: Panckoucke, 1784–88), vol. 3:566–68.

21. [François Alexandre Frédéric, duc de] la Rochefoucauld-Liancourt, *Voyage dans les États-Unis d'Amérique, fait en 1795, 1796 et 1797* (Paris: Du Pont, an VII [1799]), vol. 1:196, 202. Shamelessly, La Rochefoucauld claims to have irrefutable evidence of her heterosexuality (202–3).

22. See Catherine A. Brekus, *Strangers and Pilgrims: Female Preaching in America, 1740–1845* (Chapel Hill: University of North Carolina Press, 1998), 80–97.

23. Ferdinand-Marie Bayard, *Voyage dans l'intérieur des États-Unis, à Bath, Winchester, dans la vallée de Shenadoha, etc., pendant l'été de 1791* (Paris: Cocheris, an V [1797]), xii.

24. Ibid., 222.

25. Ibid., 270–71.

26. Ibid., 273, emphasis added.

27. Ibid., 266–67.

28. Chateaubriand, *Essai historique, politique et moral sur les révolutions anciennes et modernes, considérées dans leurs rapports avec la Révolution française de nos jours* [1797], in *Essai sur les révolutions; Génie du Christianisme*, ed. Maurice Regard (Paris: Gallimard, Bibliothèque de la Pléiade, 1978), 147.

29. Ibid., 148.

30. In a brilliant analysis of Chateaubriand's travel narratives, François Hartog shows the complexity and subtlety of a three-way interplay contrasting the Ancients to the Moderns and to the Savages, which is also, most frequently, an interplay of "two plus one: the Moderns confronting the Ancients/Savages." Hartog, *Régimes d'historicité: Présentisme et expérience du temps* (Paris: Seuil, 2003), 79.

31. Chateaubriand, *Voyage en Amérique* [1827], in *Œuvres romanesques et voyages*, ed. Maurice Regard (Paris: Gallimard, Bibliothèque de la Pléiade, 1969), vol. 1:677.

32. Ibid., 676.

33. Chateaubriand, *Mémoires d'outre-tombe* [1849] (Paris: Le Livre de Poche, 1973), vol. 1:268.

34. Chateaubriand, *Voyage en Amérique*, 872–73. This freedom, Chateaubriand explains, is an "inexhaustible source" from which "each people is invited to draw."

35. Ibid., 677.

36. Corneille de Pauw, *Recherches philosophiques sur les Américains, ou Mémoires intéressants pour servir à l'histoire de l'espèce humaine* [1772] (Paris: Jean-François Bastien, an III [1794]), vol. 1:161.

37. Volney, *Tableau du climat*, 447, 450, and 454.

38. Chateaubriand, *Voyage en Amérique*, 825.

39. Ibid., 441.

40. Ibid., 830.

41. Volney, *Tableau du climat*, 447–48.

42. Ibid., 447.

43. See Hartog, *Régimes d'historicité*, 116–19.

44. Voltaire, "Avis au public sur les parricides imputés aux Calas et aux Sirven" in *Mélanges*, ed. Jacques Van Den Heuvel (Paris: Gallimard, Bibliothèque de la Pléiade, 1961), 827.

45. Article "Puritains" in Diderot and d'Alembert, eds., *Encyclopédie*, vol. 13:581.

46. Article "Fanatisme" in *Encyclopédie*, vol. 6:393.

47. Voltaire, *Examen important de Milord Bolingbroke ou le Tombeau du fanatisme* [1736], in *Mélanges*, 1045.

48. Article "Puritains" in *Encyclopédie*, vol. 13:581.

49. Ibid.

50. Raynal, *Histoire philosophique*, vol. 8:332–33.

51. Ibid., 347.

52. Ibid., 342.

53. Ibid., 343–44.

54. Ibid., 345.

55. La Rochefoucauld-Liancourt, *Voyage dans les États-Unis d'Amérique*, vol. 3:226.

56. The author acknowledges in this last case, however, that the punishment was not applied, either because the crime was no longer committed, "or, which is more probable, because the barbarism of the laws protects the guilty from their enforcement." Ibid., 226.

57. Ibid., 230.

58. Raynal, *Histoire philosophique*, vol. 8:348.

59. Ibid., 345.

60. Chateaubriand, *Essai sur les révolutions*, 147–48. In this passage, Chateaubriand proposes to "cast a backward glance" to consider the origin of the "American empire."

61. Voltaire, *Treatise on Tolerance*, trans. Brian Masters (Cambridge: Cambridge University Press, 2000), 22.

62. Voltaire, *Questions sur l'Encyclopédie* (1772), quoted by Pierre Manent, *Les Libéraux* (1986; Paris: Gallimard, 2001), 111.

63. J. Hector St. John de Crèvecœur, *Letters from an American Farmer* (New York: Penguin, 1981), 74.

64. Voltaire, *Treatise on Tolerance*, 22. The reference is to *The Fundamental Constitutions of Carolina* (1669), which Locke, at the request of his patron Lord Ashley, the future Earl of Shaftesbury, helped to draft.

65. Voltaire, "Sixth Letter: On the Presbyterians," *Philosophical Letters*, 20.

66. See Ralph Ketcham, "James Madison and Religion: A New Hypothesis," *Journal of the Presbyterian Historical Society*, no. 2 (1960).

67. James Madison, Alexander Hamilton, John Jay, *The Federalist Papers* [1787], ed. Isaac Kramnick (New York: Viking Penguin, 1987), 321.

68. See Ibid., 10 and 51.

69. Thomas Paine, *The Age of Reason*, in *Collected Writings* (New York: The Library of America, 1994), 554–55.

70. Ibid., 548, 568.

71. Ibid., 555, unnumbered note.

2. The Rehabilitation of the Puritans

1. J. G. A. Pocock, *Barbarism and Religion*, vol. 2, *Narratives of Civil Government* (Cambridge: Cambridge University Press, 2001), 268–88. Robertson's work, *A View of the Progress of Society in Europe from the Subversion of the Roman Empire to the Beginning of the Sixteenth Century* corresponds generally to the first volume of *The History of the Reign of the Emperor Charles the Fifth*.

2. William Robertson, *The History of America* (1777; Paris: Baudry, 1828).

3. Ibid., 468, 479.

4. Ibid., 480.

5. Ibid., 503.

6. "Religion had gradually excited among the great body of the [Pilgrims] a spirit that fitted them remarkably for encountering the dangers, and surmounting the obstacles. . . ." Ibid.

7. Ibid.

8. Disciples of Robert Browne (1550?–1633), founder of the Congregationalist movement who, after studies at Cambridge and a period as an Anglican priest, denounced all forms of episcopal authority and advocated the establishment of small autonomous Christian communities.

9. Robertson, *The History of America*, 507.

10. Ibid., 509.

11. The Charter of the Massachusetts Bay Company defined the political rights of the new colonists, their trade relations with the mother country, and the prerequisites for their ownership of property. It did not give them the power to establish an autonomous government.

12. Robertson, *The History of America*, 514.

13. Ibid.

14. Ibid., "Author's Preface," [ca. 1777], i.

15. Had Tocqueville read Robertson? Probably, because the first part of *The History of America* (books 1 to 8) had been available in French since 1778 and the posthumous books since 1818. See John Renwick, "The Reception of William Robertson's Historical Writings in Eighteenth-Century France," in *William Robertson and the Expansion of Empire*, ed. Stewart J. Brown (Cambridge: Cambridge University Press, 1997), 145–63.

16. Alexis de Tocqueville, *Democracy in America*, trans. Arthur Goldhammer (New York: Library of America, 2004), 31. Joseph de Maistre refrained from making that kind of extrapolation: "America is often cited. I know of nothing so provoking as the praises bestowed on this babe-in-arms. Let it grow." *Considerations on France*, trans. Richard A. Lebrun (Cambridge: Cambridge University Press, 1994), 31.

17. The title of the second chapter of *Democracy in America* (vol. 1, part 1) is "On the point of departure and its importance for the future of the Anglo-Americans."

18. Tocqueville, *Democracy in America*, 35–37.

19. Ibid. 37.

20. Namely, Robert Beverley, *History of Virginia from the Earliest Period* (1722); George Chalmers, *Political Annals of the Present United Colonies from Their Settlement to the Peace of 1763* (1780); Thomas Hutchinson, *The History of the Colony and Province of Massachusetts-Bay* (1765); Thomas Jefferson, *Notes on the State of Virginia* (1785); Cotton Mather, *Magnalia Christi Americana: or, The Ecclesiastical History of New England* (1702); Daniel Neal, *History of the Puritans* (1732–1738); Captain John Smith, *The General History of Virginia, New England, and the Summer Isles Together with the True Travels, Adventures, and Observations* (1627).

21. Tocqueville, *Democracy in America*, 45, 48. The identification of the spirit of liberty with Protestantism was one of the commonplaces of the English and Scottish Enlightenment, as Murray Pittock has shown in reference to Hume and Robertson in "Historiography," in *The Cambridge Companion to the Scottish Enlightenment*, ed. Alexander Broadie (Cambridge: Cambridge University Press, 2003), 264–73.

22. Tocqueville, *Democracy in America*, 42–44.

23. John Murrin, "Religion and Politics in America from the First Settlements to the Civil War," in *Religion and American Politics*, ed. Mark Noll and Luke Harlow (New York: Oxford University Press, 1990), 23–43.

24. Mayflower Compact as reproduced in George Bancroft, *History of the United States* (1834; London: Routledge, 1864), vol. 1:233–34 (emphasis added).

25. The version of the Mayflower Compact presented by Tocqueville is truncated. It omits any reference to the monarchy and to the "loyal subjects" of King

James, thereby giving the compact a republican slant for the purposes of his argument.

26. Edmund S. Morgan, *Visible Saints: The History of a Puritan Idea* (Ithaca, NY: Cornell University Press, 1963), 33–63.

27. Ibid., 37–38.

28. Ibid., 35, quoting Williston Walker, *The Creeds and Platforms of Congregationalism* (New York: Scribner's, 1893), 40, 51.

29. The subtlest thinker among the Separatists, Henry Ainsworth, replied to skeptics: "Faith is in the hart. . . . The hart no man knoweth but God alone." *Counterpoyson*, quoted in Morgan, *Visible Saints*, 57–58.

30. I take the expression from Denis Crouzet, speaking of Calvin's disciples. *Jean Calvin* (Paris: Fayard, 2000), 198.

31. Morgan, *Visible Saints*, 31, 47, 65–70, 92–112; Perry Miller, "The Covenant of Grace," in *The New England Mind* (1939; Cambridge, MA: Harvard University Press, 1982), vol. 2:365–97.

32. Tocqueville, *Democracy in America*, 48. John Winthrop, the leader of the English Puritans who sailed on the *Arabella* in 1630 and author of a famous journal, was, with a few interruptions, governor of the Massachusetts Bay Company from 1630 to 1649.

33. Ibid., 46.

34. Ibid., 42, 45.

35. Ibid., 40.

36. See Lauric Henneton, introduction to William Bradford, *Histoire de la colonie de Plymouth: Chroniques du Nouveau Monde (1620–1647)* (Geneva: Labor et Fides, 2004), 30–36; Nathaniel Philbrick, *Mayflower: A Story of Courage, Community, and War* (New York: Viking, 2006), 35–47; Joke Kadux and Eduard van de Bilt, *Newcomers in an Old City: The American Pilgrims in Leiden 1609–1620* (1998; Leiden: Burgersdikj & Niermans, 2007), 44, 56–68.

37. Unlike their predecessors the Pilgrims, the Puritans around Winthrop were not Separatists. Their aim was to preserve the Church of England while "purifying" it of its vices and corruption.

38. A freeman in seventeenth-century England was the shareholder or co-owner of a commercial company with the right to vote. In the North American colonies, the freemen of a colonization company, each of which had a charter, became by extension the freemen of the whole colony.

39. Bancroft, *History of the United States*, vol. 1:267.

40. Tocqueville, *Democracy in America*, 40.

41. Bancroft, *History of the United States*, vol. 1:267.

42. Cited in Morgan, *Visible Saints*, 92, and Bancroft, *History of the United States*, vol. 1:271.

43. John Marshall, *A History of the Colonies Planted by the English on the Continent of North America* (Philadelphia: Abraham Small, 1824), 119.

44. Ibid. Very loquacious on the subject of the public liberties enjoyed by Connecticut communities, Tocqueville says not a word about the distinctly less exemplary situation of Massachusetts towns. On this strategic omission, see Robert T. Gannett, Jr., "Bowling Ninepins in Tocqueville's Township," *American Political Science Review* 97, no. 1 (2003): 7.

45. Bancroft, *History of the United States*, vol. 1:270–71.

46. Morgan, *Visible Saints*, 91.

47. Ibid., 95–96.

48. Tocqueville, *Democracy in America*, 48.

49. Gordon Wood, *The Creation of the American Republic, 1776–1787* (1969; New York: Norton, 1996), 341.

50. Thomas Paine, *The Rights of Man*, in *Collected Writings* (New York: Library of America, 1994), 492.

51. Ibid., 572.

52. Ibid., 574.

53. James Madison, Alexander Hamilton, John Jay, *The Federalist Papers* [1787], ed. Isaac Kramnick (New York: Viking Penguin, 1987), 184.

54. Letter from John Adams to Thomas Jefferson, July 15, 1813, quoted in David Brion Davis, *Revolutions: Reflections on American Equality and Foreign Liberations* (Cambridge, MA: Harvard University Press, 1990), 66.

55. John Bristed, *America and Her Resources* (London: Henry Colburn, 1818), 397.

56. François Guizot, *General History of Civilization in Europe*, ed. G. W. Knight (1842; New York: Appleton, 1896), 395.

57. Agnès Antoine, *L'Impensé de la démocratie Tocqueville, la citoyenneté et la religion* (Paris: Fayard, 2003), 193.

58. Bancroft, *History of the United States*, vol. 1:243.

59. Ibid., 1:206.

60. Ibid., 1:201.

61. Ibid. Bancroft, later a Democrat and supporter of Jackson, advocated ideas close to those of the Whig Party at the beginning of his career as a historian. See Jack P. Greene, *Pursuits of Happiness* (Chapel Hill: University of North Carolina Press, 1988), 1–5 and Lilian Handlin, *George Bancroft: The Intellectual as Democrat* (New York: Harper and Row, 1984), 125–27, 146.

62. Tocqueville, *Democracy in America*, 6.

63. Ibid., 3, 5. Unlike Guizot and Bancroft, Tocqueville, as Agnès Antoine has shown, saw no incompatibility between Catholicism and democracy, quite the contrary. Quinet, as she points out in a footnote, "criticized Tocqueville for having insufficiently shown the connection between Protestantism and democracy." *L'Impensé de la démocratie*, 195, 381, n. 82.

64. Tocqueville, *Democracy in America*, 6.

65. Ibid., note r. Draft of *Democracy in America*, Yale Tocqueville Collection, Beinecke Rare Book Library.

66. On Tocqueville's religious ideas and his romantic sensibility, see Agnès Antoine, *L'Impensé de la démocratie*, 174–77 and Cheryl Welch, *De Tocqueville* (New York: Oxford University Press, 2001), 178–85.

67. Tocqueville, *Democracy in America*, 832–33.

68. Tocqueville's numerous remarks on the aristocratic spirit of Southern elites, the economic divergence between North and South, and the practices of slavery indicate that he possessed all the elements needed to outline a parallel history of an authoritarian and antidemocratic America.

69. Tocqueville, *Democracy in America*, 38.

3. Evangelical Awakenings

1. See the excellent summary by David D. Hall, "Narrating Puritanism," in *New Directions in American Religious History*, ed. Harry S. Stout and D. G. Hart (New York: Oxford University Press, 1997), 51–83.

2. See Denis Lacorne, *L'Invention de la République américaine*, 2nd edition (Paris: Hachette, 2008).

3. John M. Murrin, "A Roof without Walls: The Dilemma of American National Identity," in *Beyond Confederation*, ed. Richard Beeman, Stephen Botein, and Edward C. Carter II (Chapel Hill: University of North Carolina Press, 1987), 333–48.

4. Jonathan Edwards, "A Divine and Supernatural Light" (1734), quoted in George M. Marsden, *Jonathan Edwards: A Life* (New Haven: Yale University Press, 2003), 157.

5. Marsden, *Jonathan Edwards*, 192–200. For Edwards, Peter was not the founder of the Roman Catholic Church. He identified the probable "beginning" of the papacy with the election of Boniface III in 607. He hinted that the Millennium would begin when the earth was six thousand years old, that is, a date close to the year 2000. Ibid., 199, 335.

6. John Wesley, the founder of Methodism, invented while at Oxford a new form of ascetic piety, noted for the rigor of its method, hence the name Methodism.

George Whitefield joined this religious movement after John Wesley left for a mission to Savannah, Georgia. See Kenneth Cracknell and Susan White, *An Introduction to World Methodism* (Cambridge: Cambridge University Press, 2005), 9–15.

7. Ibid., 15–29. See also Jon Butler, *Becoming America: The Revolution Before 1776* (Cambridge, MA: Harvard University Press, 2000), 185–224; and William G. McLoughlin, *Revivals, Awakenings, and Reform* (Chicago: University of Chicago Press, 1980).

8. Excerpt from Hymn No. 29, *Collection of Hymns for the Use of the People Called Methodists*, quoted by Cracknell and White, *An Introduction to World Methodism*, 13.

9. *Journal of John Wesley*, May 24, 1738, quoted in Cracknell and White, *An Introduction to World Methodism*, 14 (emphasis in original).

10. Ibid., 101.

11. Ibid., 102. The name of the magazine referred to the doctrine of Arminius (1560–1609), who had sought to refute the doctrine of predestination and whose disciples, the Remonstrants, were condemned by the Synod of Dordrecht (1618–19).

12. Ibid., 100–9, 44–65. See generally Sydney E. Ahlstrom, *A Religious History of the American People* (New Haven: Yale University Press, 1972), 415–54.

13. For the majority of contemporary American historians, the real beginning of the history of Christian America came with the Great Awakenings of the early nineteenth century. See John Murrin, "A Roof without Walls."

14. Robert Baird, *Religion in America, or, An Account of the Origin, Progress, Relation to the State, and Present Condition of the Evangelical Churches in the United States* (New York: Harper and Brothers, 1844), 202. Reported by Rev. C. A. Goodrich, D.D., a "distinguished professor at Yale College," who claims to have witnessed fifteen distinct revivals in the same college.

15. Richard J. Carwardine, *Evangelicals and Politics in Antebellum America* (New Haven: Yale University Press, 1993), 44.

16. Nathan O. Hatch, *The Democratization of American Christianity* (New Haven: Yale University Press, 1989), 94, n. 90; Mark A. Noll, *America's God: From Jonathan Edwards to Abraham Lincoln* (New York: Oxford University Press, 1990), 200.

17. Hatch, *The Democratization of American Christianity*, 37, 26. See also Gordon Wood, *The Radicalism of the American Revolution* (New York: Knopf, 1992).

18. Hatch, *The Democratization of American Christianity*, 10.

19. Ibid., 172.

20. Baird, *Religion in America*, 288.

21. See Harold Bloom, "The Religion-Making Imagination of Joseph Smith," in *The American Religion: The Emergence of the Post-Christian Nation* (New York: Simon and Schuster, 1992), 96–111.

22. Hatch, *The Democratization of American Christianity*, 70–71.

23. Daniel L. Dreisbach, *Thomas Jefferson and the Wall of Separation between Church and State* (New York: New York University Press, 2002), 9–17.

24. Timothy Dwight, "The Duty of Americans at the Present Crisis" (1798), quoted ibid., 19.

25. *Hudson Bee*, September 7, 1800, quoted in Dwight, "The Duty of Americans," 168, n. 50.

26. *Gazette of the United States*, September 11, 1800, quoted in Dwight, "The Duty of Americans," 18 (emphasis in original).

27. Henriette Lucie Dillon, Marquise de La Tour du Pin, *Memoirs of Madame de La Tour du Pin*, ed. and trans. Felice Harcourt (London: Harvill, 1969), 265.

28. Ibid., 265–66.

29. Ibid., 259.

30. Ibid., 267.

31. Ibid.

32. Ibid., 259.

33. Fanny Trollope, *Domestic Manners of the Americans* (1832; Dover: Alan Sutton, 1993), 77.

34. Ibid., 118–19.

35. Ibid., 121.

36. Ibid., 122.

37. Michel Chevalier, *Lettres sur l'Amérique du Nord* (Paris: Charles Gosselin, 1836), 2, 459. The author was in the United States from 1833 to 1835.

38. These two "sects," Chevalier asserts, backed by figures, "together make up more than half the population." Ibid., 2, 185, n. 2 and 459–65.

39. For the disciples of Saint-Simon, religion constituted "the true social bond" and facilitated "the fastest possible improvement of the well-being of the poorest class." See Saint-Simon *Nouveau christianisme* (Paris: Bureau du Globe, 1832), 138, 20.

40. Michel Chevalier, *Society, Manners and Politics in the United States: Being a Series of Letters on North America* (Boston: Weeks, Jordan and Co., 1839), 318.

41. Ibid., 320 (translation modified).

42. Ibid., 320–21.

43. Ibid., 321.

44. Ibid., 322. Sangrado is a character in *Gil Blas* who prescribes warm water and bleeding for every ailment.

45. Ibid., 323.

46. Alexis de Tocqueville, *Democracy in America*, trans. Arthur Goldhammer (New York: Library of America, 2004), 623–24.

47. Like Michel Chevalier, Tocqueville used the word *sect* as Americans of the time did, to mean a new Christian denomination. A *church* was a well established and recognized sect. The word *sect* at the time had no pejorative meaning.

48. Ibid., 623.

49. "Sects in America," previously unpublished manuscript, discovered and translated by James T. Schleifer, "Alexis de Tocqueville Describes the American Character: Two Previously Unpublished Portraits," *South Atlantic Quarterly* 74, no. 2 (1975): 250.

50. Ibid., 251–52.

51. Ibid., 252.

52. Tocqueville, *Democracy in America*, 623.

53. Gustave de Beaumont, "Note sur le mouvement religieux aux États-Unis," in *Marie, ou l'Esclavage aux États-Unis* (1835; Paris: Gosselin, 1850), 282.

54. Tocqueville, "Sects in America," 253–54.

55. Beaumont, "Note sur le mouvement religieux aux États-Unis," 283.

56. Ibid., 279–80.

57. Ibid., 269.

58. Ibid., 280.

59. Tocqueville, *Democracy in America*, 506.

60. Ibid., 502.

61. Ibid., 507.

62. Ibid., 507, 508.

63. Ibid., 501, 502.

64. Ibid., 503. On this subject, see the luminous commentary by Pierre Manent in *Tocqueville and the Nature of Democracy*, trans. John Waggoner (Lanham, MD: Rowman and Littlefield, 1996), 83–107. Manent writes that in Tocqueville's eyes, "the democratic horse has the bit in its teeth." Ibid., 93.

65. "Sects in America," manuscript variant cited in *De la Démocratie en Amérique*, ed. Eduardo Nolla (Paris: Vrin 1990) note h2, 123.

66. Ibid.

67. Tocqueville, *Democracy in America*, 501.

4. The Bible Wars

1. Alexis de Tocqueville, *Democracy in America*, trans. Arthur Goldhammer (New York: Library of America, 2004), 49.

2. See chapter 3 and Tocqueville's letter to Louis de Kergorlay, from Yonkers on June 29, 1831, in *The Tocqueville Reader*, ed. Olivier Zunz and Alan S. Kahan (Oxford: Blackwell, 2002), 42ff.

3. Ibid., 46.

4. Ibid.

5. *Memoirs, Letters, and Remains of Alexis de Tocqueville* (Cambridge: Macmillan, 1861), 308–9.

6. On Tocqueville and Catholicism in America, see Eugène d'Eichthal, "Tocqueville et 'La démocratie en Amérique,'" *Revue politique et parlementaire* (April–May 1896); Agnès Antoine, *L'Impensé de la démocratie: Tocqueville, la citoyenneté et la religion* (Paris: Fayard, 2003), 192–200; Cheryl Welch, *De Tocqueville* (New York: Oxford University Press, 2001), 96–101.

7. Jay P. Dolan, *The American Catholic Experience* (Notre Dame, IN: Notre Dame University Press, 1992), 79, 87.

8. Report of John Carroll to Cardinal Antonelli, quoted in Sydney E. Ahlstrom, *A Religious History of the American People* (New Haven: Yale University Press, 1972), 531. On the career of this former Jesuit, who was born in Maryland, educated at St. Omer, was a supporter of American independence, and worked with Benjamin Franklin on a diplomatic mission, see Dolan, *The American Catholic Experience*, 101–24.

9. "For example, in Boston in 1850, 62 percent of Irish-born workers were unskilled laborers, 53 percent in Sacramento, and 50 percent in Detroit. Thirty years later, a similar pattern existed in Boston, where 67 percent of Irish-born workers were unskilled laborers; in Detroit it was 42 percent, and in Sacramento, California, 46 percent." Dolan, *The American Catholic Experience*, 139. The median annual wage of an unskilled laborer was $360, which made the living conditions of a typical family extremely precarious.

10. "The Irish rabble." Quoted in Ahlstrom, *A Religious History of the American People*, 543.

11. According to a sermon by the Catholic Archbishop of New York, John Hughes, quoted in Ray Billington, *The Protestant Crusade 1800–1860: A Study of the Origins of American Nativism* (Chicago: Quadrangle Books, 1938), 291.

12. *New York Observer*, November 14, 1829, quoted in Billington, *The Protestant Crusade*, 54.

13. Samuel F. B. Morse, *Foreign Conspiracy Against the Liberties of the United States* (1841). A good analysis of this collection of articles, originally published in the *New York Observer* in 1834, can be found in Mark S. Massa, S. J., *Anti-Catholicism in America: The Last Acceptable Prejudice* (New York: Crossroads, 2003), 23–24.

14. Billington, *The Protestant Crusade*, 125–27. The most influential nativists were Samuel Morse and Reverend Lyman Beecher, famous for his fiery sermons against the "papal conspiracy" and one of the instigators of the attack against the Ursuline convent.

15. Ibid., 68–76.

16. Richard Hofstadter, *The Paranoid Style in American Politics* (New York: Knopf, 1965), 21.

17. W. Jos. Walters, "Catholic, Roman," in *An Original History of the Religious Denominations at Present Existing in the United States*, ed. I. Daniel Rupp (Philadelphia: J. Y. Humphreys, 1844), 162.

18. Maria Monk, *Awful Disclosures* (Philadelphia: T. B. Peterson, 1836), 42, 89, and 124.

19. Ibid., 147–50 and 160.

20. Ibid., 148.

21. Ibid., 82.

22. Ibid., 84.

23. Initiation ritual of a lodge of the Order of the Star Spangled Banner, quoted in Tyler Anbinder, *Nativism and Slavery: The Northern Know Nothings and the Politics of the 1850s* (Oxford: Oxford University Press, 1992), 23.

24. See the collection of articles from the *American Protestant Vindicator* and the *Long Island Star*, printed as appendices to Monk, *Awful Disclosures*, 187–92.

25. *Long Island Star*, February 29, 1836, in Monk, *Awful Disclosures*, 191.

26. Epistle Dedicatory "To the most High and Mighty Prince James, by the Grace of God, King of Great Britain, France, and Ireland, Defender of the Faith, etc." *The Bible: Authorized King James Version with Apocrypha* (Oxford: Oxford World's Classics, 1997), lxxii. On the making of this Bible, see Adam Nicolson, *God's Secretaries: The Making of the King James Bible* (New York: Harper Collins, 2003).

27. Exodus 20.4–5. King James Version. The same prohibition is formulated in similar terms at Deuteronomy 5.8–9.

28. "Even prostitutes in brothels are to be seen in more chaste and modest attire, than those images in their temples, which they wish to be accounted images of virgins." Calvin, *Institutes*, quoted by Denis Crouzet, *Jean Calvin* (Paris: Fayard, 2000), 213.

29. Ibid., 211. From the Catholic perspective, the cult of sacred images was justified from the 787 Council of Nicaea on, because "We do not pray to the crucifix or to the images and relics of the saints, but to the persons they represent." Hence, there is no violation of the prohibition in Exodus 20.3. *The Baltimore Catechism* § 223.

30. John T. McGreevy, *Catholicism and American Freedom* (New York: Norton, 2003), 7–15.

31. *American Law Register* 7 (1859): 417–26, quoted in McGreevy, *Catholicism and American Freedom*, 8.

32. McGreevy, *Catholicism and American Freedom*, 8, 9.

33. "Constitution of the American Society to Promote the Principles of the Protestant Reformation," *American Protestant Vindicator*, June 24, 1840, reproduced in Ray Billington, *The Protestant Crusade*, 437–38. Other associations, such as the American Protestant Association and the American and Foreign Christian Union, advocated the same ideas, which were later adopted by the founders of the Know Nothing Party.

34. Ibid., 437.

35. McGreevy, *Catholicism and American Freedom*, 10.

36. Horace Mann, "Twelfth Annual Report to the Massachusetts Board of Education" (1848), in *The Republic and the School: Horace Mann on the Education of Free Men*, ed. Lawrence Cremin (New York: Teachers College, Columbia University, 1957), 103.

37. Horace Mann, *Lectures on Education* (Boston: Ide & Dutton, 1855), 125.

38. Ibid., 124.

39. Ibid., 118, 120.

40. Horace Mann, "Twelfth Annual Report," 111.

41. Ibid., 105–12.

42. *New York Freeman's Journal*, July 11, 1840, quoted in Stephen Macedo, *Diversity and Distrust: Civic Education in a Multicultural Democracy* (Cambridge, MA: Harvard University Press, 2000), 69.

43. Speech by John Hughes (1840), quoted in Macedo, *Diversity and Distrust.* On this subject, see also Diane Ravitch, *The Great School Wars* (New York: Basic Books, 1974).

44. As had been proposed, in a greatly conciliatory spirit, by the educator Theodore Sedgwick, one of the most active members of the Public School Society of New York. See Macedo, *Diversity and Distrust*, 71.

45. See Anbinder, *Nativism and Slavery*, 10–12.

46. Proclamations of the American Republican Party, March 11 and May 3, 1844, quoted in Billington, *The Protestant Crusade*, 222.

47. Ibid., 224.

48. Ibid., 231.

49. Anbinder, *Nativism and Slavery*, 12–14.

50. In 1880, more than 400,000 Catholic children from families with modest incomes were registered in the country's 2,246 Catholic schools. See Noah Feldman, *Divided by God* (New York: Farrar, Straus, and Giroux, 2005), 88.

51. Message of the President to Congress, December 8, 1875, quoted in Feldman, *Divided by God*, 76. See also John T. McGreevy, *Catholicism and American Freedom: A History* (New York: Norton, 2003), 91–112.

52. Unsigned editorial, *The Princeton Review*, April 1870, quoted in Feldman, *Divided by God*, 85.

53. Tocqueville, *Democracy in America*, 510.

54. Tocqueville was in fact carrying letters of introduction to these French clergymen from a friend of the family, Monseigneur de Cheverus, former archbishop of Boston. See Jean-Claude Lamberti, *Tocqueville et les deux démocraties* (Paris: PUF, 1983), 207, n. 94. On the strong ties between French and American clergy before the great wave of Irish immigration, see René Rémond, *Les États-Unis devant l'opinion française, 1815–1852* (Paris: Armand Colin, 1962), vol. 1:158–60.

55. This is the argument presented, for example, by W. J. Walters in his history of the Roman Catholic Church in Rupp, *An Original History of the Religious Denominations*, 164–65.

56. See Ferdinand Brunetière, "Le catholicisme aux États-Unis," *Revue des Deux Mondes*, November 1898, 140–81, and especially Jules Tardivel, *La Situation religieuse aux États-Unis: Illusions et réalité* (Paris: Desclée de Brouwer, 1900). This very polemical work presents a thoroughgoing critique of "Americanism" and "Americanizing Catholics," along with a refutation of Brunetière's argument and evidence.

57. Letter to Louis de Kergorlay, in *The Tocqueville Reader*, 46. Moreover, this is why Tocqueville, who admitted he had lost his faith in his adolescence, acted "as though he believed," as Agnès Antoine writes, because he was convinced that the practice of religion corresponded to "the enlightened self-interest of any democratic person." Antoine, *L'Impensé de la démocratie*, 177.

58. Charles Marshall, open letter to Al Smith, *Atlantic Monthly*, April 1928, quoted in Mark S. Massa, S. J., *Anti-Catholicism in America*, 33.

59. *Baptist Progress*, October 4, 1928, quoted in Massa, *Anti-Catholicism in America*, 34.

5. Religion, Race, and National Identity

1. Samuel P. Huntington, *Who Are We? The Challenges to America's National Identity* (New York: Simon and Schuster, 2004), 38.

2. Ibid., 68 and 69.

3. Samuel P. Huntington, "The Hispanic Challenge," *Foreign Policy* 141 (March–April 2004): 31.

4. Ibid., 45.

5. See Alejandro Portes and Ruben J. Rumbaut, *Immigrant America: A Portrait*, 3rd edition (Berkeley: University of California Press, 2006), 117–20; Paul Starr, "The

Return of the Nativist," *New Republic*, June, 21, 2004; Francis Fukuyama, "Why We Shouldn't Worry about Mexican Immigration," *Slate*, June 4, 2004.

6. This theory, supposedly inspired by the work of Darwin, divided humanity into superior and inferior races. See Denis Lacorne, *La Crise de l'identité américaine: Du melting-pot au multiculturalisme*, revised edition (Paris: Gallimard, Tel, 2003), 135–68, and the classic American work, John Higham, *Strangers in the Land: Patterns of American Nativism, 1860–1925* (1955; New Brunswick, NJ: Rutgers University Press, 1988).

7. A brilliant analysis of German Romanticism is found in Alain Renaut's introduction to Johann Gottlieb Fichte, *Discours à la nation allemande* (1807–8) (Paris: Imprimerie nationale, 1992), 7–48.

8. François Guizot, *General History of Civilization in Europe*, ed. G. W. Knight (1842; New York: Appleton, 1896), 56, 55.

9. Ibid., 331.

10. Édouard Laboulaye, *Histoire des États-Unis* (Paris: Charpentier, 1866), 158.

11. Ibid., 255–57, emphasis added.

12. Ibid., 256.

13. Ibid., 129, n. 1. The word *Yankee*, Laboulaye explains, is an Indian corruption of *English*.

14. Michel Chevalier, *Society, Manners and Politics in the United States: Being a Series of Letters on North America* (Boston: Weeks, Jordan and Co., 1839), 115–16. The author specifies in a note that the "name of Yankee was first applied in derision, but the New Englanders, thinking they have ennobled it, have adopted it" (109, unnumbered note).

15. Ibid., 112–13.

16. Ibid., 117.

17. Élisée Reclus, *The Earth and Its Inhabitants: North America*, vol. 3, *The United States*, ed. A. H. Keane (New York: D. Appleton, 1893), 450. On the importance of Reclus's work, see *Hérodote* 117 (2005), a special issue on Reclus.

18. Reclus, *The Earth and Its Inhabitants*, vol. 3:451 (translation modified).

19. Reclus, *Géographie Universelle* (Paris: Hachette, 1892) vol. 16:676.

20. Ibid., 678.

21. Madison Grant, *The Passing of the Great Race or the Racial Basis of European History* (New York: Charles Scribner's Sons, 1916), 43–44.

22. Ibid., 45.

23. Ibid., 43.

24. The Nordic race is, according to Grant, the "white man par excellence," the purest expression of "*Homo Europeanus*" (Ibid., 150).

25. Ibid., 228.

26. In this respect, Madison Grant's argument is comparable to that of Houston Stewart Chamberlain. See Denis Lacorne, *La Crise de l'identité américaine*, 134 ff, and Christine Rosen, *Preaching Eugenics: Religious Leaders and the American Eugenics Movement* (New York: Oxford University Press, 2004).

27. Émile Boutmy, *Éléments d'une psychologie politique du peuple américain* (Paris: Armand Colin, 1902), 63–64.

28. Ibid., 68.

29. Ibid., 69–72.

30. Ibid., 102.

31. Ibid., 87–88.

32. Ibid., 103.

33. Ibid., 90, 92–94.

34. Ibid., 305.

35. Ibid., 26.

36. Ibid. This thesis was obviously influenced by the work of Frederick Jackson Turner, starting with his famous essay on "The Significance of the Frontier in American History" 1893), reprinted in *The Frontier in American History* (New York: Henry Holt, 1920), 1–38.

37. See Theodore Roosevelt, "The Backwoodsmen of the Alleghanies, in *The Winning of the West* (New York: G. P. Putnam's Sons, 1889), vol. 1:101–33. See also "Manhood and Statehood," in *The Strenuous Life: Essays and Addresses by Theodore Roosevelt* (New York: The Century Co., 1901), 245–59.

38. Boutmy, *Éléments d'une psychologie politique du peuple américain*, 13.

39. Alexis de Tocqueville, "Two Weeks in the Wilderness," in *Democracy in America and Two Essays on America*, trans. Gerald E. Bevan (London: Penguin Books, 2003), 875–927.

40. Ibid., 885–88.

41. Ibid, 888.

42. Roosevelt, *The Winning of the West*, 21.

43. On Roosevelt's conception of the race of the pioneers, see Gary Gerstle, *American Crucible: Race and Nation in the Twentieth Century* (Princeton: Princeton University Press, 2001); and Richard Slotkin, *Gunfighter Nation: The Myth of the Frontier in Twentieth-Century America* (New York: Macmillan, 1992).

44. Letter to Ernest Vinet, February 1871, quoted in Eugène d'Eichthal, "L'École libre des sciences politiques," *Revue des Deux Mondes* (December 1927): 2. On the school's founders, see Pierre Favre, *Naissance de la science politique en France, 1870–1914* (Paris: Fayard, 1989).

45. Émile Boutmy, *Essai d'une psychologie politique du peuple anglais au XIXe siècle* (Paris: Armand Colin, 1901).

46. André Siegfried, *America Comes of Age: A French Analysis*, trans. H. H. and Doris Hemming (New York: Harcourt, Brace, 1927).

47. Pierre Leroy-Beaulieu, *The United States in the Twentieth Century*, trans. H. Addington Bruce (New York: Funk & Wagnalls, 1906), 23.

48. Siegfried, *America Comes of Age*, 9, 3 (translation modified).

49. Ibid., 146 (translation modified).

50. Ibid., 145.

51. On Horace Kallen, one of the first critics of the melting pot thesis, see Lacorne, *La Crise de l'identité américaine*, 268–82.

52. Siegfried, *America Comes of Age*, 145.

53. Ibid., 142, 144.

54. Ibid., 141.

55. *The American Standard* (Ku Klux Klan bimonthly), October 1, 1925, quoted and analyzed in ibid., 138–39.

56. Ibid., 146.

57. Ibid., 6, 7, 9, 16.

58. Siegfried, *Les États-Unis d'aujourd'hui* (Paris: Armand Colin, 1927), 17.

59. Siegfried, *America Comes of Age*, 26, 27.

60. Ibid., 25.

61. Ibid.

62. Siegfried, *Les États-Unis d'aujourd'hui*, 26.

63. Siegfried, *America Comes of Age*, 20, 25, 27, 22.

64. Ibid., 20.

65. Rebecca Godchaux, letter to André Siegfried, *Archives Siegfried* [2 S I 19 dr 2], in the library of the Institut des Études Politiques in Paris. Godchaux was the author of *"Our Method" for Teaching Practical French* (San Francisco: Raphael Weill & Co., 1918). Her letter to Siegfried was written in French.

66. I deliberately adopt here the terms of Godchaux's answer to a letter from Siegfried. She thanked the author for his "letter explaining the attempt . . . made to attenuate the very painful impression caused by certain passages of [his] book." Letter of May 19, 1927, *Archives Siegfried* [2 S I 19 dr 4]. *Les États-Unis d'aujourd'hui* was reprinted up to 1951. The book's commercial success was unquestionable, with more than thirteen thousand copies sold in France in the first year, and more than twenty thousand copies of the English translation sold in America that same year. Twenty-six years later, Rita Barisse, the proposed translator of a new book by Siegfried (*Tableau des États-Unis* [Paris: Armand Colin, 1954]), which repeated

most of the offensive epithets of the 1927 book, expressed similar indignation in practically identical terms. Rather than change his style or his formulations, Siegfried chose to change translators. See Pierre Birnbaum, "*La France aux Français*": *Histoire des haines nationalistes* (Paris: Seuil, 1993), 157–59.

67. Siegfried, *America Comes of Age*, 113, 111.

68. Ibid., 109.

69. Ibid., 33.

70. Ibid., 34.

71. Weber's study was first published in two installments in the *Archiv für Sozialwissenschaft und Sozialpolitik* in 1904 and 1905. Nothing in the Siegfried Archives at the Institut des Études Politiques indicates that Siegfried had read it. But his Protestant origins and Protestant culture and his many university contacts had certainly predisposed him to use an argument that was fashionable among the sociologists and economists of his time.

72. Ibid., 36.

73. Max Weber, *The Protestant Ethic and the Spirit of Capitalism* [1904–5], trans. Talcott Parsons (1930; London and New York: Routledge, 1992), 110.

74. Ibid.

75. Ibid., 112 (referring to Baxter's *Christian Directory*).

76. Ibid., 117.

77. Ibid., 121.

78. Ibid., 112.

79. Siegfried, *America Comes of Age*, 35.

80. Ibid., 36, 50, 89.

81. Ibid., 54–90. See also Dominique Lecourt, *L'Amérique entre la Bible et Darwin* (Paris: PUF, 1992) and Michael Kazin, *A Godly Hero: The Life of William Jennings Bryan*, (New York: Alfred A. Knopf, 2006), 285–95.

82. Siegfried, *America Comes of Age*, 77.

83. Samuel P. Huntington, *Who Are We?*, chap. 7, "Deconstructing America: The Rise of Subnational Identities," 141–77.

84. Siegfried had sent a copy of his book to Madison Grant, and he received in return a laudatory commentary from this leading figure of American nativism. *Archives Siegfried* [2 S I 19 dr 4], letter of May 3, 1927.

85. Huntington, *Who Are We?*, 63.

86. Ibid., 61.

87. Ibid., 316.

88. David Lopez, "Bilingualism and Ethnic Change in California," in Tony Judt and Denis Lacorne eds., *Language, Nation, and State: Identity Politics in a Multi-*

lingual Age (New York: Palgrave Macmillan, 2004), 79–101; Portes and Rumbaut, *Immigrant America*, 204–43.

89. Tony Judt and Denis Lacorne, "The Politics of Language," in *Language, Nation, and State*, 1–16.

90. Huntington, *Who Are We?*, 324.

91. Ibid., 20.

92. On the controversy provoked by Huntington's book, see Alan Wolfe, "Native Son: Samuel Huntington Defends the Homeland," *Foreign Affairs*, May–June 2004; James W. Ceaser, "O, My America," *Weekly Standard*, May 3, 2004; Louis Menand, "The New Nativism of Samuel Huntington," *The New Yorker*, May 17, 2004; Peter Skerry, "What Are We to Make of Samuel Huntington?," *Society*, Nov.–Dec. 2005; Jack Citrin et al., "Testing Huntington: Is Hispanic Immigration a Threat to American Identity?" *Perspectives on Politics*, March 2007.

6. A Godless America

1. Jean-Louis Loubet del Bayle, *Les Non-Conformistes des années 30* (Paris: Seuil,1969).

2. There were of course a few French apostles of Taylorism or Fordism, such as the car maker Citroën, or Dubreuil, a union organizer who worked for a full year in an American factory. See André Citroën, "Speeding up the Automobile Industry," *European Finance*, June 13, 1928; Hyacinthe Dubreuil, *Standards: Le travail américain vu par un ouvrier français* (Paris: Grasset, 1929); André Philip, *Le Problème ouvrier aux États-Unis* (Paris: Felix Alcan, 1927); and, more generally, Paul Gagnon, "French Views of the Second American Revolution," *French Historical Studies* 2, no. 4 (1962): 430–49.

3. André Siegfried, *America Comes of Age: A French Analysis*, trans. H. H. and Doris Hemming (New York: Harcourt, Brace, 1927), 344.

4. Siegfried, *Les États-Unis d'aujourd'hui* (Paris: Armand Colin, 1927), 346 (emphasis added).

5. Siegfried, *America Comes of Age*, 348–50.

6. André Siegfried, preface to Philip, *Le Problème ouvrier aux États-Unis*, x and xvi (emphasis added).

7. Manifesto of *Ordre nouveau*, quoted in Loubet del Bayle, *Les Non-Conformistes des années 30*, 443. Martin Heidegger said practically the same thing in his writings on craftsmanship, which is clearly the superior form of production, because it is only through craftsmanship that the painter, the carpenter, the potter, or the great artist can demonstrate the "complete mastery" of a technique whose "science"

they have grasped. See "The Origin of the Work of Art" [1935], in *Basic Writings*, ed. David Farrell Krell (New York: Harper & Row, 1977), 179.

8. Bayle, *Les Non-Conformistes des années 30*, 442 and 443.

9. Siegfried, *America Comes of Age*, 353.

10. "Europe," according to Heidegger, "lies in the pincers between Russia and America, which are metaphysically the same, namely in regard to their world-character and their relation to the spirit." Europe faced a terrible threat: "a *disempowering of the spirit*, its dissolution, diminution, suppression, and misinterpretation." Martin Heidegger, *An Introduction to Metaphysics*, trans. Gregory Fried and Richard Polt (New Haven: Yale University Press, 2000), 47–48.

11. Robert Aron and Arnaud Dandieu, *Le Cancer américain* (Paris: Rieder, [October] 1931), 14.

12. Ibid., 16 and 18. The same argument was reiterated the following year by a contributor to *Ordre nouveau*, Henri Daniel-Rops, in *Le Monde sans âme* (Paris: Plon, 1932).

13. Aron and Dandieu, *Le Cancer américain*, 14.

14. Aron and Dandieu, *Décadence de la nation française* (Paris: Rieder, [January] 1931).

15. Ibid., 182, 297, and 213.

16. Ibid., 207. Descartes was also denounced, less extravagantly, by Emmanuel Mounier in the first issue of *Esprit*. "Refaire la Renaissance," *Esprit* 1, no. 1 (October 1932): 26.

17. I take the expression from Marcel Gauchet, *Le Désenchantement du monde* (Paris: Gallimard, 1985); *La Religion dans la démocratie* (Paris: Gallimard, 1998).

18. Aron and Dandieu, *Décadence de la nation française*, 19, 119, and 120

19. Ibid., 220 and 221. The Binet method, the authors explain, is nothing but "the extension of an *ossified and emasculated Cartesianism*" (emphasis added).

20. Ibid., 217–18.

21. Emmanuel Mounier, "Ce ne sont pas ceux qui disent: esprit, esprit," *La Nouvelle Revue française*, December 1932, 824–26, reprinted in Mounier, *Mounier et sa génération: Lettres, carnets et inédits* (Paris: Seuil, 1956), 107–9.

22. Letter to Robert Garric, January, 16, 1932, in Mounier, *Mounier et sa génération*, 81.

23. "Prospectus annonçant la fondation d'*Esprit*," February 1932, Mounier, *Mounier et sa génération*, 82.

24. Ibid.

25. Mounier, "Refaire la Renaissance," 29 (emphasis added).

26. Mounier, "Extraits d'un rapport privé sur *Esprit* à l'usage de Mgr Courbe et de l'archevêque de Paris," in *Mounier et sa génération*, 185.

27. Letter to Jacques Chevalier, September 23, 1932, Mounier, *Mounier et sa génération*, 96.

28. "Letter from France: A Personalist leader, editor of *Esprit*, sends this message to America from France," *Commonweal* 33, no. 1 (October 25, 1940). Heidegger said practically the same thing when he denounced the primacy of productive values in America and Russia, with as a result "the onslaught of what we call the *demonic* [in the sense of what we call the destructively evil]." *An Introduction to Metaphysics*, 49 (emphasis added).

29. See above.

30. Mounier, "Entretiens XII," May 18, 1941, in *Mounier et sa génération*, 300.

31. See chapter 1.

32. "Entretiens XII," May 8, 1941, *Mounier et sa génération*, 297 and 298.

33. Ibid., 298.

34. "Entretiens XII," May 18, 1941, 300.

35. Ibid.

36. "Entretiens XI," March 30, 1941, 291–92.

37. Ibid., 291.

38. Pierre Emmanuel, *Autobiographies* [1970], quoted in Michel Winock, *"Esprit"*: *Des intellectuels dans la cité* (Paris: Seuil, 1996), 393.

39. Georges Duhamel, *America the Menace: Scenes from the Life of the Future*, trans. Charles Miner Thompson (London: Allen & Unwin, 1931), viii.

40. Ibid., 110. See chapter 8, "The Kingdom of Death," describing a visit to the Chicago abattoirs, which provided inspiration for Hergé's *Tintin en Amérique*.

41. Philippe Roger, *The American Enemy: The History of French Anti-Americanism*, trans. Sharon Bowman (Chicago: University of Chicago Press, 2005), 392.

42. Duhamel, *America the Menace*, 200.

43. Ibid., 202 (emphasis added).

44. Ibid., 128.

45. Ibid., 132–33 (translation modified).

46. Ibid., chapter 15, "Meditation on the Cathedral of Commerce," 198.

47. Ibid., chapter 12, "The New Temple," 157.

48. Ibid., 196.

49. Ibid., xiv.

50. Aron and Dandieu, *Décadence de la France*, 20, 21, and 22.

51. Maurice Blanchot, *Réaction* 3 (July 1930), quoted in Loubet del Bayle, *Les Non-Conformistes des années 30*, 254.

52. Emmanuel Mounier, *Revue de culture générale* (October 1930), quoted in Bayle, *Les Non-Conformistes*, 258.

53. Georges Bernanos, *La France contre les Robots* [1944], in *Essais et écrits de combat*, ed. Michel Estève (Paris: Gallimard, Bibliothèque de la Pléiade, 1995), vol. 2:1991.

54. Ibid., 1023.

55. Ibid., 1047.

56. Bernanos, "La France devant le monde," in *La liberté pour quoi faire?* [1946–48], 7th ed. (Paris: Gallimard, 1953), 17.

57. "Révolution et liberté," in *La liberté pour quoi faire?*, 165.

58. "L'esprit européen," in *La liberté pour quoi faire?*, 239–40.

59. Ibid., 242. On the simultaneous denunciation of American and Soviet imperialism by writers as different as Alain de Benoist, Jean-Marie Benoist, Jean-Pierre Chevènement, and Michel Jobert, see Denis Lacorne, Jacques Rupnik, and Marie-France Toinet, eds., *The Rise and Fall of Anti-Americanism: A Century of French Perception* (London : Macmillan, 1990), 18–27.

60. Bernanos, "L'esprit européen," in *La liberté pour quoi faire?*, 240 (emphasis added).

61. Ibid., 241.

62. Ibid., 101, 164.

63. As Marie-Christine Granjon has clearly shown, Sartre expressed real sympathy for America in his articles for *Combat* and *Le Figaro*. See Granjon, "Sartre, Beauvoir, Aron: les passions ambiguës," in *L'Amérique dans les têtes*, 144–64.

64. Jean-Paul Sartre, "Matérialisme et révolution" (*Les Temps modernes*, June 1946), in *Situations III* (1949; Paris: Gallimard, 2003), 147 and 148.

65. "La fin de la guerre (*Les Temps modernes*, October 1945), in ibid., 51, 53, and 55. Sartre does not exclude the hypothesis of the bomb being used by a madman or a new Hitler. "We would all be responsible" for this new Führer, he writes. Sartre was thus one of the first apologists for preventive war against a tyrant in possession of weapons of mass destruction.

66. Louis-Ferdinand Céline, *Journey to the End of the Night*, trans. Ralph Manheim (New York: New Directions, 1983), 166. Paul Morand had said practically the same thing when he visited the "sanctuary of the temple": the stock exchange. He "can hear the dull, disturbing noise of all those silver dollars rolling, heaping hugely up, like sacred wafers, and slipping from one pocket into another, in an instant." Morand, *New York*, trans. Hamish Miles (New York: Henry Holt, 1930), 68.

67. Alfred Kinsey et al., *Sexual Behavior in the Human Male* (Philadelphia: W. B. Saunders, 1948); *Sexual Behavior in the Human Female* (Philadelphia: W. B. Saunders, 1953). On the importance of these investigations, see John D'Emilio and

Estella B. Freedman, *Intimate Matters: A History of Sexuality in America* (Chicago: University of Chicago Press, 1997).

68. Sartre, "Individualisme et conformisme aux États-Unis" (*Le Figaro*, March 1945), *Situations III*, 60.

69. Ibid. (emphasis added).

70. Sartre, "U.S.A. Présentation" (*Les Temps modernes*, August 1946), *Situations III*, 96.

71. Ibid.

72. Ibid.

73. Paul Bourget, *Outre-Mer: Impressions of America* (New York: Scribner, 1895), quoted by Jacques Laurent in "Paul et Jean-Paul," *Les Cahiers irréguliers* 2 (1951): 65. Laurent presents a striking parallel between the journeys and observations of Bourget and Sartre in the United States and constructs an imaginary dialogue between the two writers.

74. Simone de Beauvoir, *America Day by Day*, trans. Carol Cosman (Berkeley: University of California Press, 1999), 281.

75. Ibid., 282.

76. Ibid (emphasis added).

77. Ibid., 286.

78. Ibid., 286 and 287.

79. Bernard-Henri Lévy, *American Vertigo: Traveling America in the Footsteps of Tocqueville* (New York: Random House, 2006), 211. The book recounts a journey of fifteen thousand miles around America and presents his travel impressions, first published in *The Atlantic Monthly*.

80. Ibid., 210 and 211.

81. Ibid., 211 (emphasis added).

7. The Rise of the Religious Right

1. *La Vie*, March 13, 2003; *Le Nouvel Observateur*, February 26, 2004, quoted in Sébastien Fath, *Dieu bénisse l'Amérique: La religion de la Maison-Blanche* (Paris: Seuil, 2004), 23.

2. Jacques Sallebert, "Pèlerinage aux sources," *Le Point*, July 19, 1976.

3. Ibid.

4. *Playboy*, November 1976, quoted in Olivier Todd, "Deux champions sans punch," *Le Nouvel Observateur*, September 27, 1976.

5. Charles Lambroschini, "La ceinture de la Bible," *Le Figaro*, January 24, 1998.

6. P. Girard, *L'Événement du Jeudi*, September 17, 1998.

7. Franz-Olivier Giesbert, "Libidocratie," *Le Figaro Magazine,* January 31, 1998.

8. Editorial by Jacques Amalric, *Libération,* September 14, 1998.

9. Front-page headline of "Magazine Idées" written by Sébastien Lapaque, *Marianne,* December 20, 1999.

10. Clinton was found not guilty on both counts of the indictment: perjury and obstruction of justice. See Denis Lacorne, "Le simulacre du procès Clinton," *Justices* 1 (1999): 151–56.

11. Patrick Sabatier, *Libération* February 12, 1999.

12. Unsigned editorial, *Le Monde,* February 14, 1999.

13. Chantal de Rudder, citing the opinion of the political scientist Rogers Smith, in "Amérique: La démocratie gangrénée," *Le Nouvel Observateur,* October 22, 1999.

14. "Transcript of President Clinton's Speech at the Religious Leaders' Prayer Breakfast, September 11, 1998," in *Judgment Day at the White House,* ed. Gabriel Fackre (Grand Rapids: W. B. Eerdmans, 1999), 185–86.

15. White House Prayer Breakfast, September 28, 1999, quoted in the *International Herald Tribune,* September 29, 1999.

16. "Declaration Concerning Religion, Ethics, and the Crisis in the Clinton Presidency," in Fackre, *Judgment Day at the White House,* 2.

17. Inaugural Address of George W. Bush, January 20, 2001, http://avalon.law .yale.edu/subject_menus/inaug.asp.

18. Inaugural Address of William J. Clinton, January 20, 1993, ibid.

19. Inaugural Address of Jimmy Carter, January 20, 1977, quoting Micah 6.8, ibid.

20. Inaugural Address of Thomas Jefferson, March 4, 1801, ibid.

21. Inaugural Address of Franklin D. Roosevelt, March 4, 1933, ibid.

22. J. C. D. Clark, *The Language of Liberty, 1660–1832* (Cambridge: Cambridge University Press, 1994), 30.

23. Ibid., 383.

24. Ibid., 384.

25. Laurie Goodstein, "A President Puts His Faith in Providence," *New York Times,* February 9, 2003.

26. Peter Baker, "Bush Tells Group He Sees a 'Third Awakening,'" *Washington Post,* September 13, 2006. On the history of evangelical awakenings, see William G. McLoughlin, *Revivals, Awakenings, and Reform* (Chicago: University of Chicago Press, 1980).

27. David Aikman, *A Man of Faith: The Spiritual Journey of George W. Bush* (Nashville, TN: W Publishing Group, 2004), 81; Fath, *Dieu bénisse l'Amérique,* 103–11.

28. Sidney Blumenthal, *Pledging Allegiance* (New York: Harper Collins, 1991), 98. Pat Robertson had come ahead of George H. W. Bush in the Iowa caucuses.

29. Quoted in Aikman, *A Man of Faith*, 81–82.

30. A spectacular hagiography of Bush can be found in a film titled *George W. Bush: Faith in the White House. See How the Power of Faith Can Change a Life, Build a Family, and Shape the Destiny of a Nation*, Grizzly Adams Productions, Good Times DVD 05–50082 (2004), approximately 70 minutes.

31. Remarks Bush made to a group of evangelical preachers in January 1999 in the Texas governor's residence, quoted in *The Economist*, December 16, 2004.

32. Melinda Henneberger, "Gore and God: Spiritual Life Still Evolving," *New York Times*, October 22, 2000. Like his father, Gore is a Southern Baptist. He studied for two years at the Vanderbilt University Divinity School and considers himself a born-again Christian.

33. Louisiana, Mississippi, Alabama, Georgia, and South Carolina.

34. Quoted in Robert Dallek, *Lyndon B. Johnson: Portrait of A President* (New York: Oxford University Press, 2004), 170.

35. Earl Black and Merle Black, *The Rise of Southern Republicans* (Cambridge, MA: Harvard University Press, 2002), 204–11.

36. Quoted in A. James Reichley, *Religion in American Public Life* (Washington, DC: Brookings Institution, 1985), 316.

37. The prayer to be said at the beginning of each school day was: "Almighty God, we acknowledge our dependence upon Thee, and we beg Thy blessings upon us, our parents, our teachers, and our Country."

38. For more detail on the origin and meaning of this amendment, see chapter 8.

39. Opinion of the Court by Justice Hugo Black, *Engel v. Vitale*, 370 U.S. 421 at 431, 432.

40. Quoted in Reichley, *Religion in American Public Life*, 147.

41. *Abington School District v. Schempp*, 374 U.S. 203 (1963); *Epperson v. Arkansas*, 393 U.S. 97 (1968).

42. *Griswold v. Connecticut*, 381 U.S. 479 (1965); *Roe v. Wade*, 410 U.S. 113 (1973).

43. Quoted in Randall Balmer, *God in the White House: A History* (New York: HarperOne, 2008), 98.

44. Frank Lambert, *Religion in American Politics: A Short History* (Princeton: Princeton University Press, 2008), 201.

45. Reichley, *Religion in American Public Life*, 316–20; Karen Orren and Stephen Skowronek, *The Search for American Political Development* (Cambridge: Cambridge University Press, 2004), 152–53; Mark C. Taylor, *After God* (Chicago: University of Chicago Press, 2007), 266–73.

46. Noah Feldman, *Divided by God: America's Church-State Problem and What We Should Do About It* (New York: Farrar, Straus and Giroux, 2005), 190.

47. Black, *The Rise of Southern Republicans*, 215. On the operation of this fundamentalist college, see Susan Friend Harding, *The Book of Jerry Falwell: Fundamentalist Language and Politics* (Princeton: Princeton University Press, 2000), 106–117, 139–47.

48. Steve Bruce, *The Rise and Fall of the New Christian Right* (Oxford: Oxford University Press, 1990), 81–90; Reichley, *Religion in American Life*, 320–22.

49. *The Rise and Fall of the New Christian Right*, 81.

50. Robert W. Fowler, Allen Hertzke, and Laura Olson, *Religion and Politics in America* 2nd edition (Boulder, CO: Westview Press, 1999), 81–82.

51. Ibid., 94; James W. Ceaser and Andrew E. Busch, *Red over Blue* (Lanham, MD: Rowman and Littlefield, 2005), 137.

52. See Kevin Phillips, *American Theocracy* (New York: Viking, 2006), 186–90, and Blumenthal, *Pledging Allegiance*, 99.

53. Bob Jones University's website, quoted in an unsigned article: "The Tower of Babel: Bob Jones's Dating Tips," *New York Times*, March 5, 2000.

54. James W. Ceaser and Andrew E. Busch, *The Perfect Tie: The True Story of the 2000 Presidential Election* (New York: Rowman and Littlefield, 2001), 88–94.

55. Andrew Ward, "Democrats Miss the Dixieland Beat," *Financial Times*, November 14, 2006.

56. Scott Keeter, "Evangelicals and the GOP: an Update," Pew Research Center, October 18, 2006; "Elections 06: Big Change in Some Key Groups," Pew Research Center, November 16, 2008, www.pewresearch.org.

57. Christopher Shays, quoted in Phillips, *American Theocracy*, 217. Kevin Phillips observes that in 2004, the votes of the seven chief Republican leaders in the Senate conformed to the recommendations of the Christian Coalition 100 percent of the time.

58. Tom DeLay, quoted in Phillips, *American Theocracy*, 216.

59. Rabbi James Rudin, *The Baptizing of America* (New York: Thunder's Mouth Press, 2006).

60. In 2004, 81.5 percent of white evangelical Republicans thought Iraq had weapons of mass destruction, compared to 63 percent of nonevangelical Republicans, and 31 percent of all Democrats. See Gary C. Jacobson, *A Divider, Not a Uniter* (New York: Pearson, 2007), 153–57.

61. Morris P. Fiorina, *Culture Wars? The Myth of a Polarized America*, 2nd edition (New York: Pearson, 2006), 33–56.

62. Phillips, *American Theocracy*, 210.

8. The Wall of Separation Between Church and State

1. Régis Debray, "Êtes-vous démocrate ou républicain?" *Le Nouvel Observateur*, November 30, 1989, reprinted in *Contretemps: Éloges des idéaux perdus* (Paris: Gallimard, Folio, 1992), 23.

2. See, for example, Debray, *Contretemps*, 25, and Debray, *Le Feu sacré: Fonctions du religieux* (Paris: Fayard, 2003), 33.

3. Quoted in U.S. Treasury, "History of 'In God We Trust,'" www.treasury .gov/education/fact-sheets/currency/in-god-we-trust.shtml.

4. Act of April 22, 1864.

5. P. L. 84–10, July 30, 1956.

6. The 1892 version by Francis Bellamy read: "I pledge allegiance to my Flag and the Republic for which it stands, one nation, indivisible, with liberty and justice for all."

7. Law of June 14, 1954, emphasis added.

8. Eisenhower cited in *Newdow v. U.S. Congress*, Goodwin, J., 292 F. 3rd 597 (9th Cir. 2002).

9. Article 6 of the Constitution provides that "no religious Test shall ever be required as a Qualification to any Office or public Trust under the United States."

10. According to the remarks of a delegate to the North Carolina ratifying convention in 1788, reported by Stephen Botein, "Religious Dimensions of the Early American State," in *Beyond Confederation: Origins of the Constitution and American National Identity*, ed. Richard Beeman, Stephen Botein, and Edward C. Carter II (Chapel Hill: University of North Carolina Press, 1987), 321.

11. Amos Singletary, delegate to the Massachusetts ratifying convention, quoted by Albert Furtwangler, *The Authority of Publius* (Ithaca, NY: Cornell University Press, 1984), 108–9.

12. *New York Daily Advertiser*, quoted in Morton Borden, *Jews, Turks, and Infidels* (Chapel Hill: University of North Carolina Press, 1984), 16.

13. Ibid.

14. Articles from 1788 by "Elihu," quoted in Isaac Kramnick and R. Laurence Moore, *The Godless Constitution* (New York: Norton, 1996), 40.

15. William Van Murray, Esq., quoted in Kramnick and Moore, *The Godless Constitution*, 41.

16. John Adams, quoted in Kramnick and Moore, *The Godless Constitution*. On these questions, see also Susan Jacoby, *Freethinkers: A History of American Secularism* (New York: Henry Holt, 2005), 13–34.

17. Quoted in Ralph C. Reynolds, "In God We Trust: All Others Pay Cash," *Preserving the Wall* 3, no. 3, newsletter of the Rochester Chapter of Americans United for Separation of Church and State, http://candst.tripod.com/ingodwe.htm.

18. One example among dozens: in 1953, Vermont senator Ralph Flanders proposed this new wording for the preamble to the Constitution: "This Nation devoutly recognizes the authority and law of Jesus Christ, Saviour and Ruler of Nations through whom are bestowed the blessings of Almighty God."

19. Article 5 of the Constitution provides that amendments require approval by two-thirds of the members of both houses of Congress and three-quarters of the states.

20. *Moretum* is one of the minor poems of Virgil collected by Scaliger in 1573 in the *Appendix Vergiliana*. On the meaning of this poem, which foreshadows the American melting pot, see Denis Lacorne, *La Crise de l'identité américaine*, 2nd edition (Paris: Gallimard, 2003), 193–241.

21. Virgil, *Eclogues* 4, 5; *Georgics* 1, 40.

22. Walter Berns, *Making Patriots* (Chicago: University of Chicago Press, 2001), 32. Berns clearly shows the influence of Locke's *Letter Concerning Toleration* on the writings of the Founding Fathers, and on Jefferson in particular.

23. Jefferson, *Notes on the State of Virginia* (1785), in *Writings*, ed. Merrill D. Peterson (New York: Library of America, 1984), 285.

24. Article 4, Section 4 of the Constitution.

25. "Treaty of Peace and Friendship between the United States of America and the Bey and Subjects of Tripoli of Barbary," Yale Law School, *The Avalon Papers*, http://avalon.law.yale.edu/18th_century/bar1796t.asp, emphasis added.

26. *The Jefferson Bible: The Life and Morals of Jesus of Nazareth Extracted from the Gospels* (1804; Costa Mesa, CA: The Noontide Press, 1989), 134. A first draft was written by Jefferson in the White House with the title *The Philosophy of Jesus of Nazareth* in 1804. The complete version was finished in 1820 with the title *The Life and Morals of Jesus of Nazareth*. It was first published in 1895 by the National Museum in Washington, DC, and then reprinted by Congress in 1904 to commemorate the "Father" of the separation between church and state. Free copies were distributed to new members of Congress.

27. Jefferson, cited in Jaroslav Pelikan, "Believers-in-Chief," *New Republic*, September 4, 1995.

28. John Harris, "God gave us 'what we deserve,' Falwell says," *Washington Post*, September 14, 2001. On the secularization of American patriotism, see Denis Lacorne, "*God is Near*: L'instrumentalisation du religieux par le politique aux

États-Unis," in *Religion et politique: Une liaison dangereuse?*, ed. Thomas Ferenczi (Brussels: Complexe, 2003), 179–88.

29. According to a survey conducted in 2001, 29.4 million Americans had no religious affiliation or acknowledged denomination, amounting to 14 percent of the total population. In 1990, they had been only 14.3 million (8 percent of the population). Nonbelievers are thus a rapidly growing group. See Jacoby, *Freethinkers*, 6–7. In addition only 20 percent of Americans go to church at least once a week. Actual weekly observance is thus less than declared observance (more than 40 percent). See Bob Smietana, "Statistical Illusion," *Christianity Today*, April 2006, 85–88.

30. Here I am repeating and updating elements from the article "La séparation de l'Église et de l'État aux États-Unis," *Le Débat* 127 (Nov.–Dec. 2003), 63–79.

31. Quoted in Kramnick and Moore, *The Godless Constitution*, 54.

32. Quoted by Jean-Fabien Spitz in his introduction to John Locke, *Lettre sur la tolérance et autres textes* (Paris: Garnier-Flammarion, 1992), 40, n. 58.

33. Roger Williams, *Mr. Cotton's Letter, Lately Printed, Examined and Answered* (London, 1644), quoted in Philip Hamburger, *Separation of Church and State* (Cambridge, MA: Harvard University Press, 2002), 45. In this work, Williams was responding to John Cotton, a Massachusetts Congregationalist, who had written to him to justify the status of established Church granted by the English crown to the colony's Congregationalists.

34. See David Wootton, "Leveller Democracy and the Puritan Revolution," in *The Cambridge History of Political Thought, 1450–1700*, ed. J. H. Burns (Cambridge: Cambridge University Press, 1996), 436–44.

35. Ibid., 441.

36. Williams, *The Bloudy Tenent of Persecution*, quoted in Hamburger, *Separation of Church and State*, 44.

37. William, *Mister Cotton's Letter*, 44.

38. Kramnick and Moore, *The Godless Constitution*, chapter 3.

39. John Locke, "A Letter Concerning Toleration" (1686), in *The Selected Political Writings of John Locke*, ed. Paul E. Sigmund (New York: Norton, 2005), 129 and 138.

40. Ibid., 130 and 132.

41. Daniel L. Dreisbach, *Thomas Jefferson and the Wall of Separation between Church and State* (New York, New York University Press, 2002), 80 and 81.

42. The costly conduct of the wars of the British Empire justified certain exceptions to the rule: Catholic soldiers sent to the West Indies, Ireland, Canada, and North America, were exempted from the Protestant oath provided for in the Test Act.

43. See note 49.

44. Article "Laïcité," in *Nouveau Dictionnaire de pédagogie et d'instruction primaire*, ed. Ferdinand Buisson and James Guillaume (Paris: Hachette, 1911), http://laicite-aujourdhui.fr/spip.php?article47. This article repeats and expands the definition already given by Buisson in his *Dictionnaire de pédagogie et d'instruction primaire* (Paris: Hachette, 1882–87).

45. On the importance of Madison's petition, *Memorial and Remonstrance against Religious Assessments* (1785), see Akhil Reed Amar, *The Bill of Rights: Creation and Reconstruction* (New Haven: Yale University Press, 1998), 31.

46. "A Bill for Establishing Religious Freedom," in Jefferson, *Writings*, 346–47.

47. The first clause is generally known as the "establishment clause" (it would have been more logical to call it the "non-establishment clause"), and the second as the "free exercise clause" of the First Amendment.

48. Virginia was in advance of Connecticut and Massachusetts, which maintained oaths to established churches until 1818 and 1833 respectively.

49. "To Messrs. Nehemiah Dodge and Others, a Committee of the Danbury Baptist Association, in the State of Connecticut," January 1, 1802, in Jefferson, *Writings*, 510, emphasis added.

50. *Everson v. Board of Education of Ewing Township*, 330 U.S. 1, 18 (1947), emphasis added.

51. *Reynolds v. United States*, 98 U.S. 145, 167 (1879).

52. 98 U.S. at 164.

53. Dreisbach, *Thomas Jefferson and the Wall of Separation*, 100.

54. *Everson*, Jackson, dissenting, 330 U.S. at 19.

55. 330 U.S. at 18.

56. *Brief Amici Curiae* of the National Council of Catholic Men and the National Council of Catholic Women, *Everson v. Board of Education*, quoted in Dreisbach, *Thomas Jefferson and the Wall of Separation*, 101.

57. Stephen L. Carter, *The Culture of Disbelief: How American Law and Politics Trivialize Religious Devotion* (New York: Basic Books, 1993), 109, 272–73.

58. *Wallace v. Jaffree*, Rehnquist, J., dissenting, 472 U.S. 38, 107 (1985).

59. *Engel v. Vitale*, 370 U.S. 421 (1962); *School District of Abington Township v. Schempp*, 374 U.S. 203 (1963); *Wallace v. Jaffree*, 472 U.S. 38 (1985); *Lee v. Weisman*, 505 U.S. 577 (1992).

60. *County of Allegheny v. ACLU Greater Pittsburgh Chapter*, 492 U.S. 573 (1989). A crèche is tolerated if it is surrounded by secular objects or symbols such as a Christmas tree, a bear, reindeer, Santa Claus, and the like. See *Lynch v. Donnelly*, 465 U.S. 668 (1984).

61. *Stone v. Graham*, 449 U.S. 39 (1980); *McCreary County, Kentucky v. ACLU of Kentucky*, 545 U.S. 844 (2005).

62. *Zelman v. Simmons-Harris*, 536 U.S. 639 (2002). This kind of aid remains exceptional and is legally permitted in only a dozen states.

63. *Wisconsin v. Yoder*, 406 U.S. 205 (1972).

64. The sacrifices consisted of slitting the throats of a variety of animals, including pigeons, ducks, chickens, goats, sheep, and so on.

65. *Church of the Lukumi Babalu Aye, inc. v. City of Hialeah*, 508 U.S. 520 (1993). See generally David M. O'Brien, *Animal Sacrifice and Religious Freedom* (Lawrence: University Press of Kansas, 2004).

66. *Employment Division, Department of Human Resources of Oregon v. Smith*, 494 U.S. 872 (1990).

67. Religious Freedom Restoration Act (1993).

68. *McCreary County v. ACLU*, 545 U.S. 844, opinion of Justice Souter, citing Santa Fe Independent School Dist. v. Doe, 530 U. S. 290, 309–310 (2000), quoting Lynch v. Donnelly, 465 U. S. 668, 688 (1984) (O'Connor, J., concurring).

69. Elisabeth Zoller, "La laïcité aux États-Unis ou la séparation des Églises et de l'État dans la société pluraliste," in *La Conception américaine de la laïcité*, ed. Zoller (Paris: Dalloz, 2005), 12.

70. A lawyer by profession and an amateur Orientalist, George Sale (1697–1736) did not consider Mohammed the equivalent of Moses or Jesus Christ, but simply a great legislator in the tradition of Numa.

71. See Noah Feldman, *Divided by God: America's Church-State Problem and What We Should Do about It* (New York: Farrar, Straus, and Giroux, 2005); Christopher L. Eisgruber and Lawrence G. Sager, *Religious Freedom and the Constitution* (Cambridge,MA: Harvard University Press, 2007), Philip Hamburger, *Separation of Church and State* (Cambridge, MA: Harvard University Press, 2002) and, more generally, from a philosophical perspective: Kent Greenawalt, *Religion and the Constitution*, vol. 2, *Establishment and Fairness* (Princeton: Princeton University Press, 2008).

Epilogue

1. Barack Obama, "Call to Renewal" Keynote Address, *Sojourners News*, June 28, 2006, www.sojo.net/index.cfm?action=news.display_article&mode=C&NewsID =5454. The speech is reprinted in Barack Obama, *The Audacity of Hope* (New York: Crown, 2006).

2. Ibid.

3. Ibid.

4. Referring to Allen C. Guelzo, *Abraham Lincoln: Redeemer President* (Grand Rapids, MI: Eerdmans, 1990), Andrew Murphy explains: "Lincoln's biblically infused political rhetoric represented 'more a cultural habit rather than a religious one, to provide "lines to fit any occasion."' The sixteenth president always remained, in Guelzo's view, a child of the Enlightenment—indeed, 'our last Enlightenment politician'—who skillfully used religious symbols and biblical allusions in public utterances despite his own deep skepticism regarding questions of religious doctrine." Andrew R. Murphy, "Religion and the Presidency of Abraham Lincoln," in *Religion and the American Presidency*, ed. Gastón Espinosa (New York: Columbia University Press, 2009), 152.

5. Obama, "Call to Renewal" Keynote Address.

6. Lincoln was never a member of a Christian church. On his ambivalence toward religion, his "civil theology," his "rationalistic 'political religion,'" his enthusiastic reading of the works of Paine and Volney, and his alleged infidelity, see Murphy, "Religion and the Presidency of Abraham Lincoln," 153–58.

7. Barack Obama, Inaugural Address, www.whitehouse.gov/blog/inauguraladdress. In his "Call to Renewal" Keynote Address two years earlier, Obama had gone even further: "Whatever we once were, *we are no longer just a Christian nation*; we are also a Jewish nation, a Muslim nation, a Buddhist nation, a Hindu nation, and a nation of non-believers." Emphasis added.

8. Laura Meckler, "Obama Walks Religious Tightrope Spanning Faithful, Nonbelievers," *Wall Street Journal*, March 24, 2009.

9. Obama, quoted in Meckler, "Obama Walks Religious Tightrope," (according to his declaration at the February 2009 National Prayer Breakfast).

10. In a speech to the African Methodist Episcopal Convention in St. Louis in July 2008, Obama referred to his experience as a community organizer in Chicago and his salvation experience: "I let Jesus Christ into my life. I learned that my sins could be redeemed and if I placed my trust in Jesus, that he could set me on a path to eternal life." Quoted in John W. Kennedy, "Preach and Reach: Despite his liberal record, Barack Obama is making a lot of evangelicals think twice," *Christianity Today* 52, no. 10 (October 2008): 30. In his "Call to Renewal" Keynote Address in June 2006, Obama presented a somewhat different conversion narrative: "Faith doesn't mean that you don't have doubts. You need to come to church precisely because you have sins to wash away—because you are human and need an ally in your difficult journey."

11. This assertion, which was accepted as obvious at the time, was based on an erroneous reading of the exit polls conducted on Election Day in 2004. In fact,

according to D. Sunshine Hillygus and Todd G. Shields, "the values voter explanation appears to be only a very minor part of the citizens' voting calculus in the 2004 presidential election.... Among the most decisive groups—Independents and respondents in battleground states—gay marriage and abortion had no impact on individual vote choice once other factors were controlled for.... Values-based appeals only served to reinforce Bush's support among those already planning to vote for him, but failed to persuade new voters." Quoted in Morris P. Fiorina et al., *Culture War? The Myth of a Polarized America*, 2nd ed. (New York: Pearson Education, 2006), 156.

12. "Kneeling beneath that cross on the South Side of Chicago, I felt I heard *God's spirit* beckoning me. I submitted myself to His will, and dedicated myself to discovering His truth." Obama, "Call to Renewal" Keynote Address, emphasis added.

13. "Barack Obama's Speech on Race," *New York Times*, March 18, 2008.

14. Ibid.

15. According to Cizik, who attended an informal meeting with forty Christian leaders hosted by Obama in Chicago in June 2008, it was the first time in twenty-eight years that a Democratic presidential candidate had requested a meeting with an NAE official. See Kennedy, "Preach and Reach," 28. For a comprehensive analysis of Obama's outreach program and his 2008 electoral performance among religious voters, see Gastón Espinosa, "Religion, Race, and the 2008 Presidential Election," in *Religion, Race and the American Presidency*, ed. Espinosa, 2nd ed. (Lanham, MD: Rowman and Littlefield, 2010), 275–84.

16. Obama was first invited to meet Rick Warren at Saddleback Church in 2006 to discuss ways of fighting the AIDS crisis. He was again invited on August 16, 2008, with John McCain, to participate in a presidential forum on religion. Heavily criticized by the religious right for having invited a supporter of abortion rights, Rick Warren answered his critics: "I'm a pastor not a politician.... People always say: 'Rick, are you right-wing or left-wing?' I say 'I'm for the whole bird.'" See E. J. Dionne Jr., "A Gamble for Obama," *Washington Post*, December 23, 2008. In 2008, Warren was invited to deliver the invocation at Obama's inauguration.

17. Amy Chozick and Douglas Belkin, "Obama Courts Religious Vote in Appalachian Ohio," *Wall Street Journal*, July 2, 2008.

18. All the data referred to are from 2004 and 2008 exit polls as reported in "Pew Forum: How the Faithful Voted," November 10, 2008, http://pewforum .org/docs/?DocID=367.

19. Obama, "Call to Renewal" Keynote Address.

20. Ibid.

21. Presidential Candidates Forum, Saddleback Church, August 16, 2008, http://www.clipsandcomment.com/2008/08/17/full-transcript-saddleback-presidential-forum-sen-barack-obama-john-mccain-moderated-by-rick-warren/.

22. Aurelio Lopez, "Obama Rejects Proposed California Gay Marriage Ban," *Sacramento Bee*, July 1, 2008. For a complete analysis of the electoral campaign around Proposition 8, see Kenneth P. Miller, "The Democratic Coalition's Religious Divide: Why California Voters Supported Obama but not Same Sex Marriage," *Revue Française d'Études Américaines* 119 (2009): 42–62. As Miller points out, "The Yes-on-8 campaign also used Barack Obama to their advantage. The campaign sent a recorded telephone message to Democratic voters. The message began with a voice saying, 'Here is Barack Obama in his own words on the definition of marriage.' Obama's voice could then be heard: 'I believe marriage is a union between a man and a woman.' Another voice then urged the listener to vote yes on Proposition 8." It should also be noted that according to the NEP national exit poll, the great majority of the California ethnic electorate voted in favor of Proposition 8: 70 percent of African-American voters and 53 percent of Latinos supported the Proposition. But overall, only 36 percent of Democrats voted for it. It was approved by a margin of 52.3 percent in favor against 47.7 percent opposed.

23. "Obama's Speech in Cairo," *New York Times*, June 4, 2009. But Obama did not quote the preceding passage of the Treaty of Tripoli, analyzed in chapter 8: "*As the government of the United States of America is not in any sense founded on the Christian religion,*—as it has in itself no character of enmity against the laws, religion or tranquility of Musselmen,—and as the said States never have entered into any war or act of hostility against any Mehomitan nation, it is declared. . . ." Emphasis added.

24. Ibid.

25. Marwan Kabalan, Professor of Political Science at Damascus University, quoted in Isabel Kershner, Robert Worth, and Michael Slackman, "A Word for Every Flavor of Mideast Opinion," *New York Times*, June 5, 2009.

26. Gilles Kepel, "Barack Obama a fait de l'islam une religion américaine," *Le Monde*, June 5, 2009.

27. On the lack of neutrality of faith-based programs that favor the dominant evangelical churches over small ones (or synagogues or mosques), and the likelihood that such programs could coerce and proselytize social service recipients, see Kent Greenawalt, *Religion and the Constitution*, vol. 2, *Establishment and Fairness* (Princeton: Princeton University Press, 2008), 369–78.

28. For such a perspective, see Kent Greenawalt, *Religion and the Constitution*, and Noah Feldman, *Divided by God: America's Church-State Problem—and What We Should Do About It* (New York: Farrar, Straus and Giroux, 2005), 235–51.

29. As argued by Noah Feldman, "Acknowledging holidays like the Muslim Eid or the Hindu Divali in what has traditionally been a Christian country may validate a sense of belonging like no secular civic symbol can" (Feldman, *Divided by God*, 242–43).

30. Obama, "Call to Renewal" Keynote Address.

BIBLIOGRAPHY

Ahlstrom, Sidney E. *A Religious History of the American People.* New Haven: Yale University Press, 1972.

Aikman, David. *A Man of Faith: The Spiritual Journey of George W. Bush.* Nashville, TN: W Publishing Group, 2004.

Amar, Akhil Reed. *America's Constitution: A Biography.* New York: Random House, 2006.

————. *The Bill of Rights: Creation and Reconstruction.* New Haven: Yale University Press, 1998.

Anbinder, Tyler. *Nativism and Slavery: The Northern Know Nothings and the Politics of the 1850s.* New York: Oxford University Press, 1992.

Antoine, Agnès. *L'Impensé de la démocratie: Tocqueville, la citoyenneté et la religion.* Paris: Fayard, 2003.

Appleby, Joyce, Lynn Hunt, and Margaret Jacob. *Telling the Truth About History.* New York: Norton, 1994.

Armitage, David. *The Declaration of Independence: A Global History.* Cambridge, MA: Harvard University Press, 2007.

Aron, Robert, and Arnaud Dandieu. *Le Cancer américain.* Paris: Rieder, 1931.

————. *Décadence de la nation française.* Paris: Rieder, 1931.

Baird, Robert. *Religion in America, or, An Account of the Origin, Progress, Relation to the State, and Present Condition of the Evangelical Churches in the United States.* New York: Harper and Brothers, 1844.

Balmer, Randall. *God in the White House: How Faith Shaped the Presidency from John F. Kennedy to George W. Bush.* San Francisco: HarperOne, 2008.

————. *The Making of Evangelicalism: From Revivalism to Politics and Beyond.* Waco, TX: Baylor University Press, 2010.

Bancroft, George. *History of the United States.* 1834. London: Routledge, 1864.

————. *History of the United States of America.* 10 vols. Boston: Little, Brown, 1854–1878.

Baubérot, Jean. *Laïcité, 1905–2005: Entre passion et raison.* Paris: Seuil, 2004.

————. *La morale laïque contre l'ordre moral.* Paris: Seuil, 1997.

Baudoin, Jean and Philippe Portier, eds. *La Laïcité, une valeur d'aujourd'hui ?* Rennes: Presses Universitaires de Rennes, 2001.

Bauer, Susan. *The Art of the Public Grovel: Sexual Sin and Public Confession in America.* Princeton: Princeton University Press, 2008.

Bayard, Ferdinand-Marie. *Voyage dans l'intérieur des États-Unis, à Bath, Winchester, dans la vallée de Shenandoha, etc., pendant l'été de 1791.* Paris: Cocheris, an V [1797].

Beaumont, Gustave de. *Marie, ou l'Esclavage aux États-Unis.* 4th ed. Paris: Gosselin, 1850.

Beauvoir, Simone de. *America Day by Day.* Translated by Carol Cosman. Berkeley: University of California Press, 1999.

Beeman, Richard, Stephen Botein, and Edward C. Carter II, eds. *Beyond Confederation: Origins of the Constitution and American National Identity.* Chapel Hill: University of North Carolina Press, 1987.

Bellah, Robert N. *The Broken Covenant: American Civil Religion in Time of Trial.* 2nd ed. Chicago: University of Chicago Press, 1992.

————. "Civil Religion in America." *Daedalus* 96, no. 1 (Winter 1967): 1–21.

Ben Barka, Mokhtar. *La Droite chrétienne américaine: Les évangéliques à la Maison-Blanche?* Toulouse: Privat, 2006.

Bénichou, Paul. *Romantismes français.* 2 vols. Paris: Gallimard, Quarto, 2004.

Bennett, William J. *The Death of Outrage: Bill Clinton and the Assault on American Ideals.* New York: Free Press, 1998.

Bercovitch, Sacvan. *The American Jeremiad.* Madison: University of Wisconsin Press, 1978.

Berger, Peter L. *The Sacred Canopy: Elements of a Sociological Theory of Religion.* New York: Random House, 1990.

Bernanos, Georges. *Essais et écrits de combat.* Edited by Michel Estève. Paris: Gallimard, Bibliothèque de la Pléiade, 1995.

———. *La Liberté pour quoi faire?* 7th ed. Paris: Gallimard, 1953.

Berns, Walter. *Making Patriots.* Chicago: University of Chicago Press, 2001.

Bertrand, Jean-Claude. *Les Églises aux États-Unis.* Paris: PUF, 1975.

Billington, Ray. *The Protestant Crusade, 1800–1860: A Study of the Origins of American Nativism.* Chicago: Quadrangle Books, 1938.

Birnbaum, Pierre. *"La France aux Français": Histoire des haines nationalistes.* Paris: Seuil, 1993.

Black, Earl, and Merle Black. *Divided America: The Ferocious Power Struggle in American Politics.* New York: Simon and Schuster, 2007.

———. *The Rise of Southern Republicans.* Cambridge, MA: Harvard University Press, 2002.

Bloom, Harold. *The American Religion: The Emergence of the Post-Christian Nation.* New York: Simon and Schuster, 1992.

Bork, Robert H. *Slouching Towards Gomorrah: Modern Liberalism and American Decline.* New York: Harper Collins, 1996.

Boutmy, Émile. *Élements d'une psychologie politique du peuple américain.* Paris: Armand Colin, 1902.

———. *Essai d'une psychologie politique du peuple anglais au XIXe siècle.* Paris: Armand Colin, 1901.

Boyer, Paul. *When Time Shall Be No More: Prophecy Belief in Modern American Culture.* Cambridge, MA: Harvard University Press, 1992.

Bradford, William, *Histoire de la colonie de Plymouth: Chroniques du Nouveau Monde (1620–1647).* Edited by Lauric Henneton. Geneva: Labor et Fides, 2004.

Brekus, Catherine A. *Strangers and Pilgrims: Female Preaching in America, 1740–1845.* Chapel Hill: University of North Carolina Press, 1998.

Bristed, John. *Histoire des États-Unis d'Amérique: Tableau des mœurs et usages les plus remarquables des habitants du nouveau monde.* 2nd ed. Paris: n. p., 1832.

Broadie, Alexander, ed. *The Cambridge Companion to the Scottish Enlightenment.* Cambridge: Cambridge University Press, 2003.

Brown, Stewart J., ed. *William Robertson and the Expansion of Empire.* Cambridge: Cambridge University Press, 1997.

Bruce, Steve. *The Rise and Fall of the New Christian Right.* New York: Oxford University Press, 1988.

Brunetière, Ferdinand. "Le catholicisme aux États-Unis." *Revue des Deux Mondes,* November 1898.

Buisson, Ferdinand, and James Guillaume, eds. *Nouveau Dictionnaire de pédagogie et d'instruction primaire.* Paris: Hachette, 1911.

Burns, J. H., ed. *The Cambridge History of Political Thought, 1450–1700.* Cambridge: Cambridge University Press, 1996.

Bush, George W. *A Charge to Keep.* New York: William Morrow, 1999.

Bushman, Richard L. *From Puritan to Yankee: Character and Social Order in Connecticut, 1690–1765.* Cambridge, MA: Harvard University Press, 1967.

Butler, Jon. *Becoming America: The Revolution Before 1776.* Cambridge, MA: Harvard University Press, 2000.

Carpenter, Joel. *Revive Us Again: The Reawakening of American Fundamentalism.* New York: Oxford University Press, 1997.

Carter, Stephen L. *The Culture of Disbelief: How American Law and Politics Trivialize Religious Devotion.* New York: Basic Books, 1993.

———. *God's Name in Vain: The Wrongs and Rights of Religion in Politics.* New York: Basic Books, 2000.

Carwardine, Richard J. *Evangelicals and Politics in Antebellum America.* New Haven: Yale University Press, 1993.

Ceaser, James W. *Nature and History in American Political Development: A Debate.* Cambridge, MA: Harvard University Press, 2006.

———. *Red over Blue.* Lanham, MD: Rowman and Littlefield, 2005.

Ceaser, James W., and Andrew E. Busch. *The Perfect Tie: The True Story of the 2000 Presidential Election.* Lanham, MD: Rowman and Littlefield, 2001.

Céline, Louis-Ferdinand. *Journey to the End of the Night.* Translated by Ralph Manheim. New York: New Directions, 1983.

Chastellux, François-Jean, marquis de. *Voyages dans l'Amérique septentrionale dans les années 1780, 1781 et 1782,* 2 vols. Paris: Prault, 1786.

Chateaubriand, François-René de. *Essai historique, politique et moral sur les révolutions anciennes et modernes, considérées dans leurs rapports avec la Révolution française de nos jours,* in *Essai sur les Révolutions. Génie du christianisme.* Paris: Gallimard, Bibliothèque de la Pléiade, 1978.

———. *Mémoires d'outre-tombe,* 2 vols. Paris: Le Livre de poche, 1973.

———. *Voyage en Amérique,* in *Œuvres romanesques et voyages,* vol. 1, edited by Maurice Regard. Paris: Gallimard, Bibliothèque de la Pléiade, 1969.

Chevalier, Michel. *Lettres sur l'Amérique du Nord,* 2 vols. Paris: Charles Gosselin, 1836.

————. *Society, Manners and Politics in the United States: Being a Series of Letters on North America.* Boston: Weeks, Jordan and Co., 1839.

Chinard, Gilbert. *L'Amérique et le rêve exotique dans la littérature française au XVIIe et au XVIIIe siècle.* Paris: Droz, 1934.

Clark, J. C. D. *The Language of Liberty, 1660–1832.* Cambridge: Cambridge University Press, 1994.

Clavière, Étienne, and Jacques-Pierre Brissot de Warville. *De la France et des États-Unis ou De l'importance de la révolution de l'Amérique pour le bonheur de la France* (1787) Paris: Éditions du Comité des Travaux Historiques et Scientifiques, 1996.

Clinton, Bill. *My Life.* New York: Knopf, 2004.

Colosimo, Jean-François. *Dieu est américain: De la théodémocratie aux États-Unis.* Paris: Fayard, 2006.

Compagnon, Antoine. *Les Antimodernes: De Joseph de Maistre à Roland Barthes.* Paris: Gallimard, 2005.

Conkin, Paul. "The Religious Pilgrimage of Thomas Jefferson," in *Jeffersonian Legacies,* ed. Peter Onuf. Charlottesville: University of Virginia Press, 1995.

Cracknell, Kenneth, and Susan White. *An Introduction to World Methodism.* Cambridge: Cambridge University Press, 2005.

Crèvecœur, J. Hector St. John de. *Letters from an American Farmer* and *Sketches of Eighteenth-Century America.* New York: Penguin, 1981.

Crouzet, Denis. *Jean Calvin.* Paris: Fayard, 2000.

Daniels, Bruce, C. *Puritans at Play.* New York: St. Martin's Press, 1995.

Davis, David Brion. *Revolutions: Reflections on American Equality and Foreign Liberations.* Cambridge, MA: Harvard University Press, 1990.

Dawson, Jan C. *The Unusable Past: America's Puritan Tradition, 1830 to 1930.* Chico, CA: Scholars Press, 1984.

Debray, Régis. *Éloges des idéaux perdus.* Paris: Gallimard, Folio, 1992.

————. *Le Feu sacré: Fonctions du religieux.* Paris: Fayard, 2003.

Decugis, Henri. *Le Destin des races blanches.* Paris: Librairie de France, 1936.

Deetz, James, and Patricia Scott Deetz. *The Times of Their Lives: Life, Love, and Death in Plymouth Colony.* New York: W. H. Freeman, 2000.

Delbanco, Andrew. *The Puritan Ordeal.* Cambridge, MA: Harvard University Press, 1989.

————. *The Real American Dream.* Cambridge, MA: Harvard University Press, 1999.

Démeunier, ed. *Encyclopédie méthodique: Économie politique et diplomatique,* 4 vols. Paris: Panckoucke, 1784–88.

D'Emilio, John, and Estella B. Freedman. *Intimate Matters: A History of Sexuality in America*. Chicago: University of Chicago Press, 1997.

Diderot, Denis, and Jean le Rond d'Alembert, eds. *Encyclopédie ou Dictionnaire raisonné des sciences, des arts et des métiers*, 17 vols. http://portail.atilf.fr/encyclopedie.

Dionne, E. J. *Souled Out: Reclaiming Faith and Politics after the Religious Right*. Princeton: Princeton University Press, 2008.

Dionne, E. J., and Ming Hsu Chen, eds. *Sacred Places, Civic Purposes: Should Government Help Faith-Based Charity?* Washington, DC: Brookings Institution Press, 2001.

Dolan, Jay P. *The American Catholic Experience*. Notre Dame, IN: University of Notre Dame Press, 1992.

Dreisbach, Daniel L. *Thomas Jefferson and the Wall of Separation between Church and State* New York: New York University Press, 2002.

Dubreuil, Hyacinthe. *Standards: Le travail américain vu par un ouvrier français* Paris: Grasset, 1929.

Duhamel, Georges. *America the Menace: Scenes from the Life of the Future*. Translated by Charles Miner Thompson. London: Allen & Unwin, 1931.

Echeverria, Durand. *Mirage in the West: A History of the French Image of American Society to 1815*, 2nd ed. Princeton: Princeton University Press, 1968.

Eck, Diana L. *A New Religious America: How a "Christian Country Has Become the World's Most Religiously Diverse Nation*. San Francisco: Harper San Francisco, 2001.

Egerton, John. *The Americanization of Dixie: The Southernization of America*. New York: Harper and Row, 1974.

Eichthal, Eugène d'. "Tocqueville et 'La démocratie en Amérique.'" *Revue politique et parlementaire* (April-May 1896).

Eisenach, Eldon J. *The Next Religious Establishment: National Identity and Political Theology in Post-Protestant America*. Lanham, MD: Rowman and Littlefield, 2000.

Eisgruber, Christopher L., and Lawrence G. Sager. *Religious Freedom and the Constitution*. Cambridge, MD: Harvard University Press, 2007.

Espinosa, Gastón, ed. *Religion and the American Presidency: George Washington to George W. Bush*. New York: Columbia University Press, 2009.

———. *Religion, Race, and the American Presidency*. 2nd ed. Lanham, MD: Rowman and Littlefield, 2010.

Fackre, Gabriel, ed. *Judgment Day at the White House*. Grand Rapids, MI: Eerdmans, 1999.

Fath, Sébastien. *Billy Graham, pape protestant?* Paris: Albin Michel, 2002.

———. *Dieu bénisse l'Amérique: La religion de la Maison-Blanche*. Paris: Seuil, 2004.

Favre, Pierre. *Naissance de la science politique en France, 1870–1914.* Paris: Fayard, 1989.

Feldman, Noah. *Divided by God.* New York: Farrar, Straus and Giroux, 2005.

Ferry, Luc, and Marcel Gauchet. *Le Religieux après la religion.* Paris: Grasset, 2004.

Finke, Roger, and Rodney Stark. *The Churching of America, 1776–2005: Winners and Losers in Our Religious Economy.* New Brunswick, NJ: Rutgers University Press, 2006.

Fiorina, Morris P. *Culture Wars? The Myth of a Polarized America,* 2nd edition. New York: Pearson, 2006.

Foster, Gaines M. *Moral Reconstruction: Christian Lobbyists and the Federal Legislation of Morality, 1865–1920.* Chapel Hill: University of North Carolina Press, 2002.

Fowler, Robert Booth, et al. *Religion and Politics in America,* 3rd ed. Boulder, CO: Westview, 2004.

Fox, Richard Wightman. *Jesus in America: Personal Savior, Cultural Hero, National Obsession.* New York: Harper Collins, 2003.

Fraser, James W. *Between Church and State: Religion and Public Education in a Multicultural America.* New York: St. Martin's Press, 1999.

Furet, François. *Penser le XXe siècle.* Paris: Laffont, Bouquins, 2007.

Furtwangler, Albert. *The Authority of Publius.* Ithaca, NY: Cornell University Press, 1984.

Gauchet, Marcel. *The Disenchantment of the World.* Translated by Oscar Burge. Princeton: Princeton University Press, 1997.

——. *La Religion dans la démocratie: Parcours de la laïcité.* Paris: Gallimard, 1998.

——. *La Révolution des droits de l'homme.* Paris: Gallimard, 1989.

Gaustad, Edwin S. *Proclaim Liberty Throughout the Land: A History of Church and State in America.* New York: Oxford University Press, 2003.

Gentile, Emilio. *Les Religions de la politique: Entre démocraties et totalitarismes.* Paris: Seuil, 2001.

Gerstle, Gary. *American Crucible: Race and Nation in the Twentieth Century.* Princeton, Princeton University Press, 2001.

Gisel, Pierre, ed. *Encyclopédie du protestantisme.* Geneva: Labor et Fides, 1995.

Gleason, Philip. *Speaking of Diversity.* Baltimore: Johns Hopkins University Press, 1992.

Godbeer, Richard. *Sexual Revolution in Early America.* Baltimore: Johns Hopkins University Press, 2002.

Grant, Madison. *The Passing of the Great Race or the Racial Basis of European History.* New York: Charles Scribner's Sons, 1916.

Greenawalt, Kent. *Religion and the Constitution,* vol. 2, *Establishment and Fairness.* Princeton: Princeton University Press, 2008.

Greene, Jack P. *The Intellectual Construction of America: Exceptionalism and Identity from 1492 to 1800.* Chapel Hill: University of North Carolina Press, 1993.

——. *Pursuits of Happiness: The Social Development of Early Modern British Colonies and the Formation of American Culture.* Chapel Hill: University of North Carolina Press, 1988.

Guizot, François. *General History of Civilization in Europe.* Edited by G. W. Knight. 1842. New York: Appleton, 1896.

Hamburger, Philip. *Separation of Church and State.* Cambridge, MA: Harvard University Press, 2002.

Handlin, Lilian. *George Bancroft: The Intellectual as Democrat.* New York: Harper and Row, 1984.

Harding, Susan Friend. *The Book of Jerry Falwell: Fundamentalist Language and Politics.* Princeton: Princeton University Press, 2000.

Hartog, François. *Régimes d'historicité: Présentisme et expérience du temps.* Paris: Seuil, 2003.

Hatch, Nathan O. *The Democratization of American Christianity.* New Haven: Yale University Press, 1989.

Heclo, Hugh, and Wilfred Mc Clay, eds. *Religion Returns to the Public Square: Faith and Policy in America.* Baltimore: Johns Hopkins University Press, 2003.

Heclo, Hugh, et al. *Christianity and American Democracy.* Cambridge, MA: Harvard University Press, 2007.

Heidegger, Martin. *An Introduction to Metaphysics.* Translated by Gregory Fried and Richard Polt. New Haven: Yale University Press, 2000.

——. "The Origin of the Work of Art," in *Basic Writings.* Edited by David Farrell Krell. New York: Harper & Row, 1977.

Heimert, Alan, and Andrew Delbanco, eds. *The Puritans in America: A Narrative Anthology.* Cambridge, MA: Harvard University Press, 1985.

Henneton, Lauric. *Liberté, inégalité, autorité: Politique, société et construction identitaire du Massachusetts au XVIIe siècle.* 2 vols. Paris: Honoré Champion, 2009.

Herberg, Will. *Protestant, Catholic, Jew: An Essay in American Religious Sociology.* Chicago: University of Chicago Press, 1995.

Hervieu-Léger, Danièle. *Le Pélerin et le converti.* Paris: Flammarion, 1999.

——. *La Religion en miettes ou la Question des sectes.* Paris: Calmann-Lévy, 2001.

Heyrman, Christine Leigh. *Southern Cross: The Beginnings of the Bible Belt.* Chapel Hill: University of North Carolina Press, 1997.

Higham, John. *Strangers in the Land: Patterns of American Nativism, 1860–1925.* 2nd ed. New Brunswick, NJ: Rutgers University Press, 1988.

Himmelfarb, Gertrude. *The De-moralization of Society: From Victorian virtues to Modern Values.* New York: Knopf, 1995.

Hofstadter, Richard. *The Paranoid Style in American Politics.* New York: Knopf, 1965.

———. *Social Darwinism in American Thought.* Boston: Beacon Press, 1964.

Homes, David L. *The Religion of the Founding Fathers.* Charlottesville, VA: Ash Lawn- Highland, 2003.

Horn, James, Jan Ellen Lewis, and Peter S. Onuf, eds. *The Revolution of 1800: Democracy, Race, and the New Republic.* Charlottesville: University of Virginia Press, 2002.

Hudson, Deal W. *Onward Christian Soldiers: The Growing Political Power of Catholics and Evangelicals.* New York: Threshold Editions, 2008.

Huntington, Samuel P. *Who Are We? The Challenges to America's National Identity.* New York: Simon and Schuster, 2004.

Hutchison, William. *Religious Pluralism in America: The Contentious History of a Founding Ideal.* New Haven: Yale University Press, 2003.

Jacobson, Gary C. *A Divider, Not a Uniter: George W. Bush and the American People.* New York: Pearson, 2007.

Jacoby, Susan. *Freethinkers: A History of American Secularism.* New York: Henry Holt, 2005.

Jefferson, Thomas. *The Jefferson Bible: The Life and Morals of Jesus of Nazareth Extracted from the Gospels.* Costa Mesa, CA: Noontide Press, 1989.

———. *Writings.* Edited by Merrill D. Peterson. New York: Library of America, 1984.

Johnson, Paul E. *A Shopkeeper's Millennium: Society and Revivals in Rochester, New York, 1815–1837.* New York: Hill and Wang, 1994.

Judt, Tony. *Past Imperfect: French Intellectuals, 1944–1956.* Berkeley: University of California Press, 1992.

Judt, Tony, and Denis Lacorne, eds. *Language, Nation, and State: Identity Politics in a Multilingual Age.* New York: Palgrave Macmillan, 2004.

Kadux, Joke, and Eduard Van de Bilt. *Newcomers in an Old City: The American Pilgrims in Leiden, 1609–1620.* Leiden: Burgersdikj & Niermans, 2007.

Kengor, Paul. *God and George W. Bush.* New York: Harper Collins, 2004.

King, Desmond. *Making Americans: Immigration, Race, and the Origins of the Diverse Democracy.* Cambridge, MA: Harvard University Press, 2000.

Kinsey, Alfred, et al. *Sexual Behavior in the Human Female.* Philadelphia: W. B. Saunders, 1953.

———. *Sexual Behavior in the Human Male.* Philadelphia: W. B. Saunders, 1948.

Kramnick, Isaac, ed. *The Portable Enlightenment Reader.* New York: Penguin, 1995.

Kramnick, Isaac, and R. Laurence Moore. *The Godless Constitution: The Case Against Religious Correctness.* New York: Norton, 1996.

Kuru, Ahmed. *Secularism and State Policies Toward Religion: The United States, France, and Turkey*. New York: Cambridge University Press, 2009.

La Rochefoucauld-Liancourt, François Alexandre Frédéric, duc de. *Voyage dans les États-Unis d'Amérique, fait en 1795, 1796 et 1797*, 8 vols. Paris: Du Pont, an VII [1799].

La Tour Du Pin, marquise de. *Memoirs of Madame de La Tour du Pin*. Edited and translated by Felice Harcourt. London: Harvill, 1969.

Laboulaye, Édouard. *Histoire des États-Unis*. Paris: Charpentier, 1866.

Lacorne, Denis, Jacques Rupnik, and Marie-France Toinet, eds., *The Rise and Fall of Anti-Americanism: A Century of French Perception*. Translated by Gerry Turner. London: Macmillan, 1990.

Lacorne, Denis. *La Crise de l'identité américaine: Du melting-pot au multiculturalisme*, 2nd ed. Paris: Gallimard, Tel, 2003.

———, ed. *Les États-Unis*. Paris: Fayard, 2006

———. *L'Invention de la République américaine*. 2nd ed. Paris: Hachette, 2003.

Lambert, Frank. *The Founding Fathers and the Place of Religion in America*. Princeton: Princeton University Press, 2003.

Lamberti, Jean-Claude. *Tocqueville et les deux démocraties*. Paris: PUF, 1983.

Lecourt, Dominique. *L'Amérique entre la Bible et Darwin*. Paris: PUF, 1992.

Lehmann, Hartmut, and Guenther Roth, eds. *Weber's Protestant Ethic: Origins, Evidence, Contexts*. Cambridge: Cambridge University Press, 1993.

Leites, Edmund. *The Puritan Conscience and Modern Sexuality*. New Haven: Yale University Press, 1986.

Leroy-Beaulieu, Pierre. *The United States in the Twentieth Century*. Translated by H. Addington Bruce. New York: Funk & Wagnalls, 1906.

Lévy, Bernard-Henri. *American Vertigo: Traveling America in the Footsteps of Tocqueville*. New York: Random House, 2006.

Lieven, Anatol. *America Right or Wrong: An Anatomy of American Nationalism*. New York: Oxford University Press, 2004.

Locke, John. *A Letter Concerning Toleration*, in *The Selected Political Writings of John Locke*. Ed. Paul E. Sigmund. New York: Norton, 2005.

———. *Lettre sur la tolérance et autres textes*. Edited by Jean-Fabien Spitz. Paris: Garnier- Flammarion, 1992.

Loubet del Bayle, Jean-Louis. *Les Non-Conformistes des années 30*. Paris: Seuil, 1969.

Lowe, Janet, ed. *Billy Graham Speaks: Insight from the World's Greatest Preacher*. New York: Wiley, 1999.

Macedo, Stephen. *Diversity and Distrust: Civic Education in a Multicultural Democracy*. Cambridge, MA: Harvard University Press, 2000.

Madison, James, Alexander Hamilton, and John Jay. *The Federalist Papers*. Edited by Isaac Kramnick. Harmondsworth, UK: Penguin, 1987.

Maistre, Joseph de. *Considérations sur la France.* 1797. Brussels: Complexe, 1988.

Manent, Pierre. *La Cité de l'homme.* Paris: Fayard, 1994.

———. *Tocqueville and the Nature of Democracy.* Translated by John Waggoner. Lanham, MD: Rowman and Littlefield, 1996.

Mann, Horace. *Lectures on Education.* Boston: Ide & Dutton, 1855.

———. *The Republic and the School: Horace Mann on the Education of Free Men.* Edited by Lawrence Cremin. New York: Teachers College, Columbia University, 1957.

Mansfield, Harvey. *America's Constitutional Soul.* Baltimore, MD: Johns Hopkins University Press, 1991.

Mansfield, Stephen. *The Faith of George W. Bush.* New York: Penguin, 2003.

Marienstras, Élise. *Nous, le peuple: Les origines du nationalisme américain.* Paris: Gallimard, 1988.

Marlin, George, J. *The American Catholic Voter.* South Bend, IN: St. Augustine Press, 2004.

Marsden, George M. *Fundamentalism and American Culture.* 2nd ed. New York: Oxford University Press, 2006.

———. *Jonathan Edwards: A Life.* New Haven: Yale University Press, 2003.

Marshall, John. *A History of the Colonies Planted by the English on the Continent of North America.* Philadelphia: Abraham Small, 1824.

Martin, Jean-Pierre. *La Vertu par la loi: La prohibition aux États-Unis, 1920–1933.* Dijon: Éditions Universitaires de Dijon, 1993.

Marty, Martin E. *Modern American Religion, 1893–1941.* 2 vols. Chicago: University of Chicago Press, 1997.

Marty, Martin E., and R. Scott Appleby, eds. *The Fundamentalism Project.* 4 vols. Chicago: University of Chicago Press, 1991–94.

Massa, Mark S. *Anti-Catholicism in America: The Last Acceptable Prejudice.* New York: Crossroad, 2003.

Mathews, Donald G. *Religion in the Old South.* Chicago: University of Chicago Press, 1977.

McGreevy, John T. *Catholicism and American Freedom.* New York: Norton, 2003.

McLoughlin, William G. *Revivals, Awakenings, and Reform.* Chicago: University of Chicago Press, 1980.

Meacham, Jon. *American Gospel: God, the Founding Fathers, and the Making of a Nation.* New York: Random House, 2006.

Melandri, Pierre. *Reagan, une biographie totale.* Paris: Laffont, 1998.

Mélonio, Françoise. *Tocqueville et les Français.* Paris: Aubier, 1993.

Michelot, Vincent. *L'Empereur de la Maison-Blanche.* Paris: Armand Colin, 2004.

Miller, Donald E. *Reinventing American Protestantism: Christianity in the New Millennium.* Berkeley: University of California Press, 1997.

Miller, Perry, *Jonathan Edwards.* Cleveland: World, 1959.

———. *The Life of the Mind in America: From the Revolution to the Civil War.* New York: Harcourt, Brace and World, 1965.

———. *The New England Mind.* 2 vols. 1939. Cambridge, MA: Harvard University Press, 1982.

Miller, Perry, and Thomas H. Johnson, eds. *The Puritans: A Sourcebook of Their Writings.* New York: Harper, 1963.

Monk, Maria. *Awful Disclosures.* Philadelphia: T. B. Peterson, 1836.

Montesquieu, Charles de Secondat, baron de. *De l'Esprit des Lois,* in *Œuvres complètes.* Paris: Gallimard, Bibliothèque de la Pléiade, 1958, vol. 2.

Moore, Laurence R. *Religious Outsiders and the Making of Americans.* New York: Oxford University Press, 1986.

Morand, Paul. *New York.* Translated by Hamish Miles. New York: Henry Holt, 1930.

Morgan, Edmund S. *The Puritan Dilemma: The Story of John Winthrop.* Boston: Little, Brown, 1958.

———. *The Puritan Family.* New York: Harper, 1966.

———. *Visible Saints: The History of a Puritan Idea.* Ithaca, NY: Cornell University Press, 1963.

Morone, James A. *Hellfire Nation: The Politics of Sin in American History.* New Haven: Yale University Press, 2003.

Morton, Andrew. *Monica's Story.* New York: St. Martin's, 1999.

Mounier, Emmanuel. *Mounier et sa génération: Lettres, carnets et inédits.* Paris: Seuil, 1956.

Nicolson, Adam. *God's Secretaries: The Making of the King James Bible.* New York: Harper Collins, 2003.

Noll, Mark, ed. *America's God: From Jonathan Edwards to Abraham Lincoln.* New York: Oxford University Press, 2002.

———. *Religion and American Politics.* New York: Oxford University Press, 1990.

Nora, Pierre, ed. *Les Lieux de mémoire.* 3 vols. Paris: Gallimard, Quarto, 1997.

Nora, Pierre, and Lawrence Kritzman, eds. *Realms of Memory.* 3 vols. Translated by Arthur Goldhammer. New York: Columbia University Press, 1996–1998.

Obama, Barack. *The Audacity of Hope: Thoughts on Reclaiming the American Dream.* New York: Three Rivers Press, 2006.

———. *Dreams from My Father.* New York: Three Rivers Press, 2004.

O'Brien David M. *Animal Sacrifice and Religious Freedom.* Lawrence: University Press of Kansas, 2004.

Onuf, Peter, ed. *Jeffersonian Legacies*. Charlottesville: University of Virginia Press, 1995.

Orren, Karen, and Stephen Skowronek. *The Search for American Political Development*. Cambridge: Cambridge University Press, 2004.

Ory, Pascal, ed. *Nouvelle histoire des idées politiques*. Paris: Hachette, 2004.

Paine, Thomas. *Collected Writings*. New York: Library of America, 1994.

Pangle, Thomas L. *The Spirit of Modern Republicanism: The Moral Vision of the American Founders and the Philosophy of Locke*. Chicago: University of Chicago Press, 1988.

Pauw, Corneille de. *Recherches philosophiques sur les Américains, ou Mémoires intéressants pour servir à l'histoire de l'espèce humaine*. 7 vols. Paris: Jean- François Bastien, an III [1794].

Peacock, James L., and Ruel W, Tyson, Jr. *Pilgrims of Paradox: Calvinism and Experience Among the Primitive Baptists of the Blue Ridge*. Washington, DC: Smithsonian Institution Press, 1989.

Pena-Ruiz, Henri. *Qu'est-ce que la laïcité?* Paris: Gallimard, Folio, 2003.

Philbrick, Nathaniel. *Mayflower: A Story of Courage, Community, and War*. New York: Viking, 2006.

Philip, André. *Le problème ouvrier aux États-Unis*. Paris: Félix Alcan, 1927.

Philips, Edith. *The Good Quaker in French Legend*. Philadelphia: University of Pennsylvania Press, 1932.

Phillips, Kevin. *American Theocracy*. New York: Viking, 2006.

Pierson, George Wilson. *Tocqueville in America*. 1938. Baltimore: Johns Hopkins University Press, 1996.

Pocock, J. G. A. *Barbarism and Religion*, vol. 2, *Narratives of Civil Government*. Cambridge: Cambridge University Press, 1999.

————. *The Machiavellian Moment: Florentine Political Thought and the Atlantic Republican Tradition*. Princeton: Princeton University Press, 1975.

Portier, Philippe, "L'Église catholique face au modèle français de laïcité." *Archives de Sciences Sociales des Religions* 129 (2005).

Portes, Alejandro, and Ruben G. Rumbaut. *Immigrant America: A Portrait*. 3rd ed. Berkeley: University of California Press, 2006.

Poulat, Émile. *Liberté-Laïcité: La guerre des deux France et le principe de la modernité*. Paris: Cujas, 1987.

Prothero, Stephen. *American Jesus: How the Son of God became a National Icon*. New York: Farrar, Straus and Giroux, 2003.

Rakove, Jack. *The Annotated U.S. Constitution and Declaration of Independence*. Cambridge, MA: Harvard University Press, 2009.

Ravitch, Diane. *The Great School Wars*. New York: Basic Books, 1974.

Raynal, Guillaume-Thomas. *Histoire philosophique et politique des établissements et du commerce des Européens dans les deux Indes.* 10 vols. Geneva, 1781.

———. *A History of the Two Indies: A Translated Selection of Writings from Raynal's Histoire philosophique.* Translated by Peter Jimack. Burlington, VT: Ashgate, 2006.

Raynaud, Philippe. *Max Weber et les dilemmes de la raison moderne.* Paris: PUF, 1987.

———. *Trois révolutions de la liberté: Angleterre, Amérique, France.* Paris: PUF, 2009.

Reclus, Élisée. *The Earth and Its Inhabitants: North America,* vol. 3, *The United States.* Edited by A. H. Keane. New York: D. Appleton, 1893.

———. *Géographie Universelle,* vol. 16, *Les États-Unis.* Paris: Hachette, 1892.

Reichley, A. James. *Religion in American Public Life.* Washington, DC: Brookings Institution Press, 1985.

Reis, Elizabeth. *Damned Women: Sinners and Witches in Puritan New England.* Ithaca, NY: Cornell University Press, 1997.

Rémond, René. *Les États-Unis devant l'opinion française, 1815–1852.* 2 vols. Paris: Armand Colin, 1962.

Renaut, Alain, and Alain Touraine. *Un débat sur la laïcité.* Paris: Stock, 2005.

Richards, David A. J. *Toleration and the Constitution.* New York: Oxford University Press, 1986.

Richet, Isabelle. *La Religion aux États-Unis.* Paris: PUF, 2001.

Robertson, William. *The History of America.* 1777. Paris: Baudry, 1828.

———. *History of the Reign of Charles V.* 4 vols. Chiswick: Thomas Tegg, 1824.

Roger, Philippe. *The American Enemy: The History of French Anti-Americanism.* Translated by Sharon Bowman. Chicago: University of Chicago Press, 2005.

Roof, Wade Clark, and William McKinney. *American Mainline Religion: Its Changing Shape and Future.* 4th ed. New Brunswick, NJ: Rutgers University Press, 1992.

———. *Spiritual Marketplace: Baby Boomers and the Remaking of American Religion.* Princeton: Princeton University Press, 1999.

Roosevelt, Theodore. *The Strenuous Life: Essays and Addresses by Theodore Roosevelt.* New York: The Century Co., 1901.

———. *The Winning of the West.* Vol. 1. New York: G. P. Putnam's Sons, 1889.

Rosanvallon, Pierre. *Le Moment Guizot.* Paris: Gallimard, 1985.

Rosen, Christine. *Preaching Eugenics: Religious Leaders and the American Eugenics Movement.* New York: Oxford University Press, 2004.

Rosenblum, Nancy L., ed. *Obligations of Citizenship and Demands of Faith.* Princeton: Princeton University Press, 2000.

Rudelle, Odile, ed. *Jules Ferry: La République des citoyens.* 2 vols. Paris: Imprimerie nationale, 1996.

Rudin, James. *The Baptizing of America.* New York: Thunder's Mouth Press, 2006.

Rupp, I. Daniel, ed. *An Original History of the Religious Denominations at Present Existing in the United States.* Philadelphia: J. Y. Humphreys, 1844.

Saint-Simon. *Nouveau christianisme.* Paris: Bureau du Globe, 1832.

Sarna, Jonathan D. *Minority Faiths and the American Protestant Mainstream.* Urbana: University of Illinois Press, 1998.

Sartre, Jean-Paul. *Situations III.* 1943. Paris: Gallimard, 2003.

Schleifer, James T. *The Making of Tocqueville's Democracy in America.* 2nd ed. Indianapolis: Liberty Fund, 2000.

Shibley, Mark A. *Resurgent Evangelicalism in the United States.* Columbia: University of South Carolina Press, 1996.

Siegfried, André. *America Comes of Age: A French Analysis.* Translated by H. H. and Doris Hemming. New York: Harcourt, Brace, 1927.

———. *Deux mois en Amérique du Nord à la veille de la guerre.* Paris: Armand Colin, 1916.

———. *Les États-Unis d'aujourd'hui.* Paris: Armand Colin, 1927.

Sirinelli, Jean-François. *Sartre et Aron: Deux intellectuels dans le siècle.* Paris: Hachette, 1999.

Slotkin, Richard. *Gunfighter Nation: The Myth of the Frontier in Twentieth-Century America.* New York: Macmillan, 1992.

Smith, Gary Scott. *Faith and the Presidency: From George Washington to George W. Bush.* New York: Oxford University Press, 2006.

Starr, Kenneth W. *First Among Equals: The Supreme Court in American Life.* New York: Warner, 2002.

———. *The Starr Report.* New York: Public Affairs, 1998.

Stepan, Alfred. *Arguing Comparative Politics.* New York: Oxford University Press, 2001.

Stephanson, Anders. *Manifest Destiny: American Expansion and the Empire of Right.* New York: Hill and Wang, 1995.

Stout, Harry S., and D. G. Hart, eds. *New Directions in American Religious History.* New York: Oxford University Press, 1997.

Tardivel, Jules. *La Situation religieuse aux États-Unis: Illusions et réalité.* Paris: Desclée de Brouwer, 1900.

Taylor, Mark. C. *After God.* Chicago: University of Chicago Press, 2007.

Tocqueville, Alexis de. *Democracy in America.* Edited and translated by Harvey C. Mansfield and Delba Winthrop. Chicago: University of Chicago Press, 2000.

———. *Democracy in America.* Translated by Arthur Goldhammer. New York: Library of America, 2004.

———. *Memoirs, Letters, and Remains of Alexis de Tocqueville.* Cambridge: Macmillan, 1861.

———. *The Tocqueville Reader.* Edited by Olivier Zunz and Alan S. Kahan. Oxford: Blackwell, 2002.

———. "Two Weeks in the Wilderness," in *Democracy in America and Two Essays on America.* Translated by Gerald E. Bevan. London: Penguin Books, 2003.

Trollope, Fanny. *Domestic Manners of the Americans.* 1832. Dover: Alan Sutton, 1993.

Turner, Frederick Jackson. *The Frontier in American History.* New York: Henry Holt, 1920.

Turner, Stephen, ed. *The Cambridge Companion to Weber.* Cambridge: Cambridge University Press, 2000.

Victor, Barbara. *The Last Crusade: Religion and the Politics of Misdirection.* London: Constable, 2005.

Volney, Constantin-François de Chassebœuf, comte de. *Tableau de climat et du sol des États-Unis d'Amérique.* 2nd ed. Paris: Parmentier, 1825.

Voltaire. "Avis au public sur les parricides imputés aux Calas et aux Sirven," in *Mélanges.* Edited by Jacques Van Den Heuvel. Paris: Gallimard, Bibliothèque de la Pléiade, 1961.

———. "Examen important de Milord Bolingbroke ou le Tombeau du fanatisme" [1736], in *Mélanges.* Edited by Jacques Van Den Heuvel. Paris: Gallimard, Bibliothèque de la Pléiade, 1961.

———. *Philosophical Letters.* Translated by Prudence L. Steiner. Indianapolis: Hackett, 2007.

———. *Treatise on Tolerance.* Translated by Brian Masters. Cambridge: Cambridge University Press, 2000.

Wald, Kenneth D. *Religion and Politics in the United States.* Washington, DC: CQ Press, 2003.

Weber, Max. *The Protestant Ethic and the Spirit of Capitalism.* Translated by Talcott Parsons. 1930. New York: Routledge, 1992.

Welch, Cheryl. *De Tocqueville.* New York: Oxford University Press, 2001.

———, ed. *The Cambridge Companion to Tocqueville.* New York: Cambridge University Press, 2006.

Wiebe, Robert: *The Search for Order, 1877–1920.* New York: Hill and Wang, 1998.

Willaime, Jean-Paul. *Europe et Religions: Les enjeux du XXe siècle.* Paris: Fayard, 2004.

———. *La Précarité protestante: Sociologie du protestantisme contemporain.* Geneva: Labor et Fides, 1992.

Wills, Garry. *Reagan's America: Innocents at Home.* New York: Doubleday, 1987.

————. *Under God: Religion and American Politics.* New York: Simon and Schuster, 1990.

Wilson, Matthew J., ed. *From Pews to Polling Places: Faith and Politics in the American Religious Mosaic.* Washington, DC: Georgetown University Press, 2007.

Winock, Michel. *"Esprit": Des intellectuels dans la cité.* Paris: Seuil, 1996.

Winthrop, John. *The Journal of John Winthrop, 1630–1649.* Edited by Richard Dunn and Laetitia Yeandle. Cambridge, MA: Harvard University Press, 1996.

Wolfe, Alan. *One Nation after All: What Middle-Class Americans Really Think about God, Country, Family, Racism . . . .* New York: Viking, 1998.

————. *The Transformation of American Religion.* New York: Free Press, 2003.

Wood, Gordon. *The Creation of the American Republic, 1776, 1787.* 1969. New York: Norton, 1996.

————. *The Radicalism of the American Revolution.* New York: Knopf, 1992.

Wuthnow, Robert. *The Restructuring of American Religion.* Princeton: Princeton University Press, 1988.

Zolberg, Aristide. R. *A Nation by Design: Immigration Policy in the Fashioning of America.* Cambridge, MA: Harvard University Press, 2006.

Zoller, Élisabeth, ed. *La Conception américaine de la laïcité.* Paris: Dalloz, 2005.

————. *De Nixon à Clinton: Malentendus politiques transatlantiques.* Paris: PUF, 1999.